Save American Jobs

Save American Jobs

✦

New Business Ideas to Retain Jobs in America

Abraham K. Turkson

iUniverse, Inc.
New York Lincoln Shanghai

Save American Jobs
New Business Ideas to Retain Jobs in America

iUniverse books may be ordered through booksellers or by contacting:

iUniverse
2021 Pine Lake Road, Suite 100
Lincoln, NE 68512
www.iuniverse.com
1-800-Authors (1-800-288-4677)

ISBN-13: 978-0-595-36100-7 (pbk)
ISBN-13: 978-0-595-67330-8 (cloth)
ISBN-13: 978-0-595-80546-4 (ebk)
ISBN-10: 0-595-36100-5 (pbk)
ISBN-10: 0-595-67330-9 (cloth)
ISBN-10: 0-595-80546-9 (ebk)

Printed in the United States of America

To my wife, Florence Afful,
my son, Samuel Takor,
and my daughter Nana Adjoa Ansaba

Contents

1

INTRODUCTION

History changed on October 4, 1957 when the Soviet Union successfully launched Sputnik 1. The flight of the first artificial satellite around the Earth took only ninety minutes, but its impact was tectonic. Sputnik spooked America into fearing the satellite was the first step on the road to a ballistic missile attack by the Soviets.

Then the Soviets struck again on November 3 by launching Sputnik II, which carried a much heavier payload, including, mischievously, a dog named Laila. America was apoplectic; the end of the land of George Washington and Abraham Lincoln was now very much in sight.

In response, the United States was placed on a near war footing. Science and mathematics curriculums across the entire educational spectrum were torn into pieces and revamped by the best minds the country could offer. Satellite programs ensnared in Congress were suddenly unleashed. Government, business and academia came together as never before to galvanize the public in an unprecedented effort to successfully defeat bureaucratic red tapeism. The forces marshaled by the United States to confront the gauntlet thrown by the Soviets led to the creation of the National Aeronautics and Space Administration on October 1, 1958. It was America at her best.

As a result of the crystallization of scientific and technical resources, America was fully prepared to respond when the Russian cosmonaut Yuri Gagarin became the first human to travel into space and return successfully on April 12, 1961. But someone had to issue the clarion call. Someone had to have the wisdom, courage and foresight to reach deep down into the very soul of America to churn her blood, to overcome the naysayers and doubting Thomases, and to lead the country over troubled waters. That person was President John F. Kennedy.

He issued the call to action in a Gettysburg-like speech to Congress on May 25, 1961:

"These are extraordinary times. And we face an extraordinary challenge. Our strength as well as our convictions have imposed upon this nation the role of leader of freedom's cause. No role in history could be more difficult or more important. We stand for freedom. That is our conviction for ourselves-that is our only commitment to others. No friend, no neutral and no adversary should think otherwise. We are not against any man-or any nation-or any system-except as it is hostile to freedom. Nor am I here to present a new military doctrine, bearing any one name or aimed at any one area. I am here to promote the doctrine of freedom."

"I believe we possess all the resources and talents necessary. But the facts of the matter are that we have never made the national decisions or marshaled the national resources required for such leadership. We have never specified long-range goals on an urgent time schedule, or managed our resources and our time so as to insure their fulfillment."

"I believe that this nation should commit itself to achieving the goal, before this decade is out, of landing a man on the moon and returning him safely to earth…It will not be one man going to the moon—if we make this adjustment affirmatively, it will be an entire nation. For all of us must work to put him there."

Coming not long after his humiliation by the episode of the Bay of Pigs, his detractors howled that the call to land a man on the moon was a publicity stunt meant to whitewash his tarnished image. The seemingly prohibitive cost of the enterprise moved even some of his most loyal allies to question whether he had taken leave of his senses. But Kennedy persevered, with the delivery of a defining speech at Rice University in Houston on September 12, 1962 in which he reaffirmed America's commitment to landing a man on the moon before the end of the 1960s:

"Those who came before us made certain that this country rode the first waves of the industrial revolution, the first waves of modern invention, and the first wave of nuclear power, and this generation does not intend to founder in the backwash of the coming age of space. We mean to be a part of it—we mean to lead it. For the eyes of the world now look into space, to the moon and to the planets beyond, and we have vowed that we shall not see it governed by a hostile flag of conquest, but by a banner of freedom and peace."

"We choose to go to the moon. We choose to go to the moon in this decade and to do the other things, not because they are easy, but because they are hard, because that goal will serve to organize and measure the best of our energies and skills, because that challenge is one that we are willing to accept, one we are unwilling to postpone, and one which we intend to win."

He was cut down on November 23rd, 1963 at Dealey Plaza in Dallas. But the flame President Kennedy lit before his untimely death burned brightly in many an enterprising American soul until on July 20th, 1969, before the end of the decade of the sixties as he had vowed, Neil Armstrong uttered the most famous sentence ever spoken as he became the first man ever to set foot on the moon: "That's one small step for man but one giant leap for mankind."

But as President Kennedy had predicted, the journey was not easy. Successes were scarred by failures, budgets were bloated by waste and schedules were riddled by delays. But America had persevered, undeterred, until the dream was finally achieved.

Difficulty, rather than becoming a deterrence, motivated greater action. Hardship, rather than cause discouragement, spurred greater effort. Uncertainty, rather than cause doubt, precipitated further investigation. And failure, rather than cause defeat, became the engine for success.

And just as President Kennedy had predicted, the trip to the moon bore fruit for all of mankind. Stereotactic large-core needle biopsy reduces the pain, scarring, radiation exposure, time and expense associated with surgical breast biopsies. Laser angioplasty does not damage blood vessel walls and offers precise non-surgical cleanings of clogged arteries. Fire resistant materials are used for clothing and furniture. Advanced keyboards, customer service software, database management systems, laser surveying, aircraft controls, lightweight compact disc, microcomputers and design graphics. All these advanced technologies employing millions around the world were developed because of the decision to go to the moon.

The world owes a debt of gratitude to President Kennedy for his wisdom and foresight in launching the mission to land a man on the moon before the end of the decade of the sixties. Some men see things as they are and say 'Why?' President Kennedy dreamt of a mission never before contemplated and asked, "Why not?" He did, indeed, live by the words of his brother.

Terrorists used fuel-laden passenger planes as missiles to strike at the administrative and financial capitals of America on September 11, 2001. Hundreds of Americans and many citizens from around the world suffered harrowing deaths as the twin towers of the World Trade Center collapsed in flames. Dozens of America's bravest perished as the Pentagon was rocked to its foundation. And by all accounts, only the brave actions of stirred souls spared a traumatized nation from witnessing an attack on the White House.

In the aftermath of that day of infamy, government officials said nobody in a position of authority imagined that terrorists would employ planes as weapons to launch an attack on American soil. But someone should have done so, for the terrorists left calling cards everywhere with their intentions only slightly encrypted.

Since the first attack on the World Trade Center in February 1993 failed to bring down the building, it should have been transparent that the terrorists would attempt to bring down the twin towers using another method. A probable method for a new attack should have been discerned with the arrest in 1995 of Ramzi Yousif, a known Al-Qaida operative, and a bunch of co-conspirators in the Philippines for plotting to blow up twelve U.S. bound planes across the Pacific. Ramzi Yousif was later convicted for his role in the 1993 bombing of the World Trade Center.

Tantalizing clues to the dastardly act on September 11, 2001 were in plain sight. It required a team with a bit of imagination to put the pieces of the puzzle together to prevent the first mass scale catastrophic attack on mainland America. Unfortunately, no one or group "connected the dots" to prevent Americans from being attacked on their own soul. The consequences of that failure will persist for all time.

But, regardless of the mistakes made before that dastardly day of September 11, 2001, a man some had considered unworthy of the office he occupied was stirred into action. By his words and his deeds, President George Walker Bush strode in the path walked by his father and others before him to become the comforter-in-chief and to bear the mantle of commander-in-chief.

He started officially with these stirring words at the Episcopal National Cathedral on September 14, 2001:

"We are here in the middle hour of our grief. So many have suffered so great a loss, and today we express our nation's sorrow. We come before God to pray for the missing and the dead, and for those who loved them. On Tuesday, our country was attacked with deliberate and massive cruelty. We have seen the images of fire and ashes and bent steel."

"War has been waged against us by stealth and deceit and murder. This nation is peaceful, but fierce when stirred to anger. This conflict was begun on the timing and terms of others; it will end in a way and at an hour of our choosing."

Then in a completely unscripted moment, many in the crowd shouted they could not hear him as he spoke from atop the still smoldering remains of the World Trade Center. With a bullhorn in hand, George Bush looked out across the firefighters and volunteers and replied, "We hear you. I can hear you. America hears you. The rest of the world hears you. And the people who knocked down these buildings will hear all of us soon." Americans everywhere lifted themselves from their grief and cheered George Bush at a heroic hour equivalent to that of any president at any time in history.

On September 20, 2001, in an address to a joint session of Congress and the American people, President Bush proved emphatically that he was equal to the challenge at hand:

"Tonight we are a country awakened to danger and called to defend freedom. Our grief has turned to anger, and anger to resolution. Whether we bring our enemies to justice, or bring justice to our enemies, justice will be done."

"This is not, however, just America's fight. And what is at stake is not just America's freedom. This is the world's fight. This is civilization's fight. This is the fight of all who believe in progress and pluralism, tolerance and freedom."

"I will not forget this wound to our country or those who inflicted it. I will not yield; I will not rest; I will not relent in waging this struggle for freedom and security for the American people."

"The course of this conflict is not known, yet its outcome is certain. Freedom and fear, justice and cruelty, have always been at war, and we know that God is not neutral between them."

"Fellow citizens, we'll meet violence with patient justice—assured of the rightness of our cause, and confident of the victories to come. In all that lies before us, may God grant us wisdom, and may He watch over the United States of America."

The speech ended at 9:41 P.M. to thunderous applause. It was a speech equal in content and emotion and action to that delivered by Lincoln at Gettysburg, and it stirred a nation into action after the diabolical attack of September 11, 2001.

America is under a different kind of attack. It started slowly, but it is bound to swell into a size that will shake the economic foundation of America, if left unchallenged. The damage being done to America will mount to such a scale that it will dwarf the effects of September 11, 2001. Some vulnerable groups have already been devastated. More are sure to follow.

And even more maddening, the attack is aided and abetted by some corporate leaders holding American passports. A new generation is stripping layers of wealth from the land that has given them sustenance since their infancy, leaving gaps of vulnerability across America. A part of one group is now exporting wealth built by succeeding generations for their own benefit, leaving others to wither on the vineyard of despair. America's future is being mortgaged, with the deed held by foreigners. The attack on America is fratricidal, brother against brother.

Snippets of the attack are reported in passing, but popular American media invest more resources on sensational trials and numbing "reality shows," which are anything but real. Popular American media spent days covering the case of the so-called "Runaway Bride," even after it emerged she had gotten cold feet. But the damage being inflicted on U.S. economic infrastructure rates hardly a mention.

Or could it be that most of the media are not paying attention because the attacks are not being perpetrated with the violent cataclysm of 9/11? Be what it may, the attacks on America are about to culminate in a major disruption, if left unchecked. Let them see those that have eyes, let them hear those that have ears, and let them speak those that have voices.

Personal bankruptcies in the U.S. climbed to 1.5 million in 2002 and a record 1.6 million in 2003. The phenomenon gathering steam in the Far East could inflict much worse damage. The millions of middle class jobs in the manufacturing sector wiped out since 1998 were precipitated by ripples, not the main force, of the coming economic disruption. Use of office space across America will contract, revenue streams for local, municipal and federal governments will shrivel, and pain will spread throughout the land.

It will hurt the female and professional working populations in the same manner that a whole generation of hard-working "blue-collar" American males was jettisoned after their blood and sweat built America. Unfortunately, there will be no booming economy to lift those going to be flattened by the impact of this phenomenon.

The cost of providing services like health care and homes for the elderly will escalate as the baby-boomer population heads into retirement. How are governments going to fund these mandated entitlements in the future from a dwindling revenue base when they are struggling mightily to do so today?

The effects of this phenomenon could be worse than what happened in California, where implosion of the so-called "dot com" economy left the state with a $38 billion budget deficit, which voters passed referendum preventing taxes from being raised to close. In Santa Clara County where Silicon Valley is located, unemployment mushroomed to a painful 8.5 percent from a low of 1.8 percent in September 2000; stores closed and about 30 percent of commercial property became vacant. In the imploded dot.com enclaves in San Francisco office vacancy was as high as 40 percent. "Gleaming office parks once stuffed with start ups are see-through ghost towns," reported Newsweek.

What happened in Silicon Valley in particular and in California as a whole could pale in comparison to the effects of the coming phenomenon across the United States.

Yet, despite the impending economic crunch, most of the American media remain preoccupied with idols, bachelors, bachelorettes, fear factors, survivors, supermodels and Joe millionaires. Every now and then attention shifts from the fictional "reality" shows, a contradictory term of the highest order, to true life reality shows beamed live from Eagle County, CO featuring the fallen hero Kobe Bryant, or from Redwood City, California where Scott Peterson never uttered a word of sorrow during his trial for the murder of his wife and unborn child, or from the Santa Barbara County Courthouse in Santa Maria, California, where Michael Jackson confessed to his proclivity for hanging out with boys.

Have the American media informed Americans of the following story culled verbatim from a website?

"Phoenix Global Solutions (PGS), a technology-provider for the life insurance sector, positioned itself to become "Total Transaction Service Provider", by bundling the IT and IT-enabled services for its clients. In this connection, the company chalked out ambitious plans, including ramping up the staff-strength to 1,000 employees in both IT and IT-enabled services."

The firm, a wholly owned subsidiary of U.S.-based Phoenix Companies Inc, a 152-year old insurance and wealth management services company, provided IT services, IT-enabled services and customer care to its parent company.

The company offered a bouquet of IT solutions for insurance, mutual fund, pension fund and investment trust companies. It also focused on an array of customer requirements like managing documents, customer relationship, sales force and recruitment. It then expanded into health insurance, accident claims, property and financial service apart from business analysis.

The company increased its staff from 400 to 1,000 in the IT and IT-enabled services divisions, with plans to ramp up to 5,000 in the near term. But American corporate leaders created these jobs in India, not the United States. Phoenix set up a complete office outside the United States to handle American projects previously performed by American workers.

Extrapolating the Phoenix formula to 200 companies with each hiring 5,000 employees means 1.0 million workers would be hired in India to do the work of 1.0 million Americans. And this is exactly what is happening.

If the pace of jobs being sent overseas in just the data processing industry alone is allowed to continue unchecked, gleaming high-rises in America filled with workers will become vacant as human life is sucked out onto the wasteland of unemployment. And this is just in one industry.

It is called offshore outsourcing, the ultimate nightmare. Some of the terminology and acronyms like IT and IT-enabled services (ITES) have been introduced. Others are business process outsourcing (BPO), offshoring, external service provider (ESP), customer relations' management (CRM) and many more.

Offshore outsourcing is but only one aspect of this phenomenon hitting America like nothing it has ever seen before. Nothing is immune. When a customer calls an "800" number to dispute billing on a credit card, the person offering service could be anywhere in the world; from Manila in the Philippines, or Delhi in India, or Kingston in Jamaica. A technical call to Dell is just as likely to be answered by someone in Bismarck, North Dakota as in Bangalore, India. The thousands of paper collected by hospitals and insurance companies are for the most part being processed outside the United States.

The people in the overseas office locations have access to salary and benefit packages of Americans. They process all this information with the knowledge that somebody in America doing the same job is paid five times more, with health insurance, 401k plan and drives a car, while they have relatively little of those benefits, and cannot afford a car. And this spurs them on to work harder to deprive more Americans of their "cushy" lifestyle.

Not even doctors are immune from this phenomenon. The first person a new patient encounters after personal details have been recorded is an assistant, who measures weight, blood pressure and records other vital information. The primary care physician (PCP) follows the nurse, armed with the information collected. In reality, however, the doctor's presence in the room is dispensable.

In a budding new industry known as tele-medicine, a doctor at a remote location receives the information recorded by the assistant on his computer, and then communicates with the patient via a two-way video system hooked to the Internet. He then proceeds to perform the main duties of a PCP: probable diagnosis, test work and/or referral to a specialist. Only when an invasive procedure is necessary would the physical presence of a doctor be required. "The video doctor will see you now, please" could become commonplace in doctors' offices.

Dr. Joseph Warren, President of the Massachusetts Congress, and one of the founding fathers said, "Our country is in great danger, but not to be despared of…on you depend the fortunes of America. You are to decide the important questions upon which rests the happiness and the liberty of millions yet unborn. Act worthy of yourselves."

But the American corporate chieftains leading the charge to send American jobs overseas are not acting worthy of themselves. If they were, they would not be sending good-paying American middle class jobs to foreign lands at the expense of their fellow citizens. And these are no ordinary jobs. In every forecast from the Bureau of Labor Statistics to the Connecticut Department of Labor, these are the jobs that were predicted to create a brilliantly sunny American morning. Instead, it's turning out to be an ominous morning, with dark clouds hovering everywhere.

Nicholas Kristof of the New York Times wrote emotionally from Karapchiv, Ukraine, the birthplace of his father: "I'm so grateful to my father, and to my wife's grandparents, for leaving behind all that was familiar to them in two villages half a world apart, and thus bequeathing us the gift of America."

What kind of America is going to be bequeathed to the next generation? When Kristof's father arrived on these shores, America was bustling with opportunity. He gave America everything he had and America in return gave him everything she had. It was a fair trade. Today, many of America's children are giving her everything they have and many are getting low-paying jobs in return.

The new jobs being created are mostly in logistics, wholesale, retail, restaurants, government, healthcare and construction. Manufacturing, the bedrock of every society, is bleeding jobs by the thousands every month. The high technology industry that was supposed to be the salvation for displaced manufacturing workers is itself hemorrhaging jobs. Many American middle class jobs that were the envy of the world are slowly being moved offshore, replaced by lower paying jobs.

Americans sense all is not well, but the answers to their discomfort are buried by sensationalized media. For example, the AP-Ipsos Consumer Confidence Index for May 6, 2005 was reported to be only 78.2, the lowest since October 2003. This was despite a "rosy" jobs report of 274,000 for April 2005. For hidden in the jobs report was the fact electronics, automobile, textile, furniture and other industries were still bleeding jobs. At a time when experts claimed the U.S. economy was booming, a Gallup poll conducted between May 2-5, 2005 showed only 31 percent of Americans concurred with that assessment, while 69 percent rated the economy fair to poor. The sense of discomfort was buried deeply, among other factors, in jobs of family members and neighbors going overseas.

When the construction boom fuelled by the ditech.com refinancing phenomenon slows down and the massive amount of money being spent by the military dries up, the American media would be forced to report an economy with reduced funds to pay the nurses and healthcare professionals being employed in droves.

Every nation on earth needs a strong manufacturing base. No country can survive on transportation, warehouse, insurance, real estate and the government jobs springing up in the U.S. without a strong manufacturing catalyst. It will profit not America to gain lower paying jobs while losing manufacturing jobs.

The U.S. economy was hailed as being in good health because 274,000 new jobs had been created in April 2005. But the media failed to inform the public that 211,000 of the jobs were in the service sector as follows: 58,000 in leisure and hospitality (primarily restaurants and bars), 47,000 in construction, 29,200 in wholesale and retail trade, 28,000 in health care and social assistance, 17,300 in administrative and support services (primarily temps), 11,700 in transportation and warehousing, and 8,800 in real estate. A few jobs scattered in other service categories completed the picture.

These are the jobs globalization is creating in the United States. Gone are the manufacturing jobs that lifted America's parents and grandparents into the middle class. The better-paying jobs promised by advocates of globalization are nowhere to be found. Not knowing this was in reference to the U.S., a casual observer would have thought these were jobs in a developing country.

So this is what it has come down to. The cheaper prices at Wal-Mart are indeed being exchanged for America's middle class jobs. The only safe jobs are those in services without foreign competition. Any job that competes against another in a developing country faces the threat of being whisked via the Internet or boated to the Far East.

According to conservative commentator and former U.S. Assistant Secretary of Treasury Paul Craig Roberts, "The U.S. has ceased to create jobs in high-tech sectors and in export and import-competitive sectors." Then he added chillingly, "Offshore outsourcing of manufacturing and of engineering and professional services is dismantling the ladders of upward mobility that made the American Dream possible."

"I am so angry. My husband is 59 and lost his job four months ago. Yesterday, my sister-in-law was notified that her skip-tracing job was going to India. Hey, no problem, she's only been with the company for 21 years. I've never been so frustrated in my life. People in their 50s just can't start over. I hate life."

Americans are wailing on the Internet, but some "experts" are telling them that sending jobs overseas is good. "No pain, no gain" seems to be the message to the affected from some quarters.

Not even a speech by no less a figure than Henry Kissinger at a Computer Associates event in Las Vegas in July 2003 was enough to stir anger at jobs being moved offshore at such an accelerated pace. Mr. Kissinger asked: "The question really amounts to whether America can remain a great power or a dominant power if it becomes primarily a service economy." He answered himself as follows: "And I doubt that." He followed up by suggesting that the movement overseas called for "some careful thought of national policy of how we can create incentives to prevent that from happening." Nobody responded.

America's middle class is gradually being dismantled by the departure of millions of jobs from the manufacturing and service sectors of the economy. This is the class painstakingly constructed through the sacrifice of many who came before this generation.

As has been said by many, America is more than a country, it is an idea, which is why many from every corner of the world have made it home, and many more strive to come over. There are dishwashers who work twenty hours a day to earn enough to send money to feed their families back where they came from. There are many that forsake life with their own families to be holed up as live-in maids, cleaning bedridden alzheimer patients for enough money to help teaming extended family members. There are many who would rather die crossing the Arizona desert or the Straits of Florida in a desperate bid to claim a piece of the idea than remain in dens of destitution. There is no other country on earth with such a magnetic pull. But, now, that idea is about to be eviscerated: it's about to be converted into a nightmare.

When 500,000 financial analysts stand on the edge ready to be pushed over a cliff in the next couple of years, when competent computer programmers turn to reading gas meters for sustenance, when young college graduates are rendered redundant before they even have a chance to lay their mark on their land, not only has the land failed them, it has also extinguished an idea.

Manufacturing lost 3.3 million jobs from February 1998 to December 2004, reducing that sector's share of the labor force to 11 percent, the lowest ever. Continuation of this insanity will leave America bare and dry. Meanwhile, IBM, EDS, CSC, Dell, Microsoft, Oracle, Sun Microsystems, Hewlett Packard, Perot Systems, General Motors, Aetna, Sprint, JP Morgan Chase, GE Capital, American Express, Intel, Citigroup, and many, many more of America's so-called blue chip companies are shipping thousands of office and professional jobs overseas, the very same jobs that were supposed to replenish the souls burnt by decapitation of steel, auto manufacturing, textiles, furniture, toys, computers and other industries.

According to Kevin Rollins Chief Executive Officer of computer maker Dell Inc., the company will hire another 2,000 people by the end of 2005 to make India a hub for its *software development* and back-office work. The announcement was made on April 29, 2005 from Bangalore, India's technology hub. Rollins said Dell would increase its staff strength in India from 8,000 to 10,000 by January 2006.

"It has been a very exciting time here in India, running customer support and internal software development centers," Kevin Rollins told reporters in Bangalore. Dell planned to open more offices in India to shift technology work and to tap India's growing computer market, he said. Left unsaid but apparent to all was that the shift would come at the expense of the United States.

Of course, it's been "very exciting" for Dell in India. They are getting employees at a fraction of the wages of U.S. employees, thereby fattening their bottom line. Dell was not in danger of going under if it did not go to India. But the difference in wages between Indian and U.S. employees was, in their mind, "an offer they could not refuse."

What about the United States? Were these not the information technology jobs counted on by sanguine technocrats to fill departing "dirty" manufacturing jobs? And if the answer were affirmative, then what jobs would be left for American children?

Lou Dobbs, the CNN commentator, asked this question in his book Exporting America: "India can provide our software; China can provide our toys; Sri Lanka can make our clothes; Japan can make our cars. But at some point we have to ask, what will we export? At what will Americans work? And for what wages?" None of the avid proponents of free trade and outsourcing in government, academia, or business has been able to answer any of those questions.

The double-sided battle being waged against America is manufacturing to China and office work to India. What work would be left for American workers? What professions would be left? Nobody has the answer, because when the revenue generating components of the economy are squeezed dry, who will be taxed to pay the police, firemen, nurses, teachers, surgeons and others in the jobs supposedly immune to outsourcing? Then what will become of America?

For what will become of America, it is instructive to study what has become of America. In the very early 1970s, a band of technology hobbyists in the United States began a drive to extract some of the power available in mainframe computers for their own use. With enthusiasm the defining characteristic of all the players involved in this haphazard effort, several models of a machine capable of replicating some of the functions of the "big bad mainframe" emerged from electronics' shops. But none achieved notoriety until the January 1st, 1975 edition of Popular Electronics featured on its front page a product called MITS Altair 8800 from Micro Instrumentation and Telemetry Systems (MITS), an obscure Albuquerque, New Mexico company.

Paul Allen, one of the technology enthusiasts, was beside himself when he saw that issue of Popular Electronics. Waving his copy and jumping up and down, Allen uttered the most famous words to ever hit the computer industry, "This is it!" he exclaimed, "It's about to begin." Allen's prophetic words applied to the software that would be required to power MITS Altair, the first personal computer ever built.

Paul Allen's name is recognizable to only a few people outside the computer industry and the sports world. But Paul had a friend, a fellow technology enthusiast, who is now one of the most well known people in the world. His name is Bill Gates.

Paul and Bill were the first people to recognize that the future belonged to the brains—software—that will run the machine, and not to the nuts and bolts of the machine. So with Paul a Honeywell employee and Bill a Harvard sophomore, the two set out to modify a computer language developed by Dr. John G. Kemeny and Thomas Kurtz at Dartmouth in 1964 called BASIC, which stood for "Beginner's All-Purpose Symbolic Instruction Code." It was designed as a simple way to teach students how to program.

Working in marathon 24-hour sessions, the two technology enthusiasts adapted BASIC for MITS Altair 8800 by simulating the machine on another computer from published specifications. Although it had never been tested on an actual machine, the first software ever written for a personal computer ran perfectly on the very first try. Then in another stroke of business acumen that was to become their hallmark, the "Micro-soft" BASIC program was licensed, not sold, to MITS on July 22nd, 1975. Of course, this gave the duo the liberty to license their software to other hardware developers.

While Paul Allen and Bill Gates were focusing on software, another duo of technology enthusiasts was focusing on hardware development. On April 1, 1976, Steve Jobs and Steve Wozniak announced the development of the Apple 1 personal computer for a devilishly low price of only $666.66.

The enthusiasm for computers that burned inside Paul Allen and Bill Gates in the early 1970s led to one phenomenal software after another until in 2004, with no sign of slowing down, 57,086 Microsoft employees delivered sales of $36.85 billion in 2004. Bill Gates is still at the helm, but Paul Allen derives equal pleasure and pain while waiting for his Portland Trailblazers basketball and Seattle

Seahawks football teams to deliver Microsoft-like championship performance. He is in for a long wait, because the Seahawks have no defense, and the Trailblazers have become the Weedblazers.

Over at Apple, while Steve Wozniak has long since departed, Steve Job, after an interlude to set up the wildly successful animated company Pixar, returned to Apple to bang out the iPod, the "it" consumer product of 2004, and other zany Mac computer products. The iPod, or a similar product, will grow into a telephone, hand held computer, gamer, in addition to its original music-playing function, creating multiplying effects on the U.S. economy.

The value of Microsoft to the U.S. economy extends far beyond its immediate gigantic structure. The company acts like a magnet, attracting thousands of independent software enthusiasts whose products lead to even more employment and economic activity in the U.S.

Like Microsoft and Apple, Google, Yahoo, Oracle and the many companies nurturing America all grew out of unbridled enthusiasm of a core group of Americans for the possibilities offered by the computer industry.

It was the same enthusiasm for computers that led a young Michael Dell to dream up a new strategy for selling computers. Dell introduced "manufacturing—to—demand" strategy to the computer industry from his bedroom, laying the foundation for an empire that laudably includes three manufacturing operations in his home state of Texas, Tennessee and North Carolina.

What is the state of enthusiasm today for the computer industry among the youth of America? The Higher Education Research Institute at the University of California at Los Angeles (HERI/UCLA) conducts a survey of incoming freshmen at all undergraduate institutions to determine their major of choice. A summary of the results for 1983, 2000 and 2004 is provided in Table 1a. It shows students are forsaking the industry that gave birth to Bill Gates.

In February 2004, White House Chief Economic Advisor Greg Mankiw wrote that outsourcing would prove "a plus for the economy in the long run" and was simply "a new way of doing international trade." The data contained in Table 1a contradict Mankiw's assertion. Because, for all intends and purposes, females are about to abandon the computer science profession, and males are running away as fast as they can. Overall, the percentage of freshmen selecting computer science major has declined by about 70 percent since it peaked in 1983, and by about 60 percent from the peak of the dotcom bubble.

Table 1a			
Computer Science Listed as Probable Major Among Incoming Freshmen			
	1983	2000	2004
Males	5.8%	6.5%	2.8%
Females	4.2%	1.4%	0.3%
Total	4.8%	3.7%	1.4%
Source: HERI at UCLA			

More profits for companies who replace Americans with less expensive for-eigners cannot compensate for the loss of economic activity caused by removal of higher wages and the jobs they support from the economy. Mankiw's theory would be correct if offshore outsourcing was caused by—or caused—new tech-nology around which higher paying jobs could coalesce *in the United States.* There is no such technology in sight, and the United States would be better served if academic dogmatists lifted their eyes from textbooks and confronted reality. It's a different story for a recipient of a job departing the United States. Then, Mankiw's hypothesis applies to you.

Professions of increasing interest to freshmen students can be found in Table 1b, which shows significant leaps in freshmen students choosing teaching and medically related professions from 1983 to 2004. But particularly illuminating is that the precipitous decline in freshmen selecting computer science (Table 1a) since 2000 has been matched by a significant increase in those selecting medically related professions (Table 1b). But the importance of the healthcare profession should be tempered by the fact that it is not self-sustaining. Rather, it depends on income from revenue-generating sectors and will suffer the consequences of any adverse impact on those sectors.

Students deserting the computer science industry are flocking to medically related professions to satisfy the growing demand of an aging population and to nestle securely in the health industry perceived by students to be immune to the offshore outsourcing phenomenon. American students are voting with their brains, not wanting to enter a profession that is being severely affected by off-shore outsourcing.

The upcoming drop in computer science graduates is highlighted by a deci-sion by women as a group to leave the profession long before males. Repelled per-haps by the long lonely hours required for code writing, women's interest in computer science recovered only marginally in comparison to men even during the booming dotcom era. But whatever compensatory effect high salaries and benefits may have offered has evaporated since then. Interest in computer science among women fell about 80 percent between 1998 and 2004, and by about 93 percent since it peaked in 1982.

Table 1b Probable Majors Indicated by Incoming Freshmen			
	1983	**2000**	**2004**
Arts, Humanities, Education, Science	24%	33%	32%
Biological Sciences, (includes medical fields)	19%	18%	23%
Business	22%	17%	16%
Computer Science, Engineering, Technical	19%	15%	13%
Physical Science	3%	3%	3%
Source: HERI at UCLA			

Declining interest of freshmen women in computer science is reflected in the graduation rate, which shows (Table 1c) the profession to be one of the few in which participation by women has been reversed over the past three decades or so. Between 1976 and 2001, the proportion of females earning bachelor's degrees in all fields jumped from 45 percent to 58 percent, but the ascendancy from 20 percent to 37 percent witnessed for computer science from 1976 to 1986 had been reversed to below 30 percent by 2001. With continued steep declines predicted for women, it is improbable to envision any recovery in the number of U.S. computer science graduates in upcoming years.

Overall, the number of computer science graduates hovered around 25,000 from the early nineties till it peaked at 43,184 in 2001. According to the Computing Research Association, the number of computer science and engineering graduates will fall to an abysmally low 15,950 in 2008/2009, if the number of freshmen electing this major holds. The number of female graduates is projected at falling below 1900 in 2008/2009.

However, it is pertinent to note that the decline in freshmen choosing computer science as a major is not matched by market expectations. On the contrary, demand for computer science professionals, while it will not reach the level of the frothy dotcom era, is increasing as companies continue to integrate information systems into their business infrastructure.

Table 1c Percent of Bachelor's Degrees Earned by Women in Selected Professions						
	1976	**1981**	**1986**	**1991**	**1996**	**2001**
All Fields	45%	50%	51%	53%	55%	58%
Biological Science	40%	44%	48%	51%	53%	60%
Chemistry	22%	30%	37%	40%	42%	49%
Computer Science	20%	33%	37%	30%	28%	28%
Physics	10%	12%	15%	16%	18%	22%
Engineering	3%	11%	15%	16%	18%	20%
Source: National Center for Education Statistics						

Cognitive technology—or artificial intelligence—involves transferring functions of the brain into processes so that maximum efficiency can be derived from the created ability of machines to anticipate and fix problems. Natural order technologies involve development of products that mimic nature's ability to husband resources and survive in hostile environments. Technologists are attempting to transfer into insulation products the ability of squirrels and bears to almost completely shut down their bodily functions during hibernation. Yet others are researching characteristics of anaerobic bacteria for transfer into products for miners and divers. And more are working on ultimate preventative products capable of non-intrusively monitoring and repairing internal organs before onset of debilitating diseases.

All these nanotechnologies require advanced software for modeling and process simulation. So demand for higher-end computer programming will become more acute at precisely the time when supply of computer science professionals in the U.S. will be decelerating.

Robert Half Technology, a provider of IT professionals, confirmed increasing demand for higher-end IT professionals. Based on thousands of job orders managed by the company's U.S. offices, it predicted that, "As the economy gains momentum and businesses pursue new technology initiatives, the need for experienced IT professionals will continue to rise." However, professionals don't just become experienced. Neither do they jump immediately to the higher-end of the industry. Like everything else, the computer industry requires enthusiastic young professionals willing to do the grunt work to acquire the experience necessary for advanced work.

Bridging the projected shortage of U.S. computer science professionals from overseas may be, in the words of Greg Mankiw, "a new way of doing international trade." But losing intellectual clusters, such as those that formed in Silicon Valley in the 1990s, creates the possibility that the U.S. could cede leadership of next generation technologies and correlating economic growth to other countries, a development that would not qualify as a "plus for the economy in the long run."

So, ironically, supply shortfall of U.S. computer science professionals caused mainly by offshore outsourcing will be filled by more offshore outsourcing, bringing the kind of happiness to Kevin Rollins of Dell and others that may be short-lived.

But while interest in computer science as a profession is waning in the United States, overseas students in India in particular, but also in Russia, Bulgaria and Ukraine, are breaking down walls to enter the industry. The excitement tickling Kevin Rollins of Dell because of his company being in India, multiplied by others from his counterparts at IBM, EDS, Microsoft, Oracle and other American companies, has been transferred to overseas students.

In effect, some companies with American names, owned for the most part by Americans, and headed by holders of American passports like Kevin Rollins of Dell are, by their actions, indirectly replacing American interest in computer science with foreign interest. And this is no ordinary foreign interest. The foreign students migrating into computer science are, like Bill Gates and Paul Allen, the smartest those countries have to offer. The type of Russian scientists who were the first to send a man into space and the Indian engineers who built nuclear weapons are now sprinting to computer programming.

So where will the next Paul Allen, Bill Gates, Steve Jobs or Steve Wozniak come from? Less likely from the United States, but more likely from overseas, where enthusiasm for computer science is on the ascendancy.

Paul Baran of Rand Corporation came up with the concept of disassembling computer infrastructure systems into discrete elements to prevent the whole system from being decapitated in an attack. The concept of device files and the revolutionary C programming language came from Dennis Ritchie and Ken Thomson. The Transmission Control Protocol and Internal Protocol that serve as the backbone for information transmission on the Internet were developed in America using the same concept of discrete systems. James Gosling of Sun Microsystems developed JAVA, the de-facto Internet programming language. All these and the many more developments that came together for the Internet to be born in the U.S. were due to enthusiastic American code writers who believed in endless possibilities. Where is the likely source for the next groundbreaking computer technology? Less likely from the United States where interest in computer science is waning, but more likely from countries like India and Russia.

And since the statement in 1899 reportedly attributed to the then Commissioner of U.S. Office of Patents Charles H. Duell, "That everything that can be invented has been invented," has since been proven to be a bit off the mark, there surely is a seminal development in information technology somewhere around the corner. And it is less likely to happen in the United States.

The seeds for the development of the next MITS that will spur a group of smart students to work around the clock to develop world-changing products are being planted and nurtured overseas by some American corporate leaders. By stepping up offshore outsourcing, some leaders of the American computer industry are discouraging American students from entering the industry, while feeding high protein supplements to youths overseas. And the price the United States of America will pay for the actions of some her citizens will be deeply felt in the coming years in loss of jobs, loss of economic growth and loss of hope itself from the land that invented the computer industry, and hope.

The Institute of Electrical and Electronics Engineers (IEEE) polled 988 of its members for their views on the state of their profession. The poll revealed that an astonishing 37 percent said they considered leaving engineering entirely, and a discouraging 41 percent said they would not recommend the profession to their children, evidence of hope disappearing from the United States.

While many U.S. electrical and electronic engineers would not recommend the profession to their children, India and China are turning out 150,000 and 250,000 engineers, respectively, every year.

The reasons for the malaise among the engineers were two-fold. First, 15 percent of those unemployed said their jobs had been transferred overseas. And, second, for the first time since the Great Depression, income of those employed in electrical and electronic manufacturing dropped by 2.5 percent in 2004.

According to IEEE-USA President Gerard Alphonse, "This data supports (sic) our contention that offshoring not only contributes significantly to U.S. high-tech unemployment, but also suppresses wages." Alphonse said the concerns of the IEEE extended beyond job losses and wage suppression to the "innovation infrastructure" of the U.S. "Because innovation tends to follow jobs, key drivers of our economic prosperity could be lost," he concluded.

Projected one or two years, hollowing out of the technological infrastructure of the U.S. may seem implausible. But what about five or ten years from now? What about twenty years from now, if the current trend continues? Not only are jobs being given away, but a further consequence of goods being manufactured by many American corporate leaders in other countries is a trade deficit in excess of $600 billion for as far as the eye can see. Add to that a budget deficit in excess of $400 billion, also for as far as the eye can see. A cumulative deficit of about $1.0 trillion a year, or about $8,500 per family, for the foreseeable future will lead to financial Armageddon.

And it stems first and foremost from the fact that some companies with American names are moving manufacturing and service jobs to foreign lands at a pace that is hard to fathom. There were scowls when the trade deficit hit $617 billion in 2004, but data for the first three months of 2005 show a projected trade deficit of close to $700 billion for the entire year!

According to Business Week and other defenders of globalization, these mammoth trade deficits are defensible because "America's wealth is growing fast enough to cover its debt easily." Really? These were the same sources who predicted before the dotcom implosion that productivity—their magic word—was rising so fast that recessions had been abolished. Also lost in their argument is the indisputable fact that rising wealth is not due to any invention, but rather due to rising real estate prices. Sooner or later, the realization will strike home that the increase in valuations is ephemeral.

A true reality check on the U.S. economy is the fact that "real wages are falling at the fastest rate in 14 years," according to Newsweek. For the first time in statistical history, the U.S. has experienced a dichotomy between productivity, wages and inflation. Between 2001 and 2005, productivity rose by about 4 percent annually, while wage growth averaged only 1.5 percent and inflation averaged 2.5 percent. And offshore outsourcing or jobs being sent overseas is the reason why wages and productivity are moving in opposite directions. Cost of doing business in the U.S. is going down—which means productivity is going up—not just due to use of more efficient technology, but also because U.S. businesses are using cheaper overseas labor for everything from data processing, financial services and software development. At the same time, wages in the U.S. are being suppressed because of the presence of offshore labor.

Traditional economic hypothesis predicts that increase in productivity leads to increase in wages (or disposal income), allowing workers to purchase more goods to create more economic activity or growth. In the recent past, however, productivity growth has been accompanied by falling wages. Since disposable income is what drives purchases of more goods, this decline would have caused the economy to contract but for extra cash provided by home refinancing.

So unless wages rise in concert with increase in productivity, and there is no reason why it should happen now, the U.S. economy will contract when the home refinancing phenomenon slows down. In effect, sending jobs overseas boosts corporate profits but will also be one of the forces that drives the U.S. economy backwards.

History will also recall that productivity increased by an average of more than six percent in the six years preceding the Great Depression, and that increase in valuation—of the Stock Market then—was based on expectations, not on any invention.

One thing must be crystal clear: no blame, none, must be placed on the people of China, India and all the places where U.S. jobs are being transferred, because the people building the replacement factories in China and transferring software development jobs are predominantly Americans. Overseas countries have simply positioned themselves to receive the greatest peacetime transfer of wealth from one country to others the world has ever seen.

Many Americans live with apprehension, not knowing whether the next phone call or meeting would spell an end to their working life. According to Yale Professor Robert Shiller, "Insecurity about jobs is a defining characteristic of our age." Computer programmers, engineers, accountants, architects, customer service representatives, and an untold number of "white collar" professionals are now being shoved aside, just as their "blue collar" counterparts were—and are—being whacked.

It seems the only people in America to who Old Glory stirs patriotism are the people. To some of the corporate elite in America, it's just a piece of cloth with red and white stripes and a bunch of stars in the upper left hand corner. They swear allegiance to a flag with no country. And as their bloodletting covers Old Glory, it drags moms and dads who have worked all their lives to build small to medium companies into a ferocious hand to hand combat of survival with the likes of dragon wrestlers who pay their employees 64 cents an hour. And to avoid being flattened by the 1.3 billion pound gorilla, they do what has hitherto been unthinkable by dismissing families they break bread with to join the exodus. This is the America some multinational corporations have wrought.

Lou Dobbs, the CNN commentator, has seen the light. Though a Republican, he has seen how much damage is being inflicted on his beloved America, and is why he speaks incessantly about "Exporting America," title of the program that preceded his book of the same title. But his is a voice of exception, for there are hardly any more of his kind. Hardly any more, because an alliance of people in the media, academia and government wishes for the American people not to find out that their country is being taken to the cleaners.

The rules of the ballgame have been changed to the benefit of one class of people: some shareholders of multinational corporations. These are the people pocketing the difference in wages—labor cost differential, they call it—between American workers and those in low wage overseas countries.

Under the new rules, the $20 an hour American employee is supposed to compete against the 64 cents an hour Chinese employee, and likewise the $50,000 a year American computer programmer against the $10,000 a year Indian counterpart.

Since the winners in these competitions have already been declared, then something or some things must change to give Americans a fighting chance. For if nothing changes, suburbia could darken in the not too distant future. This is the stark, unvarnished challenge facing America today.

And the new rules are here to stay, for the people for who the new rules were enacted are not about to let go of them. The new rules will only change when overseas workers start making "too much" money. By that time, some manufacturing and educational sectors bequeathed to America by preceding generations of Americans would have been damaged beyond repair. The tool and die profession, the computer science geeks and the engineering icons would have been discouraged into insufficient numbers. And with their economies of scale entrenching their advantage, it would be nearly impossible for America to recoup.

And these new rules are only applied when it suits some of these people. Otherwise, then other rules are enacted. A meeting was held in Cancun, Mexico in 2003. It was supposed to be about extending to agriculture the same globalization principles preached incessantly for manufacturing and information technologies. If ever a terrain is made for globalization in agriculture, it is the hot humid lands of most of the developing countries in Africa, Asia and South America, where planting three crops a year on the same land is not unheard of. A hundred Floridas for lovers of mangoes, pineapples, oranges, bananas, guavas and sugarcanes to marvel at seemed to be a fair bargain for those unable to compete against industrial China under the new dispensation.

But the meeting broke up when the people from the developing world would not apparently agree to some fake new definitions and interpretations. But not many were fooled, for The Los Angeles Times tore into the hypocrites with a vengeance. The reason the meeting was unsuccessful was because some of the people benefiting from offshore outsourcing were the same ones receiving subsidized booty in agriculture from their governments in the U.S., England and Ireland, where sugar is still being produced today on those "fertile" lands.

Shove aside the agricultural workers in the developing world. Trample the computer programmers, accountants, engineers and data processing techies in the United States. And will shareholders of these multinational corporations involved in sending jobs overseas pay wages of those flocking to the medical profession in America when revenue-generating sectors of the economy are squeezed into starvation?

Is this the generation that loses a different kind of battle on American soil?

"On the other hand, the magnitude and difficulty of the trust to which the voice of my country called me, being sufficient to awaken in the wisest and most experienced of her citizens as a distrustful scrutiny into his qualifications, could not but overwhelm with despondence one who (inheriting inferior endowments from nature and unpracticed in the duties of civil administration) ought to be peculiarly conscious of his own deficiencies." The country George Washington fought to create, and gave it the first inaugural address on April 30, 1789, is under a different kind of attack, with nobody to lead her defense.

Is this the generation that extinguishes the dream?

"Let us not wallow in the valley of despair. I say to you today, my friends, that even though we face the difficulties of today and tomorrow. I still have a dream. It is a dream deeply rooted in the American dream. I have a dream that one day every valley shall be exalted, and every hill and every mountain shall be made low, the rough places will be made plains and the crooked places will be made straight and the glory of the Lord shall be revealed and all flesh shall see it together." The dream Martin Luther King spoke about on August 28, 1963 is being smothered, with nobody to keep it aflame.

Is this the generation that lets America decline?

"Fourscore and seven years ago our Fathers brought forth on this continent, a new nation, conceived in Liberty, and dedicated to the proposition that all men are created equal. Now we are engaged in a great civil war, testing whether that nation or any nation so conceived and so dedicated, can long endure…It is for us the living, rather, to be dedicated here to the unfinished work which they who fought here have thus far so nobly advanced. It is rather for us to be here dedicated to the great task remaining before us—that from these honored dead we take increased devotion to that cause for which they gave the last full measure of devotion—that we here highly resolve that these dead shall not have died in vain—that this nation, under God, shall have a new birth of freedom—and that government of the people, by the people, for the people, shall not perish from earth." Abraham Lincoln, Gettysburg address, November 19, 1863.

2

INDUSTRIALIZATION

In the minds of many, the city of Pittsburgh evokes nauseating images of pungent, acrid fumes spewing from smokestacks stretching far into the horizon. Even some who have never stepped foot in the city are convinced the description of the city's atmosphere as "hell with the lid off" by a renowned journalist is still apt.

But while elements of these images still linger, the overall reality of today's Pittsburgh could not be more different. The city of Pittsburgh has "metromorphosized," a term coined by the city's elders, into a shining light at the confluence of three mighty rivers. And to signify the transformation, it justifiably calls itself the Renaissance City.

The Delaware, Iroquois and the Shawnee were among the many Native Americans who first settled at the confluence of the Monongahela, the Allegheny and the Ohio rivers. The area provided fish, game and coal in abundance. Ease of transportation along the water routes facilitated trading with the other tribes in the area. It was prime real estate then, and it remains so today.

The French were the first Europeans to settle in the area after an expedition in 1749. Four years later, Governor Dinwiddie of Virginia sent a brash soldier named Major George Washington to investigate French activities in the area. The brilliant strategist that he was, the future president immediately recognized the importance of the converging rivers. He wrote a report urging the British to build a fort at the Point, declaring the site "extremely well situated for a fort, having command of both rivers."

In early 1754, the British acted upon his recommendation and began building a fort, but the French would have none of it. In April 1754, an alliance of French and Native troops took control of the fort without bloodshed, completed its construction and named it Fort Duquesne in honor of the French colonial governor. The settlement grew to 60 residents within a year under the umbrella of relative peace. But the peace was shattered when war broke out between the French and

Indians. The British took the Point as the price for brokering peace among the warring factions.

Supplanting the French as the new landlord in November 1758, the British built a state-of-the-art fort and named it Fort Pitt in honor of William Pitt, the Prime Minister of England. Chief Pontiac and the confederacy of Indian tribes besieged Fort Pitt in June 1763, but the siege was broken in August of that year when the Indians were defeated in the battle of Bushy Run.

A small village known as Pittsborough soon sprouted up around Fort Pitt, with the name changed later to Pittsburgh. From that small settlement of 18 acres, part of which is preserved today as Bouquet's Blockhouse, came a remarkable city unparalleled anywhere in the world for its ingenuity and resiliency. The Point was settled and formally named by the British, but its growth was fuelled by coal, at the time the most valuable commodity in the New World.

Coal is a fossil fuel formed from the remains of vegetation that grew millions of years ago. It is often referred to as "buried sunshine," because the plants that formed coal captured energy from the sun through photosynthesis to create tissues composed mostly of carbon. Most of the energy in coal is derived from carbon.

The coal in the greater Pittsburgh area was formed about 300 million years ago, when steamy swamps covered much of the earth. As plants and trees died, their remains sank to the bottom of the swampy areas, accumulating layer upon layer and eventually forming a soggy, dense material called peat.

Over long periods of time, the makeup of the earth's surface changed, and seas and great rivers caused deposits of sand, clay and other mineral matter to accumulate, burying the peat. Sandstone and other sedimentary rocks were formed, and the pressure caused by their weight squeezed water from the peat. Increasing depths and associated heat converted the material gradually to coal.

Coal is classified into four general categories, or "ranks." They range from lignite through subbituminous and bituminous to anthracite, reflecting the progressive response of individual deposits of coal to increasing heat and pressure. Anthracite coal, with the highest carbon content of between 86 and 98 percent, ranks highest in energy content. It is most frequently associated with home heating. Bituminous coal, the most plentiful form of coal in the United States, has a carbon content ranging from 45 to 86 percent. It ranks second to anthracite coal in energy content, and finds its most prolific use as a source of energy for industrial plants.

Geologic history in Pennsylvania resulted in nearly flat layers of bituminous coal deposits in the Pittsburgh area. In between the veins of coal are layers of sandstone, shale and limestone. Most of the 10 billion tons of bituminous coal produced in Pennsylvania—nearly one fourth of all coal mined in the United States—have been mined in the greater Pittsburgh area.

Coal was one of man's earliest sources of heat and light. The Chinese mined it more than 3,000 years ago. The first recorded discovery of coal in the United States was by French explorers on the Illinois River in 1679, and the earliest commercial mining occurred near Richmond, Virginia in 1750. Coal mining in Pittsburgh dates back to 1762 when the first British settlers discovered a coal seam from the southern hillside, or "Coal Hill" as it was known then. (It is known today as Mount Washington).

Like the Indians, the first settlers used coal as a cheap energy source for home heating. But the power of coal soon fuelled applications in heating forges, iron and steel manufacturing, steam engine manufacturing, shipbuilding, glass furnaces, and many other industrial activities. The industries spawned by the relatively inexpensive and abundant coal and access to distant markets accorded by the three rivers made Pittsburgh a parent to the Industrial Revolution in America.

The city also came to be known as the "Gateway to the West" for the number of people who passed through Monongahela Wharf and down the Ohio River to Cincinnati, St. Louis and as far away as New Orleans. Between 1800 and 1816 the population expanded rapidly from 1,500 to over 10,000 residents.

"Bring me your tired, your poor, your huddled masses yearning to breathe free" is inscribed on the Statute of Liberty. To this should be added, "Bring me your talented looking to enrich the land." For it was one such talented immigrant from Germany, George Anschutz, whose construction of a blast furnace in Pittsburgh in 1792 paved the way to the maturation of the nascent, coal powered iron and steel industry. The first iron produced west of the Alleghenies came from the Alliance Furnace on Jacob's Creek. The "Iron City", later changed to "Steel City", had been born.

Many more enterprising souls flocked to Pittsburgh, all attracted by the abundance of coal and other natural resources. The cumulative force of the talent led to many innovations, including the first wire rope and the first cable suspension bridge in 1841 and 1847, respectively, by local engineer, John A. Roebling.

Stoked by the labor of immigrants from Great Britain, Ireland and Germany, these innovations spurred the creation of many enterprises. It was said that many of the immigrants were dispatched from boats straight to coal mines, iron foundries, glass manufacturing plants and other places of employment, for such was the urgency to fill the burgeoning employment opportunities created by the genesis of industrialization in Pittsburgh.

In 1811 the first steamboat to ply the Mississippi River system was built in Pittsburgh, and the New Orleans steamed down the Ohio and Mississippi rivers to its namesake city in Louisiana. Pittsburgh was incorporated on March 18, 1816, followed by expansion of the Pennsylvania Mainline Canal to the city in 1837 and the Pennsylvania Railroad in 1851.

With rampant growth of commercial activity within its boundaries, not even the great fire of April 10, 1845, which destroyed 1,000 buildings in a fifty-six acre area within the heart of the city, could interrupt the population from doubling to over 46,000 between 1840 and 1850. Then the American Civil War struck in 1861, and Pittsburgh broke loose.

Abraham Lincoln was the president who refused to accede to the separatist demands of Confederate leaders. He was the one who issued the General War Order Number 1 on January 31, 1862 calling for all United States naval and land forces to begin a general advance by February 22, George Washington's birthday. General Ulysses S. Grant was the commander who led Union forces to victory. But none of these men would have been able to break the back of Confederate forces without the dynamic city of Pittsburgh.

The Allegheny Arsenal, the Fort Pitt Foundry and the shipyards of Pittsburgh supplied the Union Army with armaments, ships and armor plating during the Civil War. This feat caused another label, "Arsenal of the Union," to be slapped on the proud city. But this was by no means a charitable act: the war gave a tremendous boost to the city's economy, with increased production of coal, iron and other materials.

By the end of the war, over half of all the steel available in the U.S. was produced in Pittsburgh, economic dynamism that caused the city's population to surpass 86,000 by 1870 and 156,000 ten years later. The strategic location of Pittsburgh at the confluence of three major rivers was amazingly opportune. It provided cheap access for the many goods produced in the city through the Great Lakes, St. Lawrence, Ohio and Mississippi rivers to every part of the continent east of the Rockies. The Delaware River also boosted trade with Europe by serving as a water highway for ships coming from and going to the Atlantic Ocean.

The petroleum industry in the U.S. also witnessed its birth in Pittsburgh, with the drilling of the first well on August 27, 1859 by Edwin L. Drake in Titusville, northeast of Pittsburgh. Oil production from this field peaked between 1860 and 1870. Edwin L. Drake was the JR Ewing of his time.

Because of the abundance of cheap coal, almost every intermediary or finished product in the New World requiring massive amounts of energy to manufacture had its origins in the Pittsburgh area. So not only steel was being manufactured in prodigious quantities but also aluminum (Aluminum Company of America, now Alcoa), glass (Pittsburgh Plate and Glass, now PPG), electrical generators and appliances (Westinghouse Electric), coke-making machinery (Koppers), railroad cars and locomotives (Pressed Steel Car and Pittsburgh Locomotive) and coke and coal chemicals (H.C. Frick & Company and Pittsburgh Coal Company). For example, a third of all glass available in the U.S. in 1865 was being manufactured in Pittsburgh.

But it was steel that was dominant in the city of Pittsburgh, and it was defined by Andrew Carnegie, the man who symbolized the roaring success of Pittsburgh in the latter part of the 19th century.

Andrew Carnegie was born on November 25, 1835 in Dunfermline, Scotland, into wrenching poverty. His mother borrowed the twenty pounds needed to pay the fare for the Atlantic passage and in 1848 the Carnegies landed in Pittsburgh. He immediately began work as a bobbin boy in a cotton mill in Allegheny for $1.20 a week. Weaving was his father's profession, so it was logical he would begin his working life there.

The sheer joy of the opportunity to earn a wage to help support his family spurred him to later proclaim, "I have made millions since, but none of these gave me as much happiness as my first week's earnings. I was not a helper of the family, (but) a bread winner." He transferred shortly thereafter to another bobbin factory, the John Jay, a company with relatively more amenable working hours.

He learned fundamentals of accounting and bookkeeping at John Jay, skills that were to assist him later in life as he built his business empire. He left the bobbin industry over time for O'Reilly Telegraph Company where he was charged with the responsibility of delivering messages all across the growing city.

A keen observer, Carnegie studied "the commercial affairs of several prominent businessmen" later to become his partners. The experience he acquired in telegraphy led to a job with Pennsylvania Railroad under the tutelage of railroad official Thomas Alexander Scott.

Carnegie became the official breadwinner of the family at the tender age of twenty when his father died in 1855. The heavy burden he carried motivated him to work even harder, leading to his promotion to the prestigious position of superintendent of the Pittsburgh division of the railroad within a relatively short period of time.

Investing wisely Carnegie was worth $400,000 ($6 million in today's dollars) with an annual income of $50,000 by the age of 33. The poor boy from Dunfermline, barred from Pittencrieff, a park in his native town, because of his family's poverty, was on his way. He would later endow the park and throw its gates open to the toiling masses.

In what became the foundation for his fortune, Carnegie purchased an interest in Pullman Palace Car Company. His keen instinct in spotting lucrative opportunities led to an investment in Keystone Bridge Company, convinced, presciently, that steel would replace wood in bridge building due to the increasing weight of steel cars. Further investments in oil lands near Oil City, PA multiplied his fortune.

He served in the War Department during the American Civil War under his boss Scott, who was in charge of military transportation and government telegraphy. The U.S. would decorate these two men for their contributions during the War.

With the successful prosecution of the war, his Rolodex bulging with key government decision makers and business luminaries, he left the service of the railroad and proceeded to build his first steel mill in 1873, the Edgar Thomson Works, on the site of historic Braddock's field. His Carnegie Brothers Company acquired the Homestead Company in 1883. In 1888 his company netted a profit of $2 million, followed by $5.4 million in 1890. As a result of the profitability of his company, he bought the Allegheny Business Steel Company and merged it with Carnegie Brothers to create Carnegie Steel.

Intolerant of competition, Carnegie attempted to purchase Duquesne Steel Company. He weakened their position by spreading a vicious rumor when they balked. He then swooped in as the white knight and took over the company with an offer of $1 million in bonds.

Andrew Carnegie revolutionized manufacturing by pioneering the integrated steel mill. He increased his edge over his competitors in the 1870s by building a steel mill with all the material and equipment needed to produce steel from ore under one roof. His lead was lengthened further when his mills became the first in the U.S. to import from England the more efficient Bessemer process for making steel.

Carnegie rapidly gobbled up his weakened competitors to the point where his Carnegie Steel controlled 25 percent of all the steel produced in the U.S. in 1899. Then, in 1901, he sold it all off to the financier J.P. Morgan for $250 million and retired with the informal title of the wealthiest man in the world. J.P. Morgan renamed the company United States Steel Corporation (now US Steel).

A little known fact about Andrew Carnegie is that he was the first industrialist in the world to pay standard wages to men of African heritage, opening opportunities for viable employment. Contradictory to the end, he championed equal wages for all but collective bargaining rights for none with equal force.

In retirement Carnegie accelerated his extraordinary philanthropic activities by donating most of his time and money to educational and cultural projects. To open doors for others that were firmly slapped in his face as a boy, the man with no formal education founded Carnegie Technical Schools—now Carnegie Mellon University—in Pittsburgh, became a benefactor of Tuskegee Institute (now Tuskegee University), the legendary college of higher education for Americans of African decent founded by Dr. Booker T. Washington, and endowed over 2,800 libraries throughout the world. For the arts, he founded Carnegie Hall in New York City and the Carnegie Museums of Natural History and Art in Pittsburgh. But, instructively, Carnegie's first public gift was for simple baths in his native Dunfermline. Seared by the poverty of his youth, he never stopped trying to provide for others that which he never had.

Andrew Carnegie was the headline businessman in Pittsburgh in the late 1800s, but he was hardly the only well known entrepreneur. The terrain included many other famous industrialists and financiers. George Westinghouse, credited with development of air brake for trains and alternating current for light and power, founded over 60 companies in Pittsburgh, including Westinghouse Air Brake and Company, Union Switch and Signal, and Westinghouse Electric Company. Henry Clay Frick, who was later to join forces with Andrew Carnegie, manufactured coke, a key ingredient for steel manufacturing, at H.C. Frick and Company. In 1888, Charles Martin Hall and Alfred E. Hunt founded Pittsburgh Reduction Company (now Aluminum Company of America, ALCOA) to manufacture a new metal called aluminum. But someone had to provide nutrition and succor to toiling entrepreneurs and workers alike. And that role fell to Henry John Heinz.

Henry John Heinz was born in 1844 at Birmingham, PA to parents who emigrated from England. With a keen eye for entrepreneurship, young Henry—nicknamed Harry—bottled his own horseradish at the tender age of 15 in clear glass to display its purity. Commercial preservation was in its infancy, and competitors disguised wood fiber, turnip and leaves used for extension by packaging horseradish in opaque glass jars. Harry trumped his competitors by showing his customers he had nothing to hide, which led to official founding of his business in partnership with L.C. Noble in 1869. His founding philosophy of "heart power is better than horsepower" was perhaps not that different from the sixties hippie slogan of "make love not war."

Botulism in processed food was a common problem in America at the dawn of the 20th century. So Heinz secured the loyalty of his customers by stressing safety, quality, clarity and standards at every turn, characteristics crystallized by the use of the phrase "pure foods" to brand all Heinz products. But first, there was a failure to overcome.

The infant Heinz and Noble Company was overextended when credit collapsed with the banking crisis of 1875. Forced into bankruptcy but undeterred, he quickly picked himself up and launched F&J Heinz Company with his brother John and cousin Frederick a year later. With the strong belief that "kindly care and fair treatment" was the right and moral way to treat employees, Harry motivated his employees by showering them with lunchtime concerts, weekly manicures for all food handlers and rooftop gardens. He was also among the first businessmen of his time to provide free healthcare for his employees.

Then innovating constantly from tomato ketchup to red and green pepper sauce, followed by cider vinegar and apple butter, chili sauce, mincemeat mustard, tomato soup, olives, pickled onions, pickled cauliflower, baked beans and the first sweet pickles ever brought to market, the renamed H.J. Heinz Company grew to become America's favorite grocer.

The Company opened its first overseas office in 1896 near the Tower of London, joined in 1905 by a factory in Peckham. Several plants later, most food shoppers thought of Heinz as a British company. That philosophy of serving the taste buds of the local populace still persists as Heinz launches a major drive into China.

Concurrent with his safety-first philosophy, H.J. Heinz championed federal regulation of the production and labeling of processed foods, culminating in the passage of the Pure Food and Drug Act by Congress in 1906. It was one of his proudest achievements.

H.J. Heinz bequeathed his mother's admonition to "not live for yourself" to future generations of the family. His son Howard Heinz set up Sarah Heinz House, named after his mother, as a settlement for boys. But since 1915, this Pittsburgh landmark, together with a second, has expanded into a center offering after school activities to thousands of boys and girls between the ages of seven to eighteen.

And the company H.J. Heinz founded with the philosophy that good comes to those who do good for others—give and he shall receive—has grown into a thriving global colossus with hundreds of products in over fifty countries. HJ

Heinz Company still personifies that which the America of old stood for: Yes to profit, yes to sharing. It is hard to conceive that the man who gave his heart to his second family—his workers—would have thrown his workers on the cold fields of unemployment in pursuit of extra profit, which is why the company he founded still stands tall where many have perished. But that was another man from another era.

All the industrialists of Carnegie's era sought massive loans to build or upgrade their dream plants. And the lender of first or last resort in most cases was the bank founded in Pittsburgh in 1869 by Thomas Mellon. But Mellon was not merely a financier, but an investor as well in many of the budding enterprises mushrooming in Pittsburgh. These investments were parlayed by later generations of Mellons into dominance of Gulf Oil, ALCOA, Koppers and Pittsburgh Consolidated Coal, four of the largest companies in Pittsburgh.

The foundation built by Andrew Carnegie and others enabled Pittsburgh to leapfrog other cities to become a major educational center. The Carnegie Institute of Technology (1900), Pittsburgh Academy (1787, now University of Pittsburgh) and Duquesne University (1878) have all grown into leadership positions in the U.S. in fundamental teaching and cutting edge research. The Mellon Research Institute, at one time the largest private industrial research laboratory in the United States, is now part of Carnegie Mellon University. These strong educational institutions endowed by Carnegie and other philanthropists set in motion forces that would allow Pittsburgh decades later to transform successfully from steel to other technologies.

The successes of magnates like Andrew Carnegie and the immense opportunities spawned in the cities they helped construct boomed across the Old World. For example, the newspaper The Scotsman, described as the infant with lusty journalistic lungs when it was founded in January 1815 in Edinburgh, had a reporter permanently stationed in Pittsburgh to transmit the exploits of their famous son back home. Inspired by these stories, many in the Old World, starving and suffocating under the tyrannical rule of royalty, moved heavens to escape to the New World.

And they came from everywhere. The 1847 Potato Famine in Ireland that killed a million also caused a great exodus into the new land of opportunity. Then on January 1, 1892, the Gateway to America opened its door at Ellis Island, and the rush turned into a torrent. Coming in steam-powered ships resembling floating villages, jammed with metal-framed berths three bunks high, and in an atmosphere saturated with unwashed bodily odor, smoke and flatulence, they first saw the light, then the magnificent lady, then the famous gate. Traveling conditions were atrocious; sometimes food was served where one sat, toilet facilities were restricted, everything was piled up together in cramped quarters. And still thousands arrived everyday.

They were first inspected for disease or disability as they made their way up the steep stairs to the Registry Room, bubbling with noise. Then an officer in charge wrote down names as best he could, and if your hometown—example, Corleone—became your name, so be it, you were in America. Not even the fire of June 14, 1897 that destroyed the building could keep it shuttered forever, for it reopened on December 17, 1900.

Between 1892 and 1924, close to twelve million went through the door of opportunity. Italians, Russians, Hungarians, Austrians, Germans, Irish and English came from all over, bounded by one creed, "All for one and one for all." For this was the only creed that could bind so many from disparate backgrounds to work together for the common good. Isaac Asimov, Irving Berlin, Samuel Goldwyn and Bob Hope all went through the door of opportunity at one time or another to the betterment of mankind. Today, over 100 million Americans trace their lineage in the United States to a man, woman, or child whose name was recorded in the great Registry Room at Ellis Island.

So by the turn of the century in 1901, the face of immigration to the Pittsburgh area had changed. The nationalities of those arriving shifted to Italians, Russian Jews, Serbs, Hungarians, Poles, and Croatians. They settled in neighborhood clusters that persist today: Bloomfield (Italian), South Side and Polish Hill (Polish), and Squirrel Hill (Jewish). The population of Pittsburgh quadrupled between 1870 and 1920 to over 588,500, the majority comprised of immigrants and their children.

The consequences of uncontrolled growth were, unfortunately, horrific for Pittsburgh. Industrial waste fouled many neighborhoods, including Barefoot Square or Slab town where Carnegie used to live. Newly constructed buildings were so blackened by soot they were indistinguishable from older ones. According to Carnegie, "The smoke permeated and penetrated everything...If you washed your face and hands they were as dirty as ever in an hour. The soot gathered in the hair and irritated the skin, and for a time...life was more or less miserable."

The frenetic pace of industrial activity also exacted a steep human toll. Suffocating overcrowding exacerbated cholera epidemics of the 1830s. Ammunition exploded at the Allegheny Arsenal in 1862, killing 74, most of them young women. Harrowing disasters in the coalmines in the Pittsburgh area claimed hundreds of lives. Work and more continuous work was the order of the day, with many workers toiling 12-hour days, including Sundays, in steaming factories without any ventilation. Those who could not withstand the brutal, inhumane working conditions were summarily dismissed.

A British economist described the conditions: "Grime and squalor unspeakable, unlimited hours of work, ferocious contests between labor and capital, the fiercest commercial scrambling for money literally sweated out of the people, the utter absorption by high and low of every faculty in getting and grabbing, total indifference to all other ideals and aspirations."

The unspeakable working conditions in factories in the Pittsburgh area led to the formation of the Amalgamated Association of Iron and Steel Workers. But the desire of the union for better wages and safer working conditions was greeted with fierce resistance from business owners.

Carnegie and his partner Frick broke work stoppage in 1892, the Homestead Strike, when they unleashed hundreds of hired Pinkerton Agency detectives and the Pennsylvania State Militia on the workers. The fighting that ensued resulted in ten deaths and many more injuries. The defeat of the workers halted the formation of unions in Pittsburgh, but the distrust created between management and labor would linger long enough to play a debilitating role in the effort to resuscitate the steel industry many years down the road.

Environmental degradation in Pittsburgh continued unabated with another writer describing the city as, "A smoky, dismal city, at her best. At her worst, nothing darker, dinkier or more dispiriting can be imagined. The smoke from her dwellings, stores and factories, foundries and steamboats, uniting settles in a cloud over the narrow valley in which she is built, until the very sun looks copery through the sooty haze."

The writer was describing temperature inversion, the phenomenon that at its apogee claimed the lives of twenty people and sickened 7,000. This catastrophe, which came to be known as Donora Smog, still burns through the historical fabric of the people of Pittsburgh. A national magazine described conditions in the city as "hellish, tormenting, disease-abetting and spirit-wilting." The magazine claimed, "the very name granulate (sic) in your mouth and nostrils sting from the memory of the somehow acid quality in its air."

Pollution was so atrocious that a pall of heavy smoke required streetlights to be turned on at midday to improve visibility. In a movie of that era Groucho Marx, whether he intended to or not, pleased anti-cigar smoking and anti-pollution advocates alike when he cast a wicked eye at the rings of smoke coming from his cigar and observed, "This is like living in Pittsburgh—if you can call that living." Then in the ultimate putdown of the time, the renowned architect Frank Lloyd Wright when asked about the renewal of Pittsburgh commented, "It'd be cheaper to abandon it!"

The path to industrialization in Pittsburgh, which caused the city's immigrant population to mushroom from 1850 to 1950, was constructed primarily by the steel industry that Andrew Carnegie built. But this was not a journey unique to Pittsburgh. Starting with the city of Chicago on Lake Michigan and traveling southward to St. Louis via the combination of Illinois and Mississippi Rivers, then turning eastward along the Ohio River past the cities of Evansville, Louisville, Cincinnati, Huntington, and on to Pittsburgh, then turning north to the city of Detroit on Lake Erie, and finally turning westward back to Chicago, is the great American basin of industrialization, which later earned the derogatory epithet "Rust Belt." Detroit, Columbus, Cleveland, Gary, Indianapolis, Louisville, St. Louis, names of invention and ingenuity, were all built, just like Pittsburgh, on the backs of heavy metal or a derivative.

New and older immigrants alike streamed without end into steel mills, coal mines, automobile plants and workplaces of different stripes to give a piece of themselves to America and to receive a piece in return. More moved out of the basin of industrialization to points east and west to build their own monuments. The Hoover Dam, built to harness the potentially destructive power of the Columbia River into productive use; New York, a vibrant, resilient city, with skyscrapers that blind the eye, and an irrepressible never-say-die attitude; the magnificent Golden Gate Bridge, in its imperial color, straddling the entrance to San Francisco Bay.

And they brought forth their children; all rosy cheeked and called them Americans first and foremost. All through the Civil War and the Civil Rights strives, one thing was clear: they were all Americans and they took care, in their own way, of each other. They continued to build on the foundations laid by preceding generations block-by-block, city-by-city and state-by-state. No sacrifice was too much, no sweat too bitter and, certainly, no blood too precious: they gave everything. And they were proud. When Karl Marx and Friedrich Engels were barking about the workers having nothing to lose in "The Communist Manifesto," they vowed to teach them that capitalism and fairness could be used in the same sentence. When Vladimir Lenin and Mao Zedong rose up to confront America, they vowed to spare no resource to counter their threats. And the success they achieved was evident in the kids at Tianemen Square, who built replicas of the

Statue of Liberty and carried American flags during their eventually futile protests.

And the successes wrought by these hardened men and women gave birth to a quintessential American hero in Tampico, IL on February 6, 1911. Tough but generous, Ronald Wilson Reagan, whose mane will someday be chiseled into Mount Rushmore, bore the same motto as each of these immigrants: "All for America and Americans."

And through it all, the land the immigrants made their new home grew and grew and became the envy of the world. The official language was that of the deposed colonial master, but no two nations could be more different. One suffocated in the formality of royalty, the other bounded on the freedom of the prairies. Even those who shared direct ancestry with the colonials had no use for them, for the colonial country never gave them so much freedom or so much opportunity.

Not that it was perfect. Sometimes opportunity was dimmed for some of her peoples, like during the slave trade, when a people were brutally yanked from the land of their birth, shackled, whipped, and trudged across the sea in the most inhumane of conditions. When the slaves finally arrived they were bought and sold, just like cattle, and made to plough the land, with nothing to show for their efforts. But even then, there were others of the same origins as the slave masters who vehemently opposed the despicable practice. These men, together with the slaves, fought ceaselessly until finally the great emancipator freed the slaves.

They had been freed physically to do as they chose, but they were not full citizens yet. Denied voting rights in some areas, restricted in where they could sit on buses, banned from using the same washrooms as others, penned in like chickens where they could live, and abused on the slightest of infractions, they were considered second class citizens to be tolerated but with disdain just for the color of their black skin.

Summoning every fiber in his body, a young preacher determined he was not going to tolerate the abuses any more. Together with others, steeled by the defiance of Rosa Parks, he fought attacking dogs, arrests, intimidation, threats, until the gate of oppression broke down. In the end both the emancipator and the civil rights leader paid the ultimate price for their heroics. But nowhere else but in America would they make the birthday of Martin Luther King a national holiday. Nowhere. Abraham Lincoln and Martin Luther King, heroes of heroes, we salute you both in the same sentence.

Then there was the time during World War II, when Americans of Japanese decent were culled and incarcerated in barren conditions just because of their ancestry. Somehow, they had seized to be bearers of the light: they had returned to the land of their origins, untrustworthy and disloyal, but the same treatment was not meted out to Germans or Italians, who were also fighting against America.

But no matter what, there were always clear differences. Even if the majority acquiesced with oppression, there was always a strong minority element unafraid to confront injustice, which was why the civil rights movement had a solid white contingent. In sharp contrast to America, Nazi Germany was chilled into silence, with not a voice heard in protest at the massacre of the Jewish people. Even today, there are some who have the gull to dispute the gassing of human beings.

Scots, Irish, Poles, Croats, Blacks, Jews, Russians, Hungarians, Arabs, Italians, Greeks and Portuguese flocked in from all corners of the globe between 1850 to 1950 to claim their piece of the American dream and give a piece of themselves in return. And every one of the cities was bestowed a gift or two or three or four like Andrew Carnegie, people whose vision and indomitable spirit led to sustenance for their fellow citizens. In Detroit that gift was Henry Ford.

Ford was born on a farm near Dearborn, Michigan on July 30, 1863. At the age of 16 he left his father's farm to work as an apprentice in a Detroit machine shop. He returned home to experiment on power-driven vehicles before going back to Detroit to work as a machinist and engineer with the Edison Company. But he continued to work on his design in his spare time. In 1896 he completed his first automobile, the Quadricycle, and resigned from Detroit Edison to launch the Detroit Automobile Company, later changed to Ford Motor Company, in partnership with James Couzens, the Dodge brothers and others.

Ford introduced assembly-line strategies like interchangeable parts on a large scale for the first time in 1913. However, the monotony of mass production and high production quota resulted in labor turnover of 40—60 percent by 1914. He doubled wages from $2.5 to $5 for an 8-hr day to compensate, and instituted a profit-sharing plan that would distribute up to $30 million annually. This exercise in self-preservation—give and he shall receive in turn—was lost on his business colleagues of the time, who accused him of making life difficult for them. Undeterred, Ford saw profits at his company jump from $30 million in 1914 to $60 million in 1916.

Innovating continuously just like Andrew Carnegie, Ford introduced the Model T. in 1908. The company sold about 15 million Model T's before a more up-to-date model replaced it in 1927. Henry Ford died on April 7, 1947, leaving behind a fortune of $500 to $700 million. Like Andrew Carnegie most of his fortune went to charity, in his case to the Ford Foundation, a nonprofit organization.

Though notoriously anti-union, Ford, like Andrew Carnegie, employed men and women of all colors, which is how Motown came to be so attractive to blacks fleeing the South.

Henry Ford, Andrew Carnegie and men like them built and nurtured the great American middle class: they could be tough and uncompromising but they were for the most part fair. They were also visionaries who invested heavily in productivity enhancement.

But above all, men like Andrew Carnegie and Henry Ford were first and foremost Americans. Remembering his circumstances in his native Scotland, Andrew Carnegie said many a time that it gave him shivers just thinking about America, and that is why he did everything he could to assist his fellow Americans. They built factories in other lands, but their companies bore the stamp of their roots: they were American companies first, and they wore the label proudly. Henry Ford when asked why he was paying his workers so much famously replied, "So they can afford to buy my cars," a classic example of the saying that common sense is rather uncommon.

The memories of the land they had eschewed for America were seared through their brains. Though not from Ireland, Andrew Carnegie was close enough to suffer from the hunger that spread through the region during the potato famine in Ireland in 1847. He remembered vividly that a million Irish perished not for lack of food, but for lack of affordable food. And he would never forget that he was beneficiary of the doors of welcome opened to many like him by America. And because of the flaming memories of injustice inflicted by one person on another, Andrew Carnegie, tough to the end because he would not brook any interference to how he run his companies, would never deprive a hardworking American employee the means to sustain his family. He always found a way. But that was another generation of Americans who believed in the creed "One for all and all for one" for the benefit of America.

In Lynn, Massachusetts, sustenance arrived in 1876 in the form of an abjectly poor young black man from Dutch Guiana who barely spoke a word of English.

His name was Jan Ernst Mazeliger. Before he arrived on the scene, hundreds of inventors had failed to manufacture a complete shoe by machinery. Though there were machines that could cut, sew and tack shoes, none could *last*, and the process of stitching the upper leather to the sole was performed manually. Machines crumbled in the snow, futility scrawled over their rusting exteriors for their failure to master the art of making the basic shoe in one step.

The aristocrats of the shoe manufacturing industry, stuffy and pompous, could only manage about fifty pairs a day. Young Matzeliger, all 24 years of him, decided this was the perfect problem to solve, though he had no means, except the mechanical knowledge in his brain. So he started experimenting in secret, first with a crude wooden machine, then with a model made out of scrap iron. He toiled diligently through the winters and summers, with only derision ringing in his years.

Finally, he forwarded an application for a patent to Washington when he felt his invention was done. The reviewers sent an officer to Lynn to see the model when none could comprehend the mangled drawings and concoctions received. Jan E. Matzeliger was awarded patent number 274,207 on March 20, 1883 when the reviewer convinced himself of the efficacy of the machine made with cigar boxes, wood and wire.

Matzeliger's **Lasting Machine** turned out 200 to 600 shoes daily, compared with the best manual daily rate of 50. Unfortunately, having made Lynn the shoe capital of the world, and creating employment for thousands, the inspiration Matzeliger drew from the door of opportunity had caused him to overwork in the cold and dampness of the town. The resulting bout of tuberculosis killed him on August 24, 1887. But in between the day of his invention and the day of his death, he was nourished by the fact none ever called him by the derogatory terminology used for blacks.

In the South, help arrived in the form of George Washington Carver, a former slave. Carver was born in 1864 near Diamond Grove, Missouri. The infant George and his mother were kidnapped by a band of slave raiders. His mother was sold and shipped away but his master, Moses Carver, ransomed him in exchange for a racehorse. The fortunes of the American South were to change with that simple exchange.

He managed to educate himself under difficult conditions, including working as a janitor at Iowa Agricultural College (now Iowa State University), where he received a degree in agricultural science in 1894. He received a master's degree in

1897 in bacterial botany and agriculture from the same school and became the first African American to serve on its faculty.

In 1897 he transferred to the faculty of Tuskegee Normal and Industrial Institute for Negroes founded by Booker T. Washington, the renowned educator.

It was at Tuskegee that George Carver came into his own. Depletion of soil in the south caused by decades of growing just cotton and tobacco was compounded by unavailability of slave labor to till the land. The economy of the whole south, heavily dependent on agriculture, was on the verge of collapse. That is when salvation arrived from George Carver.

Carver had developed his crop rotation method, and he educated southern farmers to alternate cotton and tobacco with soil-enriching crops such as peanuts, peas, soybeans, sweet potato, and pecans. By 1938, pecan introduced by Carver had become a $200 million industry and a major product in Alabama. He demonstrated that 300 products could be derived from the peanut, including one of the most popular foods in America today—the peanut butter. Carver also developed 100 different products from the sweet potato.

During World War I, Carver also found a way to replace textile dyes imported from Europe. He produced 500 different shades of dye and was responsible for inventing a process for producing paints and stains from soybeans.

He received only three patents—US patents 1,522,176, 1,541,478 and 1,632,365—for his paint and dye inventions, but profited from little else. "God gave them to me," he would say of his ideas and inventions, "How can I sell them to someone else?"

For restoring southern agriculture, George Washington Carver was awarded the Roosevelt medal in 1939. For his selfness devotion to not just Americans but all of mankind, President Franklin Delano Roosevelt honored Carver with a national monument on July 14, 1943 at Diamond Grove, Missouri. It was the first national monument to be dedicated to an African American.

Other renowned African American inventors of that famous era included Norbert Rillieux (purer sugar), Elijah ("Real McCoy") McCoy (machine lubrication), Lewis Howard Latimer (carbon filament), Granville T. Woods (steam boiler furnace), Sarah Walker (hair-care products), Garret Morgan (traffic signal and gas mask) and Frederick McKinley Jones (truck refrigeration).

But then the Great Depression arrived and it threatened to not only extinguish the accomplishments of America's heroes, it jeopardized the dream itself.

There was a huge disparity in income; the rich were fabulously wealthy, while ordinary people were spending more than they earned. Between 1923 and 1929, productivity increased by 32 percent, while workers' wages grew by only 8 percent. Meanwhile, corporate profits increased by 65 percent, the stock market soared and tax on income of more than $1.0 million was slashed by two thirds.

As a result of these policies, the income of the top 0.1 percent of American families was equal to the bottom 42 percent in 1929, with the implication that most people had to purchase goods on credit. Total consumer debt eventually increased so much that people lacked enough disposal income to purchase goods from the factories, causing supply of goods to outpace demand. Meanwhile farmers, who constituted about a quarter of working people, saw prices for their goods decline significantly due to oversupply in international markets.

While the problems in the economy were hidden, the stock market became overvalued due to investors' buying shares on credit in the belief that prices would keep on rising. When the problem of oversupply of goods was exposed, investors realized that share prices exceeded profits generated by companies by a wide margin. Investors began selling their shares quickly, causing the stock market to plummet in 1929. The Great Depression had begun.

The stock market's collapse sent shock waves through the economy. Financial institutions declined to extend further credit to consumers, which led to cutbacks in factory output until eventually many factories had to close due to overstocked warehouses. Between 1929 and 1932, output from manufacturing plants in America was cut in half, leading to a steep increase in unemployment from 3.2 percent to 24.9 percent. As well as the 15 million officially unemployed people, there were many who worked part time, and the wages of the employed were cut in most instances.

Banks that had invested in the stock market depleted their reserves to the point where they could no longer service their customers. Panic reigned when many were unable to withdraw money from their savings account, and the run up caused about 5,000 banks to close their doors by March 1933. Personal bankruptcies reached record levels; banks foreclosed mortgages on many homes and farms, and the roll of the homeless swelled to breaking point. Shantytowns composed of shacks built with crates became known as "Hoovervilles," named out of bitterness after Herbert Hoover, the president at the time.

At the beginning of the Great Depression, President Hoover insisted market forces would correct the problem, and that there was no need for government intervention to restore equilibrium between supply and demand. But by 1932, as supply continued to exceed demand, investment had dropped to less than 5 percent of its 1929 level. So President Hoover decided that cutting the budget to reduce deficit would improve investor confidence, an act that had the opposite effect by reducing liquidity. Finally, as conditions worsened, Hoover's administration provided emergency loans to banks and industry, embarked on a public works program, and offered relief to states. But economic activity had shrunk too much to be improved by the feeble stimulus.

With no improvement on the horizon and more and more people going hungry, Hoover called on Americans to provide "mutual self-help through voluntary giving." Americans responded to the clarion call by stepping up donations to a record high in 1932. But charitable organizations, overwhelmed by demand, called on the government to provide direct assistance to the affected. Hoover ruled this out, claiming it would diminish recipients' self-reliance. Not even a demonstration by 20,000 World War I veterans on Washington to request early payment of bonuses could dissuade the president from his chosen path.

The unpopularity of Hoover caused his defeat at the hands of Franklin Delano Roosevelt during the elections of 1932. Roosevelt called a special session of Congress, during which many of the actions taken then and later came to be known as the New Deal. He then broadcast the first of many fireside chats on radio to reassure Americans that he had their best interest at heart.

Large amounts of federal money were pumped into construction of roads, bridges, schools and dams in an attempt to create jobs, increase demand and stimulate investment by the private sector. While the New Deal helped people survive, the trough was too deep to dig out of, and unemployment remained high through the 1930s. Not until government spending accelerated during World War II did the Great Depression begin to abate. Spending on warships, tanks, fighter planes, and other materials boosted the economy by stimulating growth, and causing unemployment to decline rapidly.

Many took their own lives, overcome by the lack of opportunity to provide for their families. Some were traumatized psychologically, causing alcoholism to explode among the population. However, all through the pain, Americans never lost sight of the need to help their neighbors. It was not uncommon for those employed to open their homes to the unemployed and provide what sustenance they could.

Having survived a test of extreme proportions, confidence began to be restored, and the victory of World War II, achieved with critical American help, erased any vestiges of gloom remaining from The Great Depression. Opportunity returned in abundance, the GI Bill was enacted to assist reintegration of GIs into regular society, demand for labor outstripped supply, and wages began to outpace inflation.

New Deal actions led to the creation of epoch-making programs and institutions. The Social Security Act of 1935 guaranteed government assistance to the unemployed, the disabled, older Americans, and women and children. A minimum wage was established, and the National Labor Relations Act of 1935 led to acceptance of labor unions as necessary components of business activity, accelerating their growth in industries such as steel and automobile manufacturing.

Women also entered the labor force in greater numbers to help support their families, a development which led to the rise of the Women's Movement decades later. New Deal figures, led by First Lady Eleanor Roosevelt, championed the cause of minorities, and programs of the era included special provisions against racial discrimination, though these were ignored in many areas in the South. In addition, a coalition of minorities and labor unions became the backbone of the Democratic Party.

Meanwhile back in Pittsburgh, suffocating pollution caused property values downtown to plummet by 28 percent between 1936 and 1946. Not even increased industrial demand created by World War II, which boosted the city's population to a peak of over 676,000 in 1950, could reverse the declining fortunes of the city. The glory days were clearly over, but abandoning the city was not an option.

With its well earned reputation as the most polluted city in the U.S., the city was threatened with the exodus of corporate offices, and even the wife of Richard Mellon, head of Pittsburgh's wealthiest clan, was said to be none too pleased to return to the grimy city after breathing much cleaner air during her travels with her husband to other cities during the Second World War.

Perhaps spurred on by his spouse's wrath, a chastised Richard Mellon joined a unique partnership of business and political leaders to champion the revitalization of the city. The group organized the Allegheny Conference in 1943 to formulate a strategy for revival, an effort classified four years later by Fortune as "Pittsburgh's last chance...to reverse the course of urban decay and industrial decline."

The Allegheny Conference elected an executive committee with the stipulation that its members, comprised of presidents and board chairmen of all leading companies, had to participate personally in the meetings. The only exception was granted to the wealthiest man Richard Mellon, but even he was represented by a powerful delegation. This rule ensured that decisions taken at the Conference had stamps of authority and could be implemented without the dithering process of "checking with the boss."

At the executive committee table sat none other than H.J. (Jack) Heinz II, grandson of the founder of H.J. Heinz Company. Continuing the legacy of his grandfather, Jack was an active participant in the campaign to spruce up his hometown, an effort that continued into the 1980s.

Blessed with the imprimatur of power, the Allegheny Conference on Community Development gave birth to Pittsburgh Renaissance in 1945, an ambitious project to form a partnership with political leaders, headed by Mayor David Lawrence, to literally dismantle the city and rebuild it.

In one of its first acts, the Conference threw its weight behind a tough anti-smoke ordinance passed by the city council of Pittsburgh in 1941 but shelved because of the onset of world war. Facing additional pressure from a broad range of civic leaders, the city council set a deadline of October 1, 1946 for industrial establishments to comply with the restrictions imposed by the ordinance. Co-opting Richard Mellon proved to be visionary when he provided financing to silence protesters from the business community who complained bitterly about the cost of complying with the ordinance.

However, in dealing with opposition from Pennsylvania Railroad, which opposed state legislation authorizing the county to restrict emissions, Richard Mellon dispensed with niceties and bluntly threatened to divert freight business of companies he controlled from Pennsylvania Railroad to other freight lines.

Just like the Godfather went to see Johnny's manager with Luca Brazi and made him "an offer he couldn't refuse,"—"My father assured him either his brains or his signature would be on the contract"—sanity prevailed as Pennsylvania Railroad, faced with the choice of folding their business or folding their opposition, chose the latter.

In 1949 a comprehensive county smoke ordinance was passed covering railroads, industries and residences, unleashing entrepreneurial activities that were to make Pittsburgh a leader in environmental remediation technologies. One of those companies, Wheelabrator Air Pollution Control of Pittsburgh, is a recognized leader even today in the industry.

In remarkably short order Pittsburgh was transformed from a soiled to a flowering city, with accolades heaped on it from all corners. In 1950 one of the strong advocates for pollution control claimed that during the first winter the ordinance was passed "the city received 39 per cent more available sunshine than the previous winter" and after three years "visibility was up by almost 70 per cent, laundry and painting bills [had] gone down, buildings [had] been cleaned, and the whole aspect of the community [was] more cheerful and bright."

In 1949 Newsweek blessed the city with the statement that it was "no longer the smoky city or the tired city, but an industrial metropolis with a new bounce, with clear skies above it and a brand-new spirit below." The Christian Science Monitor melodically chimed in: "Pittsburgh is the test of industrialism everywhere to rebuild upon the gritty ruins of the past a society more equitable, more spacious, more in the human scale."

The team embarked also on flood abatement and sewage treatment. The central business district was reconstructed; Point State Park, Gateway Center and Mellon Square were built. Traffic congestion in the city was eased with the construction of a link to the Pennsylvania Turnpike.

The impact of Pittsburgh's achievements was felt far and wide in cities across Northeast and Midwest. One writer questioned, "If benighted Pittsburgh could give birth to a renaissance, then why not Cleveland, Baltimore, or Saint Louis?" So the Greater Baltimore Committee, St. Louis's Civic Progress and the Cleveland Business Development Foundation were all modeled after the Allegheny Conference on Community Development.

So all across America, cities that were given up for dead were bathed in the sweet smell of reincarnation. Air pollution was stanched, drinking water was purified, garbage was collected and stored far away from the cities, and gargantuan, glass-encased office buildings rose into the skies. New highways snaked in and out of cities, airports sprung up to accommodate giant planes carrying passengers to locations near and far.

Manufacturing continued to grow by leaps and bounds; wages outpaced inflation, giving rise to the formation of a unique group of people called the middle class. For the most part, the middle class were not owners of capital, but, contrary to the prophecies of Marxism, they earned enough to afford some of the trappings of owners of capital, including ownership of property, excellent nutrition and good education for their children.

The middle class was comprised of two distinct groups: the white-collar who worked mostly in offices and the blue-collar who worked on factory floors. In one of the greatest social achievements of all time, the blue-collar worker, thanks to wages secured through his union, could afford to live cheek-to-jowl with the white-collar worker. The mechanics, lathe turners, and assembly line workers rubbed shoulders with teachers, middle managers, and accountants in a new neighborhood called suburbia, surrounded by trees, spacious homes with well manicured lawns and lightly traveled roads. The new neighborhood was relatively far away from city centers and the noise and congestion of industrial boroughs. More importantly, crime also became relatively infrequent.

Empowering females in the workplace meant an increase in discretionary income for families, which made vacations, dining out, and other activities of leisure more affordable to the middle class. The new industries that sprung up added more proprietors, travel agents, managers, accountants, advertisers or salespersons to the services sector of the middle class. The wealth created by the workers of industrialization generated sweet nectar for another class of employees. The five-day workweek secured by unions left weekends open to the middle class to patronize sporting activities, movies and dance halls, indulgences that until then were open predominantly to the upper class.

The nascent industry of film making, which started when Cecil B. DeMille and D.W. Griffith began making movies in Hollywood in the 1910s, took off during World War II, leading to larger than life heroes like John "Duke" Wayne, Clark Gable (King of Hollywood), Roy Rogers (King of Cowboys), Cary Grant, and their leading ladies Bette Davies, Lauren Bacall, Greta Garbo, Joan Crawford, and the incomparable "Sugar" Marilyn Monroe, who claimed she was from Sandusky, Ohio in "Some Like It Hot."

In the field of music, Elvis Presley, with his gyrating hips, delighted teenage girls while causing consternation to their parents in equal measure. Frank Sinatra, the kid from Hoboken, New Jersey, came to the fore during the "swing" era of the 1930s and 1940s and, like a chameleon, was able to transform his music to fit subsequent eras. He became ingrained forever in the hearts of New Yorkers when he gave them their anthem, "New York, New York." And with his Rat Pack, he left behind more empty bottles of whisky a night than most consumed in a year. Nat King Cole headlined an original American art form, jazz, with the first performance of its kind at the Philharmonic concert in 1944.

In baseball, the team that began in Manhattan with the name "Hilltops" when Frank Farrell and Bill Devery purchased the defunct Baltimore franchise for $18,000 became the New York Yankees in April 1913. On January 3, 1920 the Yankees laid a curse on the Boston Red Sox—broken only in 2004—when it executed one of the greatest "thefts" in sports history by buying the contract of Babe Ruth for $125,000 and a $350,000 loan against Boston's Fenway Park.

So began an era of sports championship delirium in the Bronx with Babe Ruth, Lou Gehrig, Joe DiMaggio, Mickey Mantle, and Derek Jeter leading the way. Managers nobody thought much of when they were hired won five championships in a row as Casey Stengel did, or four in five years as Joe Torre has done. Growing talent only when necessary and buying any player of consequence, the Yankees, hated by everybody else, muscled their way to 26 championships, more than any team in sports history.

The Yankees became the only team to harvest all sports' nouns of consequence in one stadium. Babe Ruth hitting 714 home runs during his career and Roger Maris hitting a single season home run record of 61 defined power. The composition of Murderers' Row inspired fear. Joe DiMaggio going on a hitting streak of 56 games portrayed consistency. Lou Gehrig playing in 2130 consecutive games illustrated endurance. The same Lou Gehrig's life cut short by amyotrophic lateral sclerosis showed frailty. Billy Martin's five stints as manager depicted chaos. Don Larsen throwing the only perfect game in World Series history characterized perfection. Reggie Jackson hitting three consecutive home runs in a World Series game painted flair. George M. Steinbrenner described resolve (The Red Sox disagree). Twenty-six championships typified success.

In athletics, Jesse Owens shattered any notion of Aryan supremacy by winning four gold medals in the 100-meter and 200-meter dashes, long jump and as a member of the 400-meter relay at the 1936 Berlin Olympic games. Rather than diminishing him, Hitler's failure to shake his hand unintentionally magnified his successes.

Boxing had many names. Rocky Marciano, the only undefeated boxing champion in history, was significant. Joe Louis, the "Brown Bomber" from Lafayette, Alabama was important. But for a time in the sixties and seventies, a brash fellow from Louisville, Kentucky, who claimed to be the "Greatest of all Time," was boxing. Nobody before or after him commanded as much attention, locally and globally, as Muhammad Ali, the name he adopted after ridding himself of his "slave" name Cassius Clay.

From the time he won the Olympic Gold Medal in 1960, to when he monumentally upset Sonny Liston in 1964, to when he refused induction into the armed services in 1967, to his three epic battles against "Smoking" Joe Frazier, to when he "rope-a-doped" George Foreman in the "Rumble in the Jungle," Ali's every move and word were consumed by an insatiable audience. "Floating like a butterfly and stinging like a bee," he danced and swayed around opponents with his body and lips to the ecstasy of his admirers and consternation of his detractors, with not a neutral soul in sight.

In the end, his greatest achievements were born not in the ring of his showmanship but in the field of his life, where he embodied the great American traditions of resistance against injustice and service in sacrifice.

Some men walk from step to step hoping to leave an impression. But it is those who choose to fly who leave indelible imprints for posterity. Muhammad Ali chose to fly.

The American middle class, solid as Mount Rushmore, strode tall on the global stage, chests bulging with pride. Between 1950 and 1980, the number of manufacturing jobs (Table 2) increased from 14 million to about 22 million, confirmation of the industrialization of the U.S. The average manufacturing wage also increased from about $9.00 an hour to about $15.00 an hour between 1950 and 1980, an increase of about 67 percent.

Employment in the service industry increased from 7.2 million to 28.8 million during the same time frame, a stunning increase of about 300 percent. It is worth mentioning, however, that this phenomenal increase in employment in the service industry did not occur in a vacuum, but rather was built on the fruits of industrialization. Burgeoning expenditures by those employed in manufacturing and the need for productivity enhancements by manufacturing plants precipitated the massive increase in employment in the service industry recorded in Table 2.

Overall, though manufacturing's share of employment had declined to 22 percent from about 32 percent between 1950 and 1980, while service's share had increased from 15 percent to 29 percent, the American middle class was in solid shape. Two-car families were the norm, and home ownership zoomed to 64.4 percent of all families in 1980 from 55 percent in 1950.

But while the American middle class was celebrating in 1980, entropic forces looming ominously on the horizon were about to spread untold havoc among its population. These forces—management incompetence, intransigent labor unions, high cost of labor—shattered not just Pittsburgh, but also Gary, Columbus, Cleveland, Toledo, Detroit, St. Louis, Buffalo, Baltimore, Wayne, East Lansing, and most of the cities in the basin of industrialization.

Table 2 Employment Data By Industry from 1950 to 1980 (millions)				
	1950	1960	1970	1980
TOTAL, 16 YEARS AND OLDER	43.31	46.88	80.7	99.3
AGRICULTURE	2.38	2.25	3.5	3.39
NONAGRICULTURAL INDUSTRIES	40.93	44.63	77.2	95.94
MINING, FORESTERS & FISHERIES	0.97	0.93	0.6	0.98
CONSTRUCTION	5.35	6.76	5.6	6.22
MANUFACTURING	14	15.5	19.4	21.94
DURABLE GOODS	6.76	8.79	11.2	13.18
NONDURABLE GOODS	7.24	6.71	8.2	8.76
TRANSPORTATION, COMMUNICATION	2.87	2.86	4.5	6.53
WHOLESALE AND RETAIL	8.70	8.96	15.0	20.19
FINANCE, INSURANCE & REAL ESTATE	0.54	0.93	3.6	5.99
SERVICE INDUSTRIES	7.24	7.48	19.4	28.75
PUBLIC ADMINISTRATION	1.26	1.21	4.6	5.34
Authors from US Bureau of Labor Statistics				

Carnegie's motto "to watch costs and the profits take care of themselves" had been completely forgotten by succeeding generations of managers, and the American Middle Class bore the brunt of their incompetence.

3

DEINDUSTRIALIZATION

In 1953 the 110 million tons of rolled steel produced by American companies was more than the steel produced in the rest of the free world combined. But like an ostrich with its head firmly buried in sand, the steel industry in America failed to confront the gathering clouds threatening its survival. Highly profitable steel companies spent the least on research and development. As one observer put it, "the industry was dominated by mindset eager to defend itself from the inconvenience of change."

Price increases for steel became automatic. Every summer U.S. Steel, the largest manufacturer, negotiated an annual wage increase with the United Steelworkers of America, followed by increase in steel price exceeding the increase in labor cost. Bethlehem Steel, the second largest manufacturer, would dutifully duplicate these wage and price increases.

Price elasticity is inapplicable only in a monopolistic scenario. But since overall demand remains the same in a competitive environment, others fill any decrease in demand for a product from one supplier due to price increase with a lower price from another supplier. And so it was with steel. Steel imports into the U.S. rose steadily from 4 million in 1963 to 10.7 million in 1966 and 18 million in 1968.

Steel production in Japan was particularly revealing. The country was nearly bereft of any of the raw materials for steel manufacturing. Yet exports of steel from Japan to the U.S. increased from 31,466 tons in 1957 to 4.5 million tons in 1967.

At this very time of heightened competition, U.S. Steel, Bethlehem and Republic all chose to raise prices in 1967.

It has been said that those that fail to learn from history live to be condemned by it. Any student of industrial history in America knows Andrew Carnegie gained a dominant position in steel by significantly reducing cost of production at his plants with introduction of the integrated steel mill and Bessemer process. His motto was "watch costs and the profits take care of themselves."

But in the most egregious decision taken collectively by Big Steel in the U.S., production capacity was increased from 100 million to 149 million tons in the 1950s using open-hearth furnaces instead of basic oxygen furnace, an Austrian invention that yielded a $5-a-ton operating advantage.

Falsely assured in its arrogance of being able to demand ever-higher prices, Big Steel sacrificed lower cost of production for the capability to generate greater volumes of steel to feed large rolling mills by the open-hearth technology. This competitive disadvantage became the albatross that eventually buried major steel manufacturing in the U.S. By the time U.S. steel manufacturers converted to the basic oxygen furnace, the even more cost-effective "mini mill" in which cheap scrap was melted down in electric arc furnaces had supplanted it.

U.S. Steel's financial vice president Robert Tyson summarized the attitude of Big Steel in 1964 when he said, "Nobody who has efficient open hearth furnaces is going to throw them out to buy oxygen furnaces. We waited until we needed to replace old capacity." Nobody reminded Mr. Tyson that Andrew Carnegie led the steel industry by pioneering innovation, not by being risk averse.

The indifferent attitude of Big Steel to innovation after the Carnegie era was demonstrated yet again by its failure to rapidly adopt continuous casting, a technology capable of achieving productivity improvements of up to twenty five percent. Claiming the technology was unproven, Big Steel stood by as innovative foreigners invested heavily to improve the technology. So by 1980 when continuous casting accounted for 46 percent and 59.5 percent of steel in West Germany and Japan, respectively, it was only 20.3 percent in American steel. By the time Big Steel was finally coerced into adopting continuous casting on a wider scale, it borrowed heavily in a futile attempt to prop up market share in an environment in which it could no longer dictate price.

While Big Steel wallowed in management incompetence and recalcitrant unions were militantly pushing for more benefits in complete disregard of competitiveness of steel, the metal was rapidly being replaced by less expensive and environmentally friendlier alternatives in many traditional applications.

Aluminum pots and pans, residential sidings, window frames, airplane frames and cans took a chunk from steel's demand base. Plastics that could withstand boiling water without distortion preceded breakthrough in kitchenware. Reinforced and pre-stressed concrete was used to build short-length bridges in the interstate highway system. Tishman Research Corporation erected a pre-stressed concrete parking garage at a Hempstead, Long Island shopping center in 1960.

The new garage was built at $1,200 per parking space, compared with $1,700 for a steel-girder structure.

As steel became more expensive, automobile companies discovered that plastics coated with a thin trim of stainless steel or other metal was a cheaper alternative. Plated plastics replaced metal in car instrument panels, dome lights, ventilation grills, and door locks.

U.S. steel manufacturers barely responded to these attacks on their product. Instead of investing in research and development to invent new applications and reduce weight without sacrificing performance, steel industry executives maintained the attitude that nothing could interfere with their prosperity.

Under the massive assault from alternative products that were literally sucking the life out of steel, the industry spent a measly 60 cents of every $100 in revenue on research and development. This compared with investments of four to six times more by aluminum, concrete, plastics and other steel substitutes.

One thing industry executives were proficient at doing was crying wolf. Using fear of plant closings and job losses, the American Iron and Steel Institute, the lobbying arm of Big Steel, tried to persuade Congress to "level the playing field" by levying a special tariff on foreign steel being "dumped" on the American market. Government complied on many occasions by imposing tariffs or quotas to help American companies compete against so-called subsidized steel.

While true that some countries engaged in dumping, this was not a universal practice. What the tariffs and quotas actually achieved was entrenchment of unsustainable inefficient methodologies. When tariffs and quotas on steel were eventually reduced or removed under threats of retaliation against other more competitive American products by America's trading partners, the steel companies collapsed under the onslaught of less expensive steel.

The scale of steel manufacturing astounded most people arriving in Pittsburgh in the sixties and seventies for the first time. One writer provided a vivid account: "Leaving Pittsburgh, heading up the Mon Valley, one reached Homestead in a few minutes, site of the immense plant of the United States Steel…Heading upriver again, one soon encountered the formidable Carrie Furnaces of U.S. Steel in Rankin. The Edgar Thomson Works of U.S. Steel came next. This plant, with its forest of tall chimneys puffing smoke like demented tobacco addicts, was the base of Andrew Carnegie's steel empire…The Duquesne Works of U.S. Steel followed. Nestled in a bend of the Monongahela, it was the site of the…Dorothy Six blast furnaces. Continuing upriver, heading out of the deep bend, one reached McKeesport, home of U.S. Steel's National Works…The Irvin Works of

U.S. Steel in West Mifflin...loomed up across the river from McKeesport...Heading upriver from Clairton, one passed the Allegheny County line into Washington County, where the Donora Works of U.S. Steel still functioned in 1963....Across the river, in unintended but outlandish contrast to everything for which Economy stood, stretched the six-mile-long 779-acre Aliquippa Works of Jones & Laughlin. And to the west of Aliquippa in Beaver County was the Midland Works of Crucible Steel."

Needless to say, the collapse of the steel industry had a calamitous effect on employment in Pittsburgh and its surrounding neighborhood, exacerbated by the reverberating effect on suppliers of raw materials like coal and coke who had to curtail output as well. With an average of 109 employees per plant compared with a national average of 52, the overdependence on manufacturing became a liability of immense proportions for the city of Pittsburgh.

The entire steel industry in Pittsburgh built over the better part of a century was decapitated in one fell swoop. Between 1982 and 1987, U.S. Steel closed its blast furnace complexes at Rankin and Duquesne, and its mills at Duquesne, Clairton, Homestead, and McKeesport. The Donora Works had been closed earlier in 1966. Jones & Laughlin (LTV Steel) closed its South Side and Hazelwood plants, J & L clamped shut the behemoth Aliquippa Works, and Wheeling-Pittsburgh closed its Monessen Works.

Steel did not suffer in isolation: it had other industries for company. The massive Westinghouse Electric and Westinghouse Air Brake Corporation plants at East Pittsburgh and Wilmerding were shuttered, throwing thousands into the streets. It had been reduced to a mere repair shop for used generator machinery by the mid-1980's.

More than 100,000 high paying steel and steel related jobs disappeared in the Pittsburgh area between 1978 and 1983. Industrial employment dropped by a staggering 44 percent, pushing unemployment in the city to a peak of 14.7 percent in January 1983, the highest since the Depression.

Gone with the shutdown of the steel industry was the way of life of several communities. The sense of cohesion, esprit-de-corps and security the steel industry provided was shattered forever. Many were those whose families stretching as far back as the days of Andrew Carnegie knew nothing else but employment by the once omnipresent industry. The sheer scale of the truncation, and the speed at which it was enforced, is unmatched in the annals of industrial organization.

The overwhelming majority of displaced workers had no skills beyond those acquired during the manufacturing of a particular product. Worse still many had never experienced the frustration of seeking employment in a difficult market.

For the most part many had never been out of a job for anything more than a few months at a time. The communality shared by the workers meant a job could be found for a "brother" through word of mouth either at any of the many U.S. Steel plants or at other Jones & Laughlin plant locations. The Edgar Thompson Works of U.S. Steel at Braddock alone employed 6,000 plentiful workers at one time at fourteen open-hearth furnaces and five blast furnaces; employment had dropped to a mere 650 jobs by the 1980s, and even those were hanging on by their fingernails. Like fish out of water, many unemployed steelworkers were left gasping for air.

A steelworker was said to have observed, "Man, I've worked since I was sixteen. I had one job after another. Before you quit one job, you had another one lined up. You never went months without work. This is all new to me, trying to find a job. I've tried like hell, there's nothing out there." A longtime steelworker was reported to have said, "Everybody felt the mill would always be there. On that basis they went out and bought cars, houses and all...We have no experience in this...For seventeen years, I went down to the shop each day and they tell you what you are doing that day. Now where I am going?"

From the day the concept of earning a living became a reality, most of the displaced workers did not have to confront the inconvenience of looking for a job. "It was easy," a former steelworker was said to have remarked. "You went to work, had a few beers after that, and then went home. You had a lot of money for the wife and kids. You had nice vacations. You bought anything you wanted." Most of these workers were traumatized to discover that their jobs had been erased permanently, and there was nothing else to fill the vacuum.

The collapse of the once preponderant manufacturing jobs meant scarcity of opportunity was the order of the day. Pittsburgh had cast its lot with the assets it was bequeathed, but those assets in the end turned out to be fool's steel: lived by steel, perished by steel.

By the mid-1990s the greatest steel making complex in the world had been reduced to only one major integrated mill (the Edgar Thomson Works); a specialty steel plant (Allegheny Ludlum); a strip mill (the Irwin Works); and two plants where coke was produced as a by-product. A haunting sight was the empty land lining the riverbanks in the Monongahela Valley where steel mills formerly stood.

The River Communities Project (RCP) of the School of Social Work at the University of Pittsburgh organized a major effort to analyze the human consequences of deindustrialization. Additional research was conducted to evaluate the effect of job evisceration on the elderly, women, children, the unemployed, and blacks. Yet another study examined a community-university effort to promote youth enterprise in the area.

The study confirmed what was already obvious: that unemployment on such a large scale had stretched the ability of the government to offer assistance to the breaking point: "Disinvestment turns vital centers of production into shrinking retirement communities" that are "increasingly sustaining themselves with social security and pension checks."

In the midst of this deprivation many turned to churches, social agencies and unions for any assistance they could garner. Churches, with their philosophy of "turn away none," were filled to the brim. Social agencies, with budgets thinned by excessive demand, offered any assistance within their means. And unions did all they could, including summoning help from far away places.

However, having a traditional scorn for those who receive public assistance, some displaced workers found it difficult, if not embarrassing, to accept so-called "freebies." The report found that pride kept many from "accepting services and goods not earned directly from their labor." It concluded that: "People of the distressed communities still cling proudly to their spirit of self-reliance. They would rather go without or borrow from a relative than apply to a social agency."

Some of the effects of the disintegration of industry were revealing: "Layoff of police officers and other municipal workers, deterioration of the B.F. Jones Memorial Library, declining revenues, and increased debt." The social fabric was disintegrating.

In his well-documented book, "Twentieth Century Pittsburgh: The Post-Steel Era," Roy Lubove wrote, "The decisive shutdown of the steel industry throughout the Pittsburgh region in the 1980s devastated a once stable and prosperous working-class way of life...The progress made by the growing number of black steelworkers in the post-1960s era abruptly ended. The tax base of the mill towns eroded at exactly the time when vastly increased health and welfare services were most needed...the cost of the transition was unevenly distributed: it fell disproportionately upon one generation of workers and their communities. It was a wrenching industrial revolution in reverse."

Meanwhile, anarchists were waging their own battle of disobedience and disorder against the corporate elite of Pittsburgh. On December 16, 1984, four masked men arrived at a Christmas pageant and proceeded to dump balloons filled with dye and skunk water on the audience, which included many top businessmen. Sacks of pennies were emptied in Mellon bank lobbies and fish was deposited in safety deposit boxes. Another group occupied a church in Clairton and had to be evicted by the sheriff.

Bankruptcies soared when many in Pittsburgh could not make mortgage payments. Divorces ballooned, crime escalated, the black middle class never recovered from the inferno that swept through Pittsburgh and a new face, the family, swamped homeless shelters.

Though steel suffered the most cataclysmic attack, it was hardly alone in being brought to its knees. The oil crisis of the seventies caught Detroit with large, gas-guzzling vehicles. Meanwhile a tiny company from Japan was fortuitous to be supplying its Hondas at about the same time. Small and fuel-efficient, Americans were surprised to discover that poor quality was not the norm for all cars. Before Honda could inflict any serious damage, however, Detroit was given a break when Americans returned to big, spacious vehicles with the passage of the oil crisis. However the battle had been joined by freshly minted competitors, Toyota and Nissan.

Not taking the new competitors seriously, Detroit continued to build vehicles that broke down all too frequently, causing baby boomers in general and females in particular to sample more and more of the vehicles from Japan. The difference between Japanese-made vehicles and those from Detroit was stark: 100,000 miles on Toyotas without a single breakdown, Hondas that rode quietly and smoothly, Nissans with superior ergonomics, Mazdas with functional signalers and Subarus that went to the bush and back in one piece. Consumers, especially on the West Coast and Northeast, were hooked and they never went back. The commute on highways across the country is revealing, with Japanese nameplates sometimes stacked three deep.

So when purchasing power declined as the effects of deindustrialization began to take hold across America, cautious consumers looking for more bang for their money shunned Detroit like a plague. With showrooms now filled with unwanted vehicles, Detroit, like Big Steel in Pittsburgh, unsheathed its weapons of mass destruction on the workers.

The Chrysler bailout in 1979-80 came at a cost of 50,000 factory employees, 18,000 office workers, and imposition of $500 million in wage cuts and other concessions. Chrysler closed five plants in the Detroit area alone, including the 5000-strong Dodge main, its largest facility, in the Detroit enclave of Hamtrack.

Record numbers of assembly plants in Detroit, Dearborn, Flint, Fort Wayne, St. Louis, etc. were closed permanently by GM, Ford and Chrysler. Half a million-factory workers were laid off between 1978 and 1999. Employees at parts suppliers, car dealerships and other ancillary businesses were also laid off.

Just like steelworkers in Pittsburgh, workers in the automobile industry were flabbergasted: they never imagined that decapitation of the plants would be so swift and on such a large scale. Again a way of life established since the days of Henry Ford had disappeared, with its attendant debilitating ramifications in many communities across America.

But the workers were not entirely blameless for their fate. Up until the crises of the eighties, the United Auto Workers Union negotiated a contract with what they perceived to be the most profitable company, and then signed the same deal with the other two manufacturers, regardless of their financial health. Of course, the logical method would have been a complete reversal: to start with the weakest, instead of the strongest. But companies and employees alike were too busy lining their pockets to realize this incongruous arrangement.

For the most part, though, the fault for the shattering of the American automobile industry lay at the door of management, whose claims of inferior workmanship by workers was disproved resoundingly when Japanese cars made in America proved to be of equal or better quality than those made in Japan.

The fact is any American given the option of choosing between vehicles of comparable quality and price will select from the Big 3 UAW—renamed because Toyota is now selling more cars in North America than Ford. But quality rankings by JD Power and Associates continue to show Toyota, Honda and Nissan ahead of the Big 3 UAW by a substantial margin.

Chrysler invented minivans and sports utility vehicles, but the Japanese, who are increasingly making more of their vehicles in America, have usurped its thunder. Muscular trucks, which have been the profit staples for the Big 3 UAW, are now increasingly carrying Japanese names, especially that of Toyota.

Honda became the first Japanese maker to assemble cars in the U.S. in 1982 at Marysville, Ohio, from where it exports cars to Japan. Toyota (Georgetown, KY), Nissan (Smyrna, TN) and others are assembling more of their vehicles in the US. By 1995, foreign carmakers sold more U.S.-made vehicles (1.9 million) than they imported (1.7 million). In 1996, foreign-owned plants employed about 40,000 Americans and built more cars than Ford Motor Co. or Chrysler.

The fact Japanese carmakers are selling more locally manufactured vehicles in an increasingly tight market is a major indictment against American management. The fact Japanese used vehicles carry far more value than second hand ones from Detroit demonstrates inability of American management to respond effectively to competitive threats by producing vehicles Americans want to buy. When a consumer's thought gravitates to the standard 4-door passenger vehicle, names like Camry, Accord and Altima readily pop to mind with nary an American nameplate to recollect. Neither is there an American-named equivalent to the Corolla or the Civic. It would seem more appropriate at this juncture for shareholders to sweep away management structures at GM and Ford, because it seems the only result from all the years of shouting "Quality is Job One" has been hoarse voices.

It seems, sadly, that the only act American management in heavy industry in those days was able to perform sufficiently well was destruction of jobs across the entire industrial landscape of America. And the carnage, for different reasons, spread to other industries.

The English and the Scots who settled in New England created the textile industry in America. Weaving is a craft passed on from one generation to another, and many came to America to give something to their new country and receive something back. The weather was congenial; not too hot, not too cold, and with appreciatively more sun than their native land.

Their enterprise led to saturation of textile mills from the Hudson Valley in upstate New York, through the shades of Connecticut, north to Boston, their spiritual capital, then along the Atlantic Ocean until the mills ended in redolent Vermont. It was for the most part like the resplendent quaint villages they had left behind, except there was more sun and a lot less rain.

Then came an offer they couldn't refuse: you will get even more sun, little to no snow, just about the same amount of rain, and a less expensive labor force. Their ancestors had braved the monsoon of India to bring back tea to the motherland. Some had gone to Africa for gold in spite of lethal malaria-bearing mosquitoes. So an odd tornado here or there was no deterrent. Welcome to the South, which is where most of the textile mills relocated in the 1930s.

But today the days of prosperity seem like a dream. Under the assault of even less expensive labor and other cost inputs, several of the mills in the South have closed, shedding jobs by the hundreds of thousands. More than 100 mills closed in 2001, with over 148,000 jobs lost. Some 1.0 million jobs in the industry disappeared between 1980 and 2005.

"It's been pretty dire," says David Link, chief economist for the American Textile manufacturers Association. "The conditions are probably worse than anything since the Great Depression."

Eight Southeastern states—Alabama, Georgia, Louisiana, Mississippi, North Carolina, South Carolina, Tennessee and Virginia—produce roughly 75 percent of the nation's textiles. About two-thirds of America's remaining 1.2 million textile and apparel workers live in the Carolinas, Georgia and Alabama.

Textile employment in the Carolinas—about a quarter of manufacturing jobs in the two states—has declined by a third in the past years. Discouraged by the pace of plant closures, the state's Chamber of Commerce no longer pursues the textile industry.

The industry is in an abysmal state despite investment of more than $2 billion in equipment upgrades over the past decade. In many plants all processes are completely automated: the human hand never touches a loom. Old shuttles that took thirteen minutes to produce the material for an average man's shirts have been replaced with air-jet looms that do it in three. And still they can't compete. Meanwhile apparel exports from the Caribbean and Mexico, where manufacturers from Taiwan have set up shop to beat their cousins from China, have increased more than 30-fold. A short detour from the Kingston airport in Jamaica into the Kingston Free Zone finds an army of manufacturers that pay no tax on goods manufactured for export. Businessmen from Taiwan own almost all the textile firms in the free zone. Shops have also been set up in Johannesburg, Durban and Cape Town to take advantage of the special agreement on textile exports from South Africa to the U.S.

China's formal admission to the World Trade Organization coincided with disappearance of 12,000 jobs from the US textile and apparel industry in January 2005 alone, the very first month of the end of tariffs and quotas. Very little of the once formidable U.S. textile and apparel industry will remain if this trend continues.

"Well, now the sort of template will be that U.S. textile and apparel companies will have management, design and these professional-type of functions performed in the United States, with their plants spread out all over the world," predicted Professor Gary Shoesmith, a Wake Forest economist. "U.S. manufacturers will have plants in China."

Mr. Shoesmith is mistaken on two counts. First, U.S. manufacturers have set up plants in China already. Second, the design can be done interactively via the web in a far cheaper location.

Shoesmith said he foresees a repeat of the cycle that began with relocation of the textile plants from New England when the industry kept head offices in the North to be closer to their main customers, but shifted workers South because of cheaper labor.

According to Shoesmith: "If an American worker has a low-skilled job within the apparel and textile industries, there's a very good chance that job won't survive the next decade. That's what it comes down to. It's a harsh reality."

The last American worker leaving the only remaining textile plant in America, please turn the lights off.

Employees with less than 10 years' service received a one-time payment of $250; those with 35 years received $1,150. The employee that gave 35 years to Richardson Brothers of Sheboygan Falls, Wisconsin received about $33 for every year of employment in June 2003. Then the tears flowed, the goodbyes were said and the crowd thinned out, for Richardson Brothers had moved its wood-furniture production to a Chinese plant where employees were paid 50 cents to 75 cents an hour, benefits included.

Joseph Richardson founded J. Richardson Sawmill in Sheboygan Falls, Wisconsin in 1848. Then his son Joe Two, as he was popularly known, took over and expanded the company into baronial furniture, the type fit for mansions everywhere. Then Joe Three took over and expanded even more. At its height, the company employed 262 craftsmen whose skills had been patiently developed over several generations of continuous familial employment. Now all 262 were gone, and with them the type of skills unique to production of high end wood furniture.

The wood-furniture industry in the U.S., like steel, automobiles, textiles and others, is being gorged like never before, with America's children and their children abandoned on the shores of Lake Superior on a cold winter morning with no clothes on their back.

It wasn't always like this. About a decade ago, imports claimed only about 20 percent of the U.S. wooden furniture. Then China came along, bulldozed the competition aside, and imports soared to 55 percent of the market.

Joe Three cried, too. He had tried to turn the company around through years of losses. He had looked at every business model, but in the end, the $13.30 an hour wage plus health insurance, pension plan and other benefits proved insurmountable at Sheboygan Falls. He was faced with either joining the exodus or shutting down permanently. He knew not only the employees, but their parents, children, brothers and sisters as well: Richardson Brothers was not only for the Richardson family; it was for the family of Sheboygan Falls. This is what made it so hard for Joe Three to shut the door: he was throwing out his own family. But he had no choice.

Many others have no choice, too. The wood-furniture industry, unlike the steel and automobile industries, has been felled simply by the cost of labor, not the incompetence typical of steel and automobile companies. Some in the industry accumulate savings of up to 40 percent shipping wood from the U.S. to China to be converted and returned.

It is estimated that a third of the wood-furniture plants in the United States have been closed since 2000, with their production shipped overseas. Employment in the industry has fallen by about 34,000, or 27 percent of the workforce, with no end in sight.

The last person leaving the last American plant to manufacture wooden furniture in the United States, please turn off the lights.

The U.S. high technology sector lost 900,000 workers between 2001 and 2004, or about 18 percent of its workforce, with the 612,000 jobs lost in 2002 being the highest. The losses were divided almost evenly between software workers and those in electronics manufacturing.

A great number of those losses were due to the collapse of the dotcom bubble. But it hasn't escaped attention that imports of electronic goods manufactured previously by U.S. workers have increased dramatically since 2000. Economy.com estimates 40 percent of those jobs were sent to developing countries.

In the meantime, according to the BLS data released in April 2005, employment in the leisure and hospitality sector has expanded by 823,000 since June 2002, with four fifths of the gain occurring in food services.

"Made in USA" signs are being replaced by signs saying, "Gone from USA." Steel, automobiles, textiles, furniture, chemicals, paper, etc; the rate of attack on American industry is unprecedented. Meanwhile, McDonalds can't hire people fast enough.

A study conducted by the Political Economy Research Institute (PERI) of the University of Massachusetts, Amherst found the share of imported inputs in the U.S. had increased by 9.8 percent for all manufactured goods between 1987 to 2002, with 14.1 percent increase for textiles, 13.5 percent for apparel, 12.4 percent for motor vehicles and parts, 12.2 percent for computer and electronic products and 9.9 percent for electrical equipment and appliances.

Increased productivity and contraction of export markets are contributing factors to loss of manufacturing jobs in the U.S. But the example of Richardson Brothers in Sheboygan Falls, Wisconsin and thousands of others show increase in foreign inputs is causing manufacturing to hemorrhage jobs as well.

Decline in manufacturing employment from 21 million in 1980 to 18 million in 1983 to 14.1 million in April 2005 shows deindustrialization in the United States is in full bloom across automobiles and related parts, heavy metals, toys, furniture, electronics, computers, heavy machinery and textiles.

The United States is amputating the fingers that have provided sustenance to this country since its birth. If not arrested, both hands will disappear soon, and gone will be the proud industrial heritage of the United States of America.

The American Middle Class built by the sweat, imagination and ingenuity of people like Andrew Carnegie, Henry Ford, Joe Richardson and millions of workers who sacrificed everything they had is being dismantled gradually right before our eyes, with not a finger lifted in support by people in positions of authority.

What about Homeland Security? Manufacturing is an intricate process relying on many inputs, some of which may seem inconsequential. So as deindustrialization sweeps the land, the day will dawn when America wakes up to the realization that critical parts for weapons of national security and manufacturing skills have been abandoned to the care of hostile foreigners. That day will come, if the current exodus continues to rage.

The sermon from the alter of business is that the economy of the U.S. is transitioning from manufacturing to "services, with the service sector now heavily represented by health, education and communication technology activities." This mantra continues to be preached despite the stark fact health and education depend exclusively on taxation from revenue generating enterprises, of which manufacturing is predominant, to survive. Health and education will tumble into the vacuum left behind by a disappearing manufacturing sector. But, then, even "communication technology activities" are disappearing from America.

The North American Free Trade Agreement and other free trade activities have been pursued on the premise that manufacturing jobs that migrate overseas are replaceable by service jobs. The rude awakening is that some multinational corporations are attacking both manufacturing and service jobs with the same ferocity, rendering both incapable of supporting the American middle class to the same extent as in years past.

4

RENAISSANCE

The city of Pittsburgh produced Carnegie, Heinz, Westinghouse, Mellon, Frick, Hall and Hunt, the greatest aggregate of industrialists of all time. It is the city of Andy Warhol, the most prolific American artist ever. It gave birth to Fred Rogers, the man whose neighborhood brought sunshine to many homes around the world. It is the city of the Steelers, who won four Super Bowls when anchored by Chuck Knox, Jack Ham, Terry Bradshaw and Mean Joe Green. Pittsburgh is the city whose adopted children Willie Stargell and Mario Lemieux overcame discrimination and cancer, respectively, to lead their teams to sporting excellence.

So while it may have been knocked flat on its back, Pittsburgh, the city of monumental heroes, had within its boundaries some of these same men of steel ready to wage battle to prevent their beloved city from giving up its soul. It was about to stage a stirring resurrection and, yes, like the Phoenix, Pittsburgh was about to rise from the ashes dumped by all the years of industrial activity.

The first arsenal in the weapons for the war of resurrection was created decades earlier when Carnegie and his fellow industrialists bequeathed excellent educational institutions to the city of Pittsburgh. These contained the seeds that gave birth to the army of intellectual foot soldiers that would wage the war.

The second arsenal was the Pittsburgh Renaissance formed by the public and private partnership in 1945 of Mayor David Lawrence and Richard King Mellon. The spruced up city shed its reputation as the "armpit of the world," thereby stemming the outflow of people and resources, and attracting intellectual capacity. The success of their efforts contributed to the construction of the third set of weapons—attractive environment—that would be needed decades later for the war to come.

Every successful war requires prescient, resolute, passionate, courageous and uncommon leadership. In Pittsburgh it also required someone who breathed and lived the city, someone who was a witness to the Donora Smog, as well as the glory days. It found all these qualities and more in one of its own children, Richard Salvatore Caliguiri.

Dick Caliguiri was born on October 20, 1931 in Pittsburgh. He spent his adolescence in the joyful Italian neighborhood of Greenfield. Like Carnegie, he could not afford higher education, so he began working in the city's parks department as a laborer. In time, he was rewarded for his hard work with a promotion to Acting Director of Public Works under Mayor Flaherty.

In 1970, he was named to a vacant seat on City Council, revoked later when he joined the Mayor in opposing a mass transit system called "Sky Bus." In 1971, he went on to lead the Council slate election. After making amends with the Democratic Party machine, he was endorsed to oppose Mayor Flaherty's bid for re-election in 1973. He lost, but became Mayor in 1977 when, as Council President, he ascended to the office vacated by Flaherty.

He ran successfully as an independent in the General Election. The man for the incredible challenges ahead was at the helm of the listing ship.

With the formula for the success of the first renaissance firmly in his mind, one of the first acts by Caliguiri was restoration of the public and private partnership abrogated by his predecessor. In what has come to be known since then as "metromorphisis," he used his considerable conciliatory skills to launch Renaissance II.

It began with the formation of the Urban Redevelopment Authority (URA), an enabling organization that was the initiator, planner, catalyst, coordinator, catalyst, funding agent and provider of technical assistance and land assembly. It continued with the Allegheny Conference, a group committed to the public-private partnership and downtown renewal and improvement.

Renaissance II undertook nine major projects. These were One Oxford Center, One Mellon Bank Center, Two Chatham Center, Riverfront Center, Liberty Center, PPG Place, Penn Station, CNG Tower, and Fifth Avenue Place.

At the center of Renaissance II was none other than the same Jack Heinz of Renaissance I, this time in charge of revival of a cultural area for downtown Pittsburgh. His efforts led to the creation of Heinz Hall for the Performing Arts, the city's version of Carnegie Hall, and home to the Pittsburgh Symphony. The Heinz Gallery, located in the Carnegie Museum of Art, and the Benedum Center, a two-year restoration of Pittsburgh's historic Stanley Theater, were all fruits of his leadership. Unfortunately, Jack Heinz did not live to see the opening of the Benedum Center, but his benefaction to his hometown lives on for posterity.

The Historic Review Commission, created to incorporate historical assets in Renaissance II, Station Square and the Strip District all came about in 1979.

Miles of aging streets, water and sewer lines were replaced, and the historic Grant Street was reconstructed. The Highland Park Zoo was refurbished, bringing joy to the many animal lovers in the city. It was one phenomenal project after another.

The successes of sporting teams in Pittsburgh during the period of turmoil, fear and uncertainty provided a major boost to the flagging spirits of its citizens. Between 1975 and 1980, the Pittsburgh Steelers football team, personified by an uncompromising set of hardened men, won four football Super Bowl trophies. Even today, though the Steelers have not won a championship in a while, the chiseled square jaw of their coach Bill Cowher on the sidelines is a continuation of the defining characteristic of the Steelers.

The Pittsburgh Pirates, led by the humble Willie "Pops" Stargell, won the World Series of baseball in 1979, using family and togetherness as their theme. The Pitt Panther football team won the collegiate national championship in 1976.

The resurrection of Pittsburgh from what was thought by many to be terminal decline was universally recognized when Rand McNally's Places Rated Almanac declared Pittsburgh to be "America's Most Livable City" in 1985. Accepting the honor on behalf of its proud citizens, a beaming Mayor Caliguiri never took credit for himself, instead praising others for their efforts.

The selflessness and the immense courage of Richard Caliguiri were on display on June 11, 1983 when he risked his own life to save a nine-year-old girl. Kelly Rogers was unintentionally knocked down by a van in view of the Mayor. Without any thought for his own life, Caliguiri immediately rushed in front of the van and pounded on the windshield for the driver to stop, saving Kelly's life.

The General Assembly of Pennsylvania recognized Richard Caliguiri for these heroic actions with a citation on June 11, 1983. As usual a misty eyed Caliguiri tried to deflect praise to others, but this time there was no one else to whom he could transfer the honor: he stood alone.

Richard Caliguiri was entreated by many politicians to seek higher office, but his response as always was blunt, "There is no higher office than serving the people of Pittsburgh." He was said to have been the rarest of all creatures, a politician nobody hated. The U.S. News and World Report selected him one of the 21 best mayors in the United States. Popular, and immensely successful, he seemed assured of a long political dynasty like that of Richard Daley of Chicago.

Then in a press conference on October 1, 1987, Richard Caliguiri stunned his constituents and all of the United States when he disclosed that he was suffering from primary amyloidosis, a rare fatal disease in which abnormal deposits of proteins invade the body's organs.

When Lou Gehrig announced at Yankee Stadium on July 4, 1939 that he had amyotrophic lateral sclerosis, his terminal condition was not immediately assimilated. With Richard Caliguiri, the realization was stark: he had not much time to walk on the surface of the earth.

And so with the abnormal proteins relentlessly attacking his heart, Richard Caliguiri died on May 6, 1988. On the day of his burial, the casket carrying his body was drenched with tears from all his beloved citizens. Pittsburgh had lost Pittsburgh, for that was what Richard Caliguiri had become. Though departed, the legacy of the victory won by Mayor Richard Caliguiri in the war of resurrection of Pittsburgh continued to sustain the citizens of Pittsburgh and beyond till this day.

To honor his memory, a Chair in Urban and Environmental History has been established in his name at Carnegie Mellon University. A statue of his likeness by master sculptor Robert Berks, something he would have strenuously frowned upon, graces the steps of the City-County Building on Grant Street.

While Mayor Richard Caliguiri was leading the charge to reconstruct the city, a wave of researchers, entrepreneurs and venture capitalists, some natives, others attracted by the enthusiasm pervasive in the city, were engaged in a cacophony of energized activity at the hub of the many fine educational and research institutions that made Pittsburgh their home.

The old coalition of people, steel and rivers that launched Pittsburgh into the industrial age was in the process of being replaced by a new alliance of intellect and computers for another journey on a new information highway. And like all journeys on uncharted terrain there were false starts and accidents, but it was the only way out of the wilderness, and the army of foot soldiers was readying for the many battles within the war of resurrection.

James Colker, a gritty graduate of the University of Pittsburgh, led one of the battles within the war. James Colker received a B.S. degree in physics and worked in various engineering and management capacities for RCA, General Electric, Union Switch and Signal Division of Westinghouse Air Brake, the venerable Pittsburgh company. He later joined J.W. Fecker Division of American Optical Company.

In 1964 Mr. Colker and two associates purchased the Goerz Optical Company of Inwood, New York, a transaction financed by Pittsburgh industrialist Henry Hillman. In 1969 Goerz Optical was merged with the Kollmorgen Corporation and Mr. Colker assumed the role of President and later Chairman of the Board of Contraves Goerz Corporation, a subsidiary of a Swiss conglomerate, Oerlikon Buehrle Holding.

Under his direction, the company purchased the Goerz-Inland Systems Division from Kollmorgen and the Fecker Systems Division from Owens-Illinois. Under Mr. Colker's direction, the operation grew to approximately 1,000 employees with annual sales of $90 million in 1987.

Mr. Colker founded Colker and Newlin Management Associates and CEO Venture Fund in 1987 with his good friend William Newlin. As director of CEO Venture Fund portfolio investments in software services, enterprise software and networked computer products, Mr. Colker was to play a critical role in the 80s and 90s in guiding many of the companies starting on the information highway in the Pittsburgh area to safety and profitability.

For this and his many other accomplishments, Mr. Colker was listed in the February 1985 issue of Business Week as one of the top 50 business leaders in the United States. He also received Venture Magazine's Entrepreneur of the Year Award in 1985.

However, the broadest influence of James Colker was felt in the Pittsburgh area when he was named the first President of the Pittsburgh High Technology Council, an organization formed in March 1983 on the suggestion of Jay Aldridge, at the time the President of Penn's Southwest Association (since merged with Pittsburgh Regional Alliance).

As President of the Pittsburgh High Technology Council, Mr. Colker became to business development in the Pittsburgh area what Richard Caliguiri was to infrastructure reconstruction. Cajoling, inspiring, browbeating, Colker was a dynamo in partnering hundreds of entrepreneurs launching new ideas and products with mentors and financiers in the established business community.

From information technology, to biomedical technology, to advanced materials, to environmental technology, many incubating technologies hatched to successful enterprises, creating thousands of high-paying jobs in the Pittsburgh area. For his achievements, Colker received the Renaissance Leader of 1985 award from the Pittsburgh Chapter of Public Relations Society of America.

Today, the renamed Pittsburgh Technology Council boasts 1,500 members, making it the largest trade association of its kind in the United States, thanks largely to James Colker who relinquished the chairmanship of the Council in 1999.

Whether by design or accident, the abandoned sprawling site of the Jones and Laughlin Hot Strip Mill, one of the largest of its kind in the world, was selected in 1985 for the construction of the Pittsburgh High Technology Center, symbolizing the transformation of Pittsburgh's economy from heavy manufacturing to one centered more on high technologies.

Along with the rest of the United States, the economy of Pittsburgh experienced dramatic growth in the 1990s as the shift from heavy manufacturing to high technology continued with new businesses sprouting up in information technology, software development, robotics, the nascent Internet, biomedical technology, advanced materials and environmental technology.

Computer Enterprises Inc., founded in 1992, achieved sales of $40 million with over 400 employees by providing programming, technical project management and eBusiness integration services to clients across the United States, including over 60 percent of the Fortune 60. FreeMarkets Inc., the original global sourcing company formed in 1995, saw sales grow beyond $10 million within 5 years. Tollgrade Communications, a designer of electronic equipment used to test telecommunications systems, saw sales increase to about $60 million after an initial public offering in 1995.

Seeds planted at the University of Pittsburgh's biomedical research department and Carnegie Mellon University's Engineering and Robotics Institutes also contributed significantly to the transformation of Pittsburgh's economy.

In 1998 alone, fifteen new companies emerged that had started life as research projects at Carnegie Mellon University. One of these is Carnegie Learning, Inc., a software development company that develops educational problem-solving products based on cognitive science.

Dr. John Anderson, a preeminent psychologist and computer science professor at the Carnegie Mellon University and his team of researchers, had studied the phenomenon of how the mind works for twenty years. Eventually, Dr. Anderson and his team configured their research into concrete, easy-to-use products that have motivated students of diverse backgrounds in many schools across the United States to achieve dramatic results in mathematics.

For example, Upper Darby High School in the Philadelphia area, with 3,700 students speaking 40 different languages, used cognitive-based products from Carnegie Learning to increase students' understanding of geometry, improve problem-solving skills, and engender newfound excitement for mathematics.

Another success story is found in New York City, where students from two schools at polar opposites of the economic spectrum employed cognitive-based technologies to achieve comparable improvement in their students' comprehension of mathematics. A solid contributor to the Pittsburgh economy, Carnegie Learning had sixty employees in 2003.

The Pittsburgh Technology Council's list of top 50 technology companies in 2000 contained at least 10 companies with annual revenues of over $100 million. Rapidigm, a provider of software consulting services, systems design and programming founded in 1968, has grown to over 2,000 employees with revenue in excess of $260 million.

The Pittsburgh Technology Council conducted a benchmark study of the high technology industry in the Pittsburgh area for the year ending 2001. The study quantified the impact of the region's technological resources in order to elicit a deeper understanding of the sector's contribution to the southwestern Pennsylvanian economy.

Data were collected across the 13 contiguous counties broadly defining the region that is southwestern Pennsylvania, as well the six county subset of Pittsburgh MSA, Allegheny, Beaver, Butler, Fayette, Washington and Westmoreland.

The study focused on the following industry clusters: information technology, biomedical and biotechnology advanced manufacturing, advanced materials and environmental technology. Data on wages and employment over the 1997-2001 period were collected, as well as business incorporations, venture capital, initial public offerings, university technology transfer activity and many other indicators.

For the 6-county MSA, the data revealed that a core of 2,261 companies in all the technology clusters employed 70,478 people with a total payroll of about $3.7 billion and an average salary of about $52,000.

Further analysis revealed, however, that one sector, information technology, had a disproportionate effect on the prospects of the high technology group. Furthermore, within the information cluster, the data showed that the software subcluster experienced the most dramatic growth.

In the 6-county MSA, the study showed that the number of information technology establishments increased by 64 percent from 946 to 1,552 between 1997 and 2001. The number of persons employed increased by 39.6 percent from 26,809 to 37,438, with a corresponding increase in total annual payroll from over $1.2 billion to over $2.0 billion within the same time frame. Average wages also increased by 19.7 percent from $45,623 to $54,632.

Undoubtedly, information technology contributed to increase in income and property taxes and other revenue streams for governments at all levels. Upon closer scrutiny, however, the study revealed the software subcluster, comprised of prepackaged, customized, embedded, enterprise and Internet software, had a disproportionate effect on the information technology cluster in the MSA as well as the technology sector as a whole.

Within the period of the study, the MSA experienced an increase of 66.7 percent in the number of software establishments from 656 to 1094, 58.9 percent increase in the number of employees from 9,487 to 15,076, 100.7 increase in total payroll from over $502 million to over $1.0 billion, and a 26.8 percent expansion from $52,986 to $67,236 in average wage increase.

In contrast, the study showed that manufacturing in the 6-county Pittsburgh MSA grew relatively moderately during the period evaluated. The number of manufacturing establishments increased by 6.9 percent from 3,161 to 3,381, the number employed declined by a marginal 1.9 percent from 136,433 to 133,805, total payroll increased by 7.6 percent from over $5.7 billion to over $6 billion and average wage increased by 9.7 percent from $42,050 to $46,136.

However, and this is critical, though manufacturing has in general been maligned, it is pertinent to note that by the end of 2001 the total number of establishments, total number employed and total payroll in the Pittsburgh MSA were still formidable. The average wage, though low in relative terms, still provided more than adequate sustenance for many.

In the rush to proclaim America's economy service-based, it must be remembered that the 3,381 manufacturing establishments in the MSA by the end of 2001 provided a rich avenue of nutrition for the information technology industry and revenue extractors everywhere.

The information technology industry exploded in large part by assisting the manufacturing industry improve efficiency, productivity, profitability and competitiveness. The weakening of the symbiotic relationship between manufacturing and information technologies due to maturation of productivity gains by the former was one of the underlying causes for the severe contraction of the latter at the dawn of the 21st century.

The study revealed that the environmental services subcluster, the industry that helped release the MSA from the lethal grip of pollutants, was hopping sprightly along in the midst of the condescending attitude cast upon the manufacturing sector. The number of establishments, total payroll and average wage all grew at a healthy clip. Only employment was relatively stagnant, demonstrating the utilization of advanced technologies by the industry.

Contributions of universities and research institutions to the growth of southwestern Pennsylvanian communities and beyond were documented by the study. Research activities in life sciences at the University of Pittsburgh and computer science at the Carnegie Mellon University produced seminal results.

The tissue engineering research program at the University of Pittsburgh ranked high among institutions in the U.S., while the federal government rewarded computer science excellence by placing the Department of Defense's Software Engineering Institute at the Carnegie Mellon University. The study reported that the Software Engineering Institute should focus exclusively on advancing the practice of software engineering, because software was such a critical part of U.S. defense systems.

Andrew Carnegie, the industrial genius without formal education, contributed to the defense of his country with his service during the Civil War. Now the university he founded is making its own contribution to the defense of the united country.

The State of the Industry Report prepared by the Pittsburgh Technology Council concluded that the Pittsburgh region had "transformed itself from an economy based on large, traditional and older manufacturing-oriented employers, primarily in the steel and other metals and materials industries, to one based on a diversified mix of technology, services and advanced manufacturing businesses."

The Report concluded further, "Beginning in the 1990s, the region began to reach a critical mass in several technology clusters, and the jobs created within these industries have more than offset those that were lost in steel and other industry downsizing a decade earlier." To validate this conclusion the Report stated, "More than 250,000 jobs have been created directly and indirectly by the region's technology companies."

Furthermore, the Report observed that "Technology jobs generally pay above average wages, and the growth potential for companies within the technology sector is far higher than more mature and established industries."

Transformation of the economy in the Pittsburgh area reported by the Pittsburgh Technology Council was validated by the sharp decline in the rate of unemployment by June 1999, standing at 4.3 percent compared to a national average of four percent. Overall, though the technology based companies had fewer employees per company compared to the heavy industries of old, the diversity and sheer numbers of these companies were thought to be mitigating factors against negative changes in the economy.

The newly constructed economic system in Pittsburgh, like that of other metropolitan areas, was thought to be relatively immune to the debilitating forces that had caused disintegration of heavy industry. In addition to paying higher wages, the new technology was of a different stripe: it did not produce the massive pollution that besmirched and poisoned older Pittsburgh.

Transformation of the U.S. economy as a whole from a dependency on manu-facturing to a more diversified base was confirmed by a summary provided by the US Department of Commerce, Bureau of Economic Analysis. It showed that between 1985 when the economy was showing signs of recovery and the end of 2000 when the economy was bubbling, employment in manufacturing fluctuated only slightly between 19 and 20 million jobs. For the services sectors, however, employment roared from about 31 million to over 53 million. In percentage terms the figures were even more startling. The share of total employment pro-vided by manufacturing over that period had dropped from 15.88 percent to 11.41 percent, while that of services had increased from about 25 per cent to 31.81 percent.

These were the numbers that drove public policy in the U.S. in the eighties. Promulgation of the North American Free Trade Agreement between the U.S., Canada and Mexico and the leadership position of the U.S. in the World Trade Organization were predicated on the prediction that the decline of employment in manufacturing would be more than compensated for by an increase in employment in services. The "why me worry" attitude to jobs transferring to China, Malaysia and Vietnam from the U.S. was dependent on more than a com-pensatory increase elsewhere.

Unfortunately, U.S. policy makers were (and are) sadly mistaken, because employment in the service industry was (and is) being attacked by a new phe-nomenon made possible by developments in data transmission, the Internet and telephony. And because of the contraction of the new information technology sector, revenue base of governments shrunk, exacerbated by a continuation of the deindustrialization phenomenon.

The following was extracted from an announcement made by Mayor Tom Murphy of Pittsburgh on August 6, 2003:

"I am announcing today cuts that must be made to ensure that the City remains solvent through the end of the year…The cuts I am announcing today will ensure that we can put gasoline in our Police cruisers and pay our critical public safety personnel through the end of this year…To be sure we have enough cash on hand, we will take the following actions:

• Layoff 731 employees

• Eliminate 113 currently vacant positions

• Close 26 swimming pools effective close of business on Friday, August 8.

- Close 4 Senior Centers, and

- Close all 19 Recreation Centers.

Of necessity, we are cutting our support of some of our most cherished community activities, such as the Great Race *(named after Richard Caliguiri)."*

Most of Pittsburgh's citizens were stunned by the severity of the cuts announced by Mayor Murphy. A drumbeat of bad news had predated the announcement, so even the most casual of observers expected cuts, but no one anticipated closure of a large number of swimming pools and recreational centers in the middle of an exceptionally humid summer.

And the large number of employees furloughed just before the costly back-to-school shopping season seamed callous, but some of the alternatives, including cutting the public safety budget, would have been even more unpleasant.

Mayor Murphy was not unaware of the effects of the cuts he announced. As he put it, "While I believe that these cuts are necessary, I hate doing this. I hate doing this because of what it means to the quality of life of our City and our neighborhoods. I hate it because of what it means to the lives of the hard working men and women who serve our City every single day. These cuts are difficult and painful for our community."

What Mayor Murphy was saying in effect was that he had no choice. It was either the cuts or the City tumbling into fiscal insolvency, with attendant negative repercussions on everything from public safety, to increased taxation on an already frightened small business community, to the credit rating of the City.

It was not supposed to happen like this, not after the proclamation by the pundits of the supposedly successful transformation of the economy of the city of Pittsburgh from one based on heavy industry to one based on high technology. After all, every known expert predicted the new economy would protect the city from such traumatic cuts.

True, the population of Pittsburgh had declined from 670,000 in 1960 to 350,000 while the cost of city government had risen from $34 million to $340 million a year. True as well that costs of expenses like health care for employees had risen rapidly. But of equal effect today but excessively so tomorrow is the fact that generation of jobs by the new economy, especially the glamorous information technology sector, is being hijacked by a new phenomenon.

And the dangerous phenomenon stalking Pittsburgh and all America today is offshore outsourcing.

Pittsburgh paid a heavy price in environmental degradation when it gave America much of its industrial goods and technologies. The city paid a heavier price in human cast off when the incompetents to whom its heritage had been entrusted failed to nurture it with the same devotion as those who created it. Through it all the children of Pittsburgh girded their loins at every turn since the city was founded to confront and overcome seemingly insurmountable obstacles.

But it may be impossible even for the hardened and ingenious people of Pittsburgh to overcome the new wave of jobs being shifted overseas. And Pittsburgh is not alone. Pain will be felt across America on a scale perhaps not seen since the Great Depression. True, budgets are being squeezed by other events happening in Washington, but most local and state governments had anticipated that growing employment in the amorphously defined service industry would come to their rescue. What most policy makers have not publicly acknowledged is that the high technology service sector is not quite living up to expectations.

Education is being squeezed across the U.S. The New York Times reported on August 24, 2003: "At many public universities grappling with record budget cuts and enrollments at the same time, the classroom is no longer being spared. After whittling away at staff, coaxing faculty members to juggle more classes, stripping sports teams and trusting aging roofs to hold out a few years longer, many public universities have reluctantly begun chopping away at academics, making it harder for students to graduate on time."

The report in the Times continued, "The University of Illinois has canceled 1,000 classes on hundreds of subjects this year...The University of Colorado has eliminated academic programs in journalism, business and engineering. The University of California has put off opening an entire campus."

The Times reported, "At the California State University, up to 30,000 students will be turned away come spring." An administrator was quoted by the Times: "The academic cuts are probably the most severe I've seen."

Cancellation of an engineering program is like amputating one's hands, but it has been done. The nursing degree program at the University of Missouri was canceled, this in the face of a severe nursing shortage.

Tuition fees have been hiked by up to 30 percent in some states; students are paying more but receiving far less. California has slashed $2.5 billion from the K-12 schools budget, with more to come. Tennessee shaved $102 million from higher education.

Health care is taking a beating. Newsweek reports that pharmacies in Washington State have stopped accepting Medicaid coupons after the state lowered its reimbursement. Due to an $804 million budget gap, LA County closed 16 health clinics and two hospitals.

Just like manufacturing jobs in Pittsburgh and many other locations across the country were brutally slashed in the eighties, so too are high technology service jobs being siphoned away in the thousands from the shores of the U.S. to places many have never heard of like Bangalore, Kolkotta and Mumbai.

The difference this time is there are no physical structures like steel plants to which workers can focus the public's mind to their plight. And if strong unions at the steel plants could not save steelworkers from being butchered, the defenseless high technology service workers, who have built a chorus of not belonging to unions, will be swatted away like flies.

Unlike the men of steel who had the fraternity of unions and communality of extended steel families to rely on for sustenance, the service workers of today are for the most part cocooned in suburbia with not even their neighbors, with whom they hardly interact, available for words of solace.

The information super highway that was supposed to lead America's children to the promised land of great-paying high technology jobs has turned instead into one on which offshore outsourcing is killing computer programming, engineering, accounting and other professional jobs at high speed. And the carnage has not hit rush hour, yet.

Some defenders of globalization would have people believe that the millions of jobs in manufacturing and information technology mushrooming overseas are not being created at the expense of the United States. Those that confess to the truth engineer the excuse that these job losses are actually good for the economy, since the invisible hand of the market will lead to creation of replacements. But so far, the only visible manufacturing-related jobs are those at McDonalds: quality jobs remain invisible.

5

INTERNET-ENABLING TECHNOLOGIES

The dependence of the global economy on information technologies is due to a seminal invention by two American heroes, Dennis Ritchie and Kenneth Thompson. These two men were the alpha "geeks" who built the foundation for the later generation of "geeks" who invented Internet, Windows, and many other systems taken for granted today.

In the early days of the computer industry, each vendor wrote an operating system designed specifically for the features of their computers. This made it difficult, if not impossible, for communication among researchers and companies alike. Plus, not only were operating systems large and complicated, only one user at a time was allowed, much like a hand-held telephone.

These problems caused frustration, agony and anger among researchers in particular, because progress in research, achieved through sharing and block building by different research groups, was being hamstrung by the poor communication infrastructure.

As the frustrations of the computer industry began to boil over, computer vendors contributed teams to a group effort to develop a more efficient enabling operating system. This responsibility was assigned to a team of engineers, including Ritchie and Thompson.

The project was given the unwieldy name of MULTiplexed Information & Computing Science (MULTICS). The complexity of the name proved prophetic as the project failed, the main reason being the antiquated software in existence at the time. The software failed to interact effectively with the hardware, causing repeated collapses of the entire system. Bell Laboratories, a partner in the project, pulled out in frustration, convinced it was an exercise in futility.

However, Ritchie, Thompson and a few colleagues were convinced elements of MULTICS, like how to build a file system, could be salvaged to build a successful operating system. The boys were also without a machine to play a game Thompson had written called Space Travel, involving an attempt to land a ship on the various planets and moons in a simulated Solar System.

Ritchie and Thompson designed a new software package to run Space Travel on a PD-7 computer, which had an excellent display processor. Proving the adage that "All work and no play makes Jack a dull boy," the software developed to provide entertainment became a roaring success, to the amazement of their superiors.

Kenneth Thompson was the brainchild behind the concept of a file system, which was at the heart of the new operating system, while Dennis Ritchie contributed the idea of device files. Making files the core of every operation executed by the new operating system was a simple yet revolutionary concept that attracted the immediate attention of the computing industry. By having several file systems, instead of one large memory, the operating system achieved the flexibility to undertake and execute several different functions efficiently and simultaneously. A malfunctioning part that would have ground the old system to a halt could be circumvented since it was isolated into a file.

The operating system that eventually grew out of the efforts of Thompson and Ritchie in 1969 was named Uniplexed Information & Computing Science, a pun on the name of the previous effort. A quick-thinking individual in the group changed the new acronym from UNICS to UNIX, perhaps attempting to sever linkage with the ill-fated MULTICS.

The success of UNIX was due to its simplicity, but the assembly language was limited in its ability to provide development tools. Systematic improvements were made until the team hit a jackpot with "C" language, completed by Dennis Ritchie for UNIX in 1973. It proved to be seminal.

C language offered a revolutionary approach to software design by connecting simple tools, rather than the large stand-alone application programs of old. It was small in size and made extensive use of pointers for memory, array, structures and functions. It produced efficient programs and could be compiled on a variety of computers. It could handle programs from the simplest to the most complicated.

UNIX C provided what is known as a consistent application interface. In this environment, a software developer could write an application on one computer with the high degree of confidence that it would run on another computer. Portability is taken for granted today, but it was not feasible before UNIX C.

UNIX C allowed a computer to run even when a new application was installed or upgrades were made to an existing application, because the hardware's resources were managed by the operating system and not the application.

It acted like a Godfather by being ruthless with those who wished to break "omerta," and soft and gentle with those who towed the line.

The functional capabilities of UNIX C were nirvana to programmers everywhere: their job had been simplified beyond their wildest imagination. Programmers who run rampant with the new toy at their disposal created most of the applications in existence today: they drove the vehicle fast, long and hard and still it would not collapse. The many applications developed for Windows without clearance from Microsoft was made possible by the use of the basic UNIX C concept.

One of the demands in the early days by organizations seeking a new operating system was that it should operate like the utilities, which are shared by many at the same time without usually encountering any problem. The ability to simultaneously print a file, download a file from the Internet while working with Word—multi-tasking—is made possible by the features incorporated in UNIX, which husbands the resources of the hardware to generate maximum efficiency.

Micro-computers, super computers, workstations, computing affordability, Palm, cell phones and the Internet were all made possible by the operating system designed initially to provide entertainment for two kids at heart.

In 1999 President Bill Clinton presented the National Medal of Technology to the two bearded aristocrats of information technology for making our lives so much easier and improving our quality of life in such a dramatic way.

During his introductory remarks, President Clinton summed up the monumental achievements of Dennis Ritchie and Kenneth Thompson as follows, "I'd like to take just a moment to reaffirm something that is obvious to all of you, but needs to be equally clear to your fellow Americans. In an age when the entire store of knowledge doubles every five years, where prosperity depends upon command of that ever-growing store of knowledge, the United States is the strongest it has ever been, thanks in large measure to the remarkable pace and scope of American Science and Technology."

Before Thompson and Ritchie began toiling away on B, C and other languages, a gaping hole in US defenses had been exposed in 1957 when the Soviets launched Sputnik, the first artificial earth satellite. An apoplectic Defense Department responded by forming the Advanced Research Projects Agency (ARPA), later changed to Defense Advanced Research Projects Agency (DARPA), to establish U.S. lead in science and technology applicable to the military.

To counter the threat posed by Sputnik, Paul Baran of Rand Corporation was awarded a contract by the U.S. Air Force to device a survival strategy by which the U.S. could maintain command and control over its missiles and bombs in the event of a military strike by the Soviets. The objective was to build a network that allowed the military infrastructure to survive a military strike and retain enough functional capacity to launch an effective counter attack.

Baran's recommendation in 1962 was a strategy based on breaking data into smaller packets, tagging the packets to indicate origin and destination, and then forwarding the data not on a monolithic system but rather from one computer to another until it reached its final destination. A further provision was that if transmission was lost at any given point it could be re-routed from its point of origin.

The proposal to deviate from a monolithic system to one linked together by discrete and independent systems was, of course, identical to the philosophy behind UNIX. So, uncannily, two projects launched by independent teams with different objectives had been initiated with identical core principles. It came as no surprise, therefore, that the two projects would intersect to launch the Internet. But that was to come later.

In the meantime, an unresolved problem was to make the computers communicate ("talk"} with one another: the concept of networking was worthless if this was not feasible. So in 1965 a team connected a computer in Massachusetts to another in California with a low speed dial-up telephone line, creating the first wide-area computer network ever built. After a maddeningly long period still typical of dial up, data transmission and retrieval between the computers at opposite coasts of the U.S. were successfully executed. No doubt the teams at both ends of the network hoisted a glass or two in celebration.

In late 1966 Lawrence G. Roberts, a participant in the formation of the network, went to DARPA to translate the proposal submitted by Paul Baran into reality. The result was the birth of a localized Internet known as Advanced Research Projects Agency Network (ARPANET).

The Internet is a loose association of millions of computers and thousands of networks working together across the world to share and transmit information. However, a group of main lines, known as Internet backbone and owned by Internet Service Providers (ISP), carries the bulk of the traffic. Today, there are five points or core stations in the United States where these lines intersect: San Francisco, San Jose, Chicago, Pennsauken (New Jersey) and Washington, D.C. These stations use high-speed networking equipment to connect the backbone to other networks owned by smaller regional and local ISPs, which in turn lease access to companies and individuals in their service domain. But this network of universal continuity was to be formed much later.

In the beginning, though, the node at UCLA was linked with only three others to form the initial ARPANET. More computers were quickly added; the protocol for data transmission along the network called Network Control Protocol (NCP) was formulated, spurring the development of applications to transform the Internet into a living, breathing, and functioning beast.

In March of 1972, motivated by the need to improve communication among the developers, Ray Tomlinson of BBN wrote a "send and read" software and demonstrated its feasibility by sending the first e-mail across the Internet. In July Lawrence Roberts developed new software empowering the e-mail system with more useful features such as the capability to not only read and send, but to file, forward and respond to messages. It was also during this period that ARPA was renamed DARPA.

Just like the original UNIX, the source code of which was shipped free of charge by Kenneth Thompson with the notation Love, Ken, ARPANET was based on accessibility: it was designed in such a way that subsets could be manipulated, cleaned and dirtied so far as certain basic and practical rules were followed. And just like UNIX, innovators everywhere transformed the Internet beyond even the wildest dreams of its founders by loading on several applications. But this was to come later: there were still bugs to be expunged from the system.

One of these bugs was the inability of NCP to establish communication beyond one of the core stations on the ARPANET, which broke the end-to-end continuity demanded by DARPA, so a new protocol called TCP/IP was proposed.

TCP/IP refers to two separate parts of one system: the Transmission Control Protocol (TCP) and the Internet Protocol (IP). TCP breaks down every piece of data such as e-mail message or a web page into packets, the same concept enunciated by Baran and others for the infrastructure. The IP then maps out a strategy to forward the data to its final destination through a series of routers. Each router examines the packet, determines its origin and final destination before sending it to another router. The process continues until the packet reaches its final destination. Meanwhile, the other packets from the disassembled e-mail travel to the final destination, but not necessarily along the same route: each packet travels along the most efficient route available. The TCP reassembles all the packets upon arrival at the set destination. But first the TCP/IP had to be developed.

It is uncanny how at almost every turn the development of the Internet paralleled that of the UNIX. The UNIX broke down the storage system into many files, each unique yet dependent on the others. Each file was important yet not so much it could bring the entire system to a halt. It was the same thinking that went into the development of the TCP/IP: each network would be a distinct stand-alone entity, playing an important part in the transmission process but not so critical a part to shut down the entire system.

The inventors of the Internet and the UNIX both shared the key philosophy of having a platform for sharing resources on a wide scale, with Dennis Ritchie taking every opportunity to remind his audience of this feature.

The formal change from NCP to TCP/IP occurred on January 1, 1983. It was an event carefully planned over a three-year period. All hosts converted successfully at the same time, but not before engineers and operators alike had been subjected to a severe case of the jitters.

Programmers everywhere began to formulate ways to sort and index the massive amount of information transmitted across the network. Search engines started to appear and Tim Berners-Lee implemented a system to organize and provide convenient access to information in 1992. It allowed documents to include pointers and links to other documents, leading to the birth of the World Wide Web (WWW).

In 1993 Marc Andreessen created a graphical user interface allowing multimedia information to be transmitted and received and interactions with the network within a single program. Thus was born commercial web browsers, with its flexible access contributing to the explosive growth of the network.

Microsoft's software, especially the Windows family, made the personal computer user-friendly and Intel's chips enhanced the power of the personal computer. But Sun Microsystems, led by CEO Scott McNealy, designed and built cost effective UNIX-based workstations, allowing the use of the Internet to propagate to all corners of the world.

The U.S. Federal Networking Council (FNC) officially proclaimed the Internet, together with its mode of operations and critical components, into existence on October 24, 1995 and launching the major medium of global communication into existence. But just because Vice President Al Gore presided over the proceedings does not mean he invented the Internet

The evolution of the Internet as the major medium of global communication held profound implications for workers everywhere. Because blending global interconnectivity with internet-enabling technologies had the potential to shatter distance as a barrier to commerce to such a degree that a colleague next door would practically be the same as one 6,000 miles away. But for this to be achieved, the cost of communication had to be reduced significantly. And along came broadband to make this feasible.

Bit is a pulse characterizing how information is transmitted along a communication line. The number of bits per second is a measure of bandwidth (the total information flow over a given time) on a telecommunications medium. When the Internet was launched, the link between the end-user and their network service provider was achieved by using dial-up analog modems with speeds ranging up to 56 thousand bits per second (Kbps), which was slow and subject to multiple interruptions. Then came Integrated Services Digital Network (ISDN), which increased speeds to 64 Kbps and 128 Kbps, but these were still insufficient to carry massive amounts of data. Everything changed with development of Digital Subscriber Line (DSL), which converted existing telephone lines into access paths for multimedia and high speed data at speeds up to 7 million bits per second (Mbps).

DSL started slowly, with connections initially restricted within countries. All that changed when the now-defunct WorldCom launched fiber optic cables across the Oceans, connecting countries to the high-speed world. DSL and satellite, which uses a satellite dish to connect to the Internet, were codenamed broadband to differentiate the new high-speed world from the old, antiquated system.

Data and voice transmission were accelerated by broadband, reducing cost of communication between far-flung countries to a fraction that of dial-up systems. Thus was born a new world in which distance was obliterated as a barrier to communication. It mattered not whether two people were separated by a street or by an ocean: cost and time were virtually the same. Telephone calls initiated within the United States carried almost the same cost as one between the United States and India. A telephone call from the United States could be routed instantaneously to India at virtually no additional cost, allowing a worker in India to walk a customer through the workings of a new computer, cell-phone, dishwater and television set, a service previously restricted to a US worker. With the Indian worker paid only a fraction that of an American worker, a new era of offshore outsourcing in the call industry was born.

Combination of broadband and technologies specially adapted to the Internet (Internet-enabled technologies) allowed massive amounts of data to be transmitted and processed in far-flung locations at virtually no additional cost. One of these, Optical Character Recognition (OCR), is in the process of wiping out thousands of office workers who inhabit gleaming high rises across the urban landscape of the U.S.

Optical Character Recognition is the technology that allows transformation of paper documents to computer files. It converts a magazine page, newspaper, fax, press-clippings, printer, photocopy or page from a book into digital form.

OCR eliminates the need to recreate a document from scratch, a tedious assignment when legibility is problematic. It provides the best alternative to manual data entry and typing. It is far more advanced than the conventional scanner routine in many offices and homes.

The process of using OCR is quite simple: place the document into the scanner and press "Scan & Read" wizard, verify the recognition result and export it to one of the office applications (MS Word, MS Excel, email, etc.) or save it in a computer format (HTML, PDF, TXT, etc.) supported by the host system.

Thus, all the process of data input from paper to computer (i.e. from scanning to export of recognition results) takes less than a minute, and the electronic document looks just like the original.

OCR can be installed on a network server and on local workstations. Once the program has been installed on the server, it can be installed remotely on local workstations anywhere over the network.

Businesses can host a number of workstations sharing OCR work, allowing multiple users on the network to process, recognize, and proofread the same batch of documents simultaneously—essentially creating an OCR production line.

OCR allows electronic dictionaries to be shared by all users. It also supports multiple language formats, allowing for documents received in one language to be translated into others for transmission to multiple destinations.

OCR includes a FormFiller, an application for completing and printing out forms. Extremely useful for bank transfers, tax forms, customs document, etc., this application transforms a scanned form into a digital form, which can be defined and then saved as a template. Users simply open the image, define fields, enter the required information and print it out. This eliminates the need to fill out the forms by hand or with a manual typewriter.

OCR recognizes odd shapes, multicolumn pictures, and wrap-around text, ideal for recognizing magazine articles and marketing brochures. It can filter out so-called background "noise" such as color and texture, increasing accuracy and format retention. OCR changes the compression ratio or resolution of pictures when exporting to PDF, HTML and RTF file formats to increase transmission speeds via email.

Hitherto setting up an office has meant purchasing an elaborate array of computers and associate software and hiring staff to handle, among other functions, inter-company data communication like receiving and processing purchase orders, invoicing, warehousing, deliveries, etc. Not only can the cost be excessive, it is also time consuming, perhaps even to the point of delaying start up due to snarls in software integration. Now, switching to web-based electronic data interchange (EDI) can generate substantial cost and time saving.

Web EDI allows a company to trade documents electronically with other companies without buying any software: only a web browser and Internet access are required to begin operations. It sends and receives data in any format, and is exceedingly less expensive than conventional EDI. It is independent of platforms, Mac or Windows, and does not require any software maintenance. A host company handles all transactions, making web EDI the least expensive in this field. In addition, company employees with security clearance can access transactions from any location with Internet access.

Implications of web EDI are stupendous, the most potent of which are accessibility and manipulation of data by a contracted worker located anywhere in the world with access to the Internet.

With web EDI and other Internet-enabling technologies, the flow of suddenly higher priced American workers into the chill wind of unemployment will turn into a torrent.

The Internet funded by U.S. taxpayers, invented by Americans and gifted to the world is now being used by other Americans to deprive U.S. citizens of their livelihood. Who would have "thunk" that?

6

BUSINESS PROCESS OUTSOURCING (BPO)

With the advent of easy to use and inexpensive communication tools facilitated by the Internet, a new corporate global philosophy has been unofficially enacted that says basic research will be done anywhere in the world, but manufacturing will be in Asia and back offices will be in India. America will wake up to desolation if this philosophy goes unchallenged.

Jordan Times, March 9, 2003, contained the following: "The first wave of globalization saw multilateral institutions from the US, Europe and Japan move the production of clothes, appliances and cars abroad. A significant part of the production chain was outsourced from low wage countries. The second wave of globalization and one of the biggest trends reshaping the global economy is the outsourcing of business support services from developing countries who have English-speaking workforce with a good number of university graduates and where the salary structure is way below that of the rich countries. The work is normally shipped electronically in what has become known as IT enabled services or teleworking."

An example provided said: "This is a small Jordanian company specialising in animation and digital media production, who has entered recently in a partnership with Fat Rock Entertainment, a Los Angeles based film and animation company." The agreement called for Fat Rock to build the facility in Jordan, procure contracts from the US, and participate in joint animated productions.

The paper continued: "The global market for outsource business is still small but it is likely to grow at double digit rates in the coming few years. First-world companies still do most of their back office and support activities in house, even though these tend to be expensive and are not related to the core competence of companies."

To reduce cost the paper said: "For example, it is estimated that a typical bank in the US or Europe can outsource 25 per cent of its support and back office activities, reduce its cost to income ratio and achieve greater efficiency and higher productivity. The trend is likely to continue with a global market for IT-related outsourced services estimated by the research firm Bradstreet to exceed $200 billion this year."

The paper mentioned that, "Employees in India or Costa Rica are now responding to people in Europe and the US who inquire about bank balances, credit card payments, airline reservations and upgrading and how to install software on newly purchased computers. The value of outsourced business here is forecast to exceed $5 billion in 2005."

"Second in importance," the paper said, "is data entry and conversion which include medical transcription. Companies in Philippines, India and elsewhere convert dictation by doctors in America into written medical reports. The value of outsourcing of medical transcription coming from the US is estimated to reach $4 billion by 2005. Third in importance is the outsourcing of problem solving. Here services such as processing insurance claims, selling stocks, analysing companies and evaluating credit ratings can all be outsourced for one third of their cost in the US or Europe. By utilising databases over the web, offshore staff can offer independent research on companies, sectors or individuals Finally, expert knowledge services that require specialists is also being outsourced. These include architectural work, animation and computer graphics, design work and technical analysis among others."

The industrial landscape in many advanced countries has undergone a radical transformation in recent decades. Relocation of manufacturing overseas has reduced that sector's share of business activity, while the service sector in general has seen a corresponding growth. In the US, for example, manufacturing's share of the employment market dropped from 15.3 percent to 12.7 percent between 1990 and 2000, while that of business services increased from 22 percent to 27 percent. The Bureau of Labor Statistics (BLS) projected the decline of manufacturing to continue to 11.4 percent by 2010, but this was achieved in a relatively short time in July 2003.

With increase in growth of business services projected to continue, policymakers everywhere raced to rearrange priorities to increase share of this lucrative market for their geographical areas. Federal, state and local governments across the board made growth in the services industry the cornerstone of economic revival strategies.

One of the reasons for growth in business services has been the trend towards more outsourcing of non-core activities by organizations to reduce cost and increase concentration of people and resources on core competencies. However, the traditional definition of outsourcing whereby one company contracted another to execute part of its business process is now almost obsolete. In its place is a relatively new phenomenon called business process outsourcing (BPO) where not just part but an entire non-core business process of a company is transferred to an outside company. This transforms the fixed cost of undertaking the activity in terms of people, time and resource-devotion to a variable cost, which can be lowered through competitive bidding.

In addition to cost reduction, companies gain the flexibility to react quickly to changing market conditions. If demand necessitated outsourced service to be increased, the external service specialist has the capability to respond much quicker than if the service was being executed internally. The service provider, in effect, becomes a partner capable of making decisions otherwise difficult within the organization. So BPO is an indisputable tool for productivity enhancement.

The first companies to exploit the opportunities offered by BPO were those partnered with their clients in traditional outsourcing programs. Automatic Data Processing (ADP), the Roseland, N.J.-based leader in payroll outsourcing in the U.S, branched into BPO human resources, including benefits, payroll and task administration. The added opportunities emanated from a trusted position as long time payroll partners of their clients.

Rochester, NY-based Paycheck, the second-largest payroll processing company in the U.S. owned by the billionaire Thomas Golisano, started by delivering an efficient traditional outsourcing service by processing client payrolls faster and cheaper than the client could handle internally. Then Paycheck expanded into the behemoth it is today by offering additional services in accounting, finance and human resources.

Introduction of personal computers and servers, with their attendant software packages, in the work place generated a new form of business process outsourcing. Many companies perplexed by the new machines and systems found it more cost effective, and less of a headache, to outsource installation of hardware and software, troubleshooting, system integration of new software, training and other information technology functions to an outside company. EDS, the company founded by the billionaire Ross Perot in Plano, Texas, was the first to offer these services on a large scale.

As information technologies grew in complexity, the traditional outsourcing pioneered by EDS increased exponentially, with old and new companies like

IBM, Microsoft, Sun Microsystems and Oracle jumping into the fray. It made sense to outsource IT operations to the providers of the servers and software.

In time IBM, for example, acquired the capability to offer integrated services across all systems, platforms and languages whether IBM manufactured them or not. Focusing IBM on delivery of information technology services was the strategy the Mineola, NY-born Lou Gerstner, appointed CEO and Chairman of the Board in April 1993, employed to reverse the declining fortunes of the company headquartered in his home state.

Outsourcing continued to claim new avenues for growth. In 2000, Hewlett-Packard was looking for a BPO partner with expertise in provision of services over the Internet in order to reduce its $800 million annual travel budget. GetThere, a company acquired by Sabre in October 2000, won the online travel procurement contract. The system allowed HP employees ready access to travel information without the usual time-consuming interaction with travel agents. With their own in-house Expedia.com, HP realized savings of about $120 million in their travel budget.

An official at Sabre explained the transaction as follows: "Travel is important to our clients but not core. Partnering with us lets them take advantage of our technology and travel domain expertise. This allows them to concentrate on investing their talent in their core competencies."

Even companies offering BPO relinquished non-core processes to other external service providers. IBM formed a partnership with supply chain management company, i2 Technologies, to pursue web-based supply chain management, CRM and product cycle management.

However, IBM then turned around and delegated its Windows Millenium Upgrade project to iLogistix based in Fremont, CA. So while IBM still provided the product, iLogistix was responsible for all other processes related to fulfilling online orders. iLogistix processed the order and responded to questions from customers via phone and e-mail.

Microsoft awarded a BPO contract to Hewlett-Packard to provide centralized end-user technical support for 61,000 Microsoft employees, vendors and contractors in up to 68 countries. The multi-million dollar agreement made Microsoft one of the largest clients of the HP Services division, which provides consulting, and system integration, customer support and BPO services.

The same cost saving and core competency forces driving the BPO industry caused Microsoft to relinquish this part of its operations. Still, Microsoft remains one of the largest providers of BPO in its own core competencies of customized software development and systems integration.

EDS said BPO represented its sweet spot for growth as it realigned some of its business lines and shored up more operating cash. In a BPO agreement announced in June 2003, EDS teamed up with electronic procurement and logistics company World Wide Technology to help it hire and manage professional contract workers.

In a similar BPO deal, EDS signed real estate management firm Realm Business Solutions to help the company improve its own rent collection and property management technology platform. EDS and Realm said they planned to combine Realm's patent pending rent collection technology platform with EDS' processing and depository lines. The companies said the relationship would enable Realm to expand its COLLECT rent collection management software, while using EDS' check processing services. Both companies planed to open a new processing center in El Segundo, CA to serve West Coast markets.

Overall, there is no non-core business process, however obscure, that is not a candidate for BPO. For that matter, there is no business too small and none too large to escape the tentacles of a BPO.

Even state and local governments are turning increasingly to BPO to extract the value accrued by third-party management of specific services. The federal government, by its very size and sheer volume of contractors, directly and indirectly employs BPO to deliver cost savings in an era of increasing budget deficits. Non-governmental organizations are flocking to BPO to help compensate for reduced public funding.

Gartner, a consulting firm, projected the global BPO industry to grow from $122 billion in 2003 to $248 billion in 2005. North America's share was projected at 57 percent in 2003.

The effect of BPO on employment is not transparent. It can be negative if the client dismisses staff and the external service representative absorbs additional workload without a corresponding increase in its work force. Or it can be positive if the client improves efficiency without dismissing staff, while the ESP increases its work force with the acquisition of additional workload. There are shades of possibilities between the two scenarios.

However, the implications of an extensive BPO are breathtaking. Taken to its limit, only a CEO and his coterie of very top managers and critical plant staff will be left to directly manage the affairs of a manufacturing company

Manufacturing, shipping and receiving, payables and receivables, basic research and development, purchasing, accounting and advertising are all susceptible to BPO treatment.

IBM purchased the BPO unit of PricewaterhouseCoopers' in 2002 with an eye on the projected increase in billings in the finance and accounting BPO industry from $40 billion in 2002 to $65 billion in 2006, a 12.3 percent, five year annual compounded growth rate.

The capability of the BPO industry has increased dramatically from the old standard "debits on the left and credits on the right" to sophisticated products like "trend data analysis—information that will help the chief financial officer (CFO) make better decisions."

Supply chain management was among the first BPO to reach maturity. Oracle's e-business suite is a popular software package with capabilities to be integrated with third party products like Freight Logic and Clear Orbit to deliver, in industry jargon, "supply chain design, forecasting, demand requirement management and supply planning, warehouse and distribution management, transportation logistics, supply chain systems integration (bolt-on) with existing systems, electronic data interchange with customers and vendors."

Supply chain management ESP has the capability to interact with the client in order to direct purchasing, receiving and storage of raw materials according to order patterns and actual orders on the books. The ESP can turn around and store the finished product for scheduled delivery to the client's customers. Wal-Mart was among the first companies to master this process through systems integration with suppliers.

Human resource (HR) BPO is another mature industry. The ESP receives and analyzes payroll data, report and pay payroll taxes, issue payments (via check or electronic payment) and reports to employees. Hiring and training according to industry and company specific needs, bringing new hires on board, relocation and expatriation administration, labor management and local compliance issues are all within the capability limits of many ESPs.

Market specific databases, sales analysis and reporting, sales management, sales force automation, follow-up reminders, e-mail campaigns, lost customer conversions, are BPO-specific functions. An ESP using web-based software platforms can perform these functions hitherto performed by in-house internal sales staff more efficiently and at less cost.

Sales reports and orders can be verified by a manager, who in turn can relay questions to a sales manager from his house. Proprietary technologies can be installed allowing the entire manufacturing process to be monitored offsite.

An ESP can monitor quality continuously and take corrective actions in many instances without the knowledge of the plant's staff. In the words of the industry,

"A proprietary application performs cross-database correlation on coded and image databases and scans all records for errors."

Equipment performance history allows the ESP to schedule maintenance of individual unit operations, instead of conventional maintenance shut downs. The result is less downtime, increased productivity and enhanced profits.

Taken to its fullest potential, business process outsourcing on a large scale has the capability to cause negative impact on employment. But the impact on employment could be even more devastating if a relatively new phenomenon—offshore outsourcing—continues to march through the U.S.

In effect business processes in human resources, financial services, customer service, data processing and manufacturing can all be done overseas, with the result being transfer of attached jobs from the U.S. This is the phenomenon known as offshore outsourcing or offshoring.

It began in manufacturing with overseas relocation of labor intensive and lower valued products like shoes, toys, clothing and basic furniture. The wooden furniture industry, for example, has been completely rationalized by business process outsourcing of the offshore variety, with most manufacturing done in China and skeletal staff left in the United States for marketing, product development and design and sales.

Since workers in higher valued industries earn higher wages, it was only logical that employers would transfer manufacture of products like automobile parts, machinery and computers overseas to obtain even greater benefits. So began the climb up the food chain, which is still in progress. This is the reason why manufacturing in the U.S. is still being gorged, and why the process will only accelerate if fundamental changes are not made to balance the cost scales in the U.S.

The exodus of "white collar" business process outsourcing to overseas locations was born with the advent of information technology and broadband. Just like manufacturing, it began with lower end products like customer service, marketing and data processing. And following in manufacturing's footsteps, the phenomenon is moving up the food chain to higher value added services, and will gorge "white collar" professionals on the same scale as their manufacturing counterparts.

This is the logical progression of the attack on the labor infrastructure of the United States. What jobs will replace the higher valued manufacturing jobs leaving the United States? What jobs will replace the professional jobs leaving the United States? Is there any guarantee that a product developed in the United States will be manufactured in the United States? How in the world can the exodus of all these higher paying jobs be good for the United States?

The people who say this phenomenon is good for the U.S. are using historical development as a reference. In the past, destruction of jobs has always been replaced by new and better jobs. This phenomenon is no different. But the new jobs do not have to be in the United States. Because of the big difference in wages between China, India and the United States, employers have less of an incentive to keep employing American workers. Until the time arrives when American workers are ready to accept the same wages as workers in developing countries, the direction of jobs will be towards developing countries.

The force driving jobs overseas obeys laws of gravity and thermodynamics, which are two fundamental mechanisms of nature. Because of gravity, a ball placed on a tilted board rolls down the incline, not upwards. In a similar manner, a hotter object gives up its heat until equilibrium is established. In the same manner, employers are moving jobs to lower wage countries after prying open those markets. And unless there is a mitigating force, this motion will continue until equilibrium is established.

Professor Daniel Trefler of the University of Toronto is telling American workers not to worry, because rising wages will cause China to cede its advantage. Of course, this is completely illogical. The reason why wages in previously low wage countries like Taiwan, South Korea and Malaysia did not materially affect U.S. wages is because of relatively low populations. Also, wages in Japan were kept artificially low during the Second World War. But the Japanese economy was productive enough to support higher wages by producing goods for both internal consumption and export.

But when the labor pool of the lower wage country is about five times that of the United States, and the overwhelming majority of the local population cannot afford goods being manufactured, it is pure wishful thinking to assume wages will rise in China without any adverse consequences in the United States. Indeed, the fact that wages are already falling in the United States and the jobs being created in the U.S. are not internationally competitive present enough proof of the damage being done to U.S. labor.

The reality is that without any mitigating force, wages in the United States will continue to decline in four ways. First, the size of the labor pool in the U.S. will be cut by direct unemployment. Second, new plants will simply be built overseas. Third, retiring workers in the U.S. will not replaced in the U.S. Fourth, wages and benefits of remaining employees will be reduced. All four phenomena are happening in the United States and will accelerate unless something else is done to stem the flow.

One thing is certain; a river will flow inexorably towards an ocean. Only damming slows its flow. Likewise, offshore outsourcing will turn into a flood, if not dammed.

As the information technology industry exploded with introduction of a dizzying array of products and services, the demand for qualified workers in the U.S. outstripped supply.

The U.S. Immigration and Naturalization Service (INS) responded by raising the number of "H-1B" visas to 115,000 in 1998 to allow qualified foreigners to be employed legally in the U.S. to fill this gap.

With the clamor by the technology industry for more foreign workers growing to a crescendo in the wake of the fear engendered by the Y2K phenomenon, both the U.S. House and Senate on October 2, 2000 overwhelmingly approved legislation to increase the "H1-B" visas to 195,000 annually for the next six years.

"This bill was intended to keep America on top of the high-tech industry," intoned Senator Phil Gramm, R-Texas, after the 96 to 1 vote. Gramm predicted the visas would allow U.S. companies to use the "brain power" of non-Americans to "help promote more jobs, more growth and more opportunity."

"This will help give growing high-tech American companies the workers they need to be competitive," said Senator Harry Reid, D-Nevada.

There are "perhaps as many as one million unfilled positions in the high-tech industry today," proclaimed Sen. Spencer Abraham, R-Michigan. "Training programs, high school programs are not producing enough workers prepared to take these jobs," he said.

But Abraham admitted, "immigration is only a stop gap solution to these problems," and he called for better U.S. education and training to fill the long-term high-tech gap.

While the technology industry was euphoric by the increase in the "H1-B" visa allocation program, labor groups were incensed. Labor groups protested that the program was being championed by the technology industry as a Trojan horse to force wages down in the U.S. and take jobs away from Americans.

Supporters countered that because U.S. educational institutions were not producing qualified graduates fast enough, increasing the number of "H1-B" visas was a short-term solution necessary to stop U.S. companies from relocating overseas to find qualified employees.

The high-tech industry drowned dissenting voices, mostly in the House. "I am disappointed that the Senate would increase the number of foreign high-tech workers without including any safeguards for American workers," moaned Rep. Lamar Smith, R-Texas, who sponsored an amendment, approved by the House

Judiciary Committee, that would have required companies using the visas to increase the median pay of their U.S. workers in addition to establishing job protections.

The bill approved by the Judiciary Committee would have lifted the ceiling on the visas while requiring that the immigrants be paid at least $40,000 annually and not be used to replace U.S. workers. The bill was defeated under vehement opposition from the technology industry.

Implosion of the high-tech bubble in 2001 resulted in a severe contraction in employment across the length and breadth of the information highway. Even the heralded services market was not spared the whiplash unleashed across the industry. With decrease demand came a demand to reduce costs.

Thus was a hitherto little known nugget called offshore business process outsourcing, or offshore outsourcing, discovered in 2001 as one company after another scoured the marketing jungle for opportunities. By then two things had changed that would launch offshore outsourcing into the stratosphere.

First was the pleasant discovery by the technology industry through the "H1-B" visa program that the less expensive foreign workers were just as competent as those in the U.S. Second, fiber optics and broadband communications had expanded so rapidly that employees in far-flung places could provide services through the Internet via a secure dedicated satellite link.

In the industry jargon pronounced in 2001, "Early inhibitors to BPO were security risks, bandwidth shortcomings and general technological immaturity. But recent improvements in collaborative technology and interconnectivity strongly encourage it."

A project in Washington D.C. could be executed by a team based in Anaheim, overseas or by multiple teams in different countries. The need to bring a foreign worker to the U.S. through the H1-B program and the headache attendant with the process had been obviated.

It was a Eureka-type moment for the IT industry, and with it came the release of the bulls, just like in Pamplona. And the bulls began gouging workers in the communication, information technology, accounting, engineering, data transmission and all manner of industries. And the gouging is leaving flesh and blood splattered across the United States.

The negative impact of offshore outsourcing on employment in the U.S. is not in dispute. The only questions are the extent of the damage and strategies needed by policymakers to fill the vacuum created by jobs leaving for offshore destinations. Policymakers have targeted knowledge-based occupations and industries as the new drivers for the new economy. But the high wages attached to these occupations make them even more attractive to replacement by offshore alternatives. Also, these occupations being internet-friendly make them more susceptible to replacement with the very same tools of their employment.

Offshore outsourcing poses additional risks besides loss of employment in host communities. It can also lead to a withering of skills within organizations in particular and host communities as a whole, placing the U.S. at risk should the external service provider default either consciously—to hold to ransom—or unconsciously due to external factors.

There has also been a multiplication of confusion in definition of core competencies. The pharmaceutical industry has outsourced key operations to contract research organizations (CROs). The CROs conduct clinical trials, contract specialist sales staff, and even conduct research and development, the very basis for the existence of pharmaceutical companies. Offshore outsourcing of research and development to CROs is done with the objective of shortening developing cycles, but could also hasten the path to a generic alternative overseas.

Delivery of effective customer service requires a certain amount of dedication and commitment to the cause of the company. Offshore outsourcing could have a negative impact on service and quality because of workers with less commitment to outcomes and success of a particular company.

The ultimate risk posed by offshore outsourcing is that transfer of knowledge and processes overseas would eventually result in the customer replacing the client as the predominant purveyor of service. Having lost control over the means to undertake functions critical to an organization, and battered by the cost pressures imposed by an erstwhile partner, offshore outsourcing could lead to the eventual extermination of an organization. And a country!

Valuable skills built over generations are disappearing from the United States. Valuable industries built over generations are disappearing from the United States. Valuable technologies built over generations are disappearing. Valuable financial assets built over generations are disappearing from the United States. Valuable communities built over generations will disappear from the United States. But do not blame the peoples of China and India that are beneficiaries of this incredible largesse.

Andrew Carnegie, Henry Ford, George Washington Carver and the many illustrious Americans of bygone generations who loved being Americans and who *found* a way against incredible odds to provide for their fellow citizens must be turning in their graves.

Professions previously thought to be one-way tickets to the middle class are suddenly under siege. Strides made by the female population towards self-fulfillment, independence and closure of the male-female wage gap are under siege. First steps on the ladder to the middle class provided by data transmission and call center jobs are being yanked away, leaving many workers to tumble into the abyss of hopelessness.

The old beautiful face of hope and reassurance of the United States is gradually being replaced by a new ugly face of anger and rejection towards her own children.

7

OFFSHORE OUTSOURCING IN CLERICAL OCCUPATIONS

The call-center industry was among the first to exploit improvements in fiber optics, broadband communications, web-based software products, and secure and dedicated satellite links to relocate operations away from the United States and deliver BPO service.

Characteristics of recipient nations of call center businesses are an educated English-speaking workplace and cheap labor. Given names like Kim, Ashley, and Jennifer, employees at the offshore location are trained in American accents and cultural dispositions in order to disguise their true origin. Unsuspecting customers receive service without knowing where it originated.

With wages in the delivering country a fraction of those in the United States, call centers are ideal businesses to be relinquished to an external service provider (ESP). Telephone operators, banks issuing credit cards, establishments with 800 numbers, catalogue companies and information technology companies have jumped on the offshore offloading bandwagon, unloading thousands of American jobs.

This was a no-brainer. It was akin to the proverbial kid in a candy store. No more in-house training, reduced costs, no more phone hassles and definitely no more angry customers spitting four letter words and slamming down phones. Unshackled, the establishments could focus on high end, must-do businesses by employees not flustered after a confrontation with one of those hissing dragons.

Even welfare program help-lines in 48 states have been farmed offshore. Calls to the 800-number are routed offshore for service execution. According to the New York Daily News, "New Jersey's welfare department was surprised to learn earlier this year that when their welfare recipients called with a question, they were speaking to an e-funds call center in India,"

General Electric, Fedex, Citibank and Shutterbug.com have moved major portions of their support operations overseas. Someone sitting at a computer terminal offshore takes calls and answers e-mails from customers in the United States on everything from computers, washers, blow dryers, gifts in transit and cameras.

Outsourcing call center operations are not a new development. Starting in the mid-nineties, U.S. organizations began to outsource their back-office service operations to companies like Convergys, Truedial and Teletech to reduce costs.

The difference is that most of the pioneering companies initially employed American-based workers. Then as hardware, routing technologies, software, web-based architecture and broadband width expanded, calls placed from the United States could be answered efficiently and instantaneously by an operator based outside the country. To the customer there was no discernible difference between a call answered by an operator in the United States or one based overseas: an unfamiliar accent could be attributed to a recent immigrant.

Offshore relocation of call centers jumped when external service providers combined the cumulative effect of new technologies with far lower cost of most overseas operators. Convergys has 48 contact centers in many countries including the US, Philippines, Australia and Malaysia.

Compaq canceled its consumer product contract with the Answer Group, a Florida-based company, when it merged with HP. In addition HP failed to renew its expired customer support contract with The Answer Group. These terminations placed 1,500 jobs at The Answer Group in jeopardy. HP confirmed offshore relocation of some of its call center support operations. The goal announced by the company was to eliminate redundancies.

The Miami News reported that The Answer Group executive vice president Dennis Quinn felt defrauded by Compaq. Apparently, he had been given an aggressive forecast of future work. He had started hiring and training new staff in anticipation of the increased work volume.

Abrupt cancellation of the contract left the family-owned company scrambling to find new work to fill the void created, and a strong dose of mouth wash to rinse the sour taste left in Mr. Quinn's mouth. Mr. Quinn claimed to have received interest from potential customers who would like their customers to be serviced in the United States by an "American company with American workers."

According to Call Center CRM Solutions magazine, the operational cost at an offshore location is $2 to $4 a call, compared to $12 in the United States, making it impossible for a company like The Answer Group to sustain its American-based business model. Indeed, Precision Response Corp., neighbor to The

Answer Group, relocated part of its operations offshore to take advantage of the lower-cost labor pool and advanced telecommunications services.

Enterprise Florida said the 35 call center operations in Florida had created 17,000 jobs statewide and accounted for nearly $300 million in projected capital investment in 2002. Many of these jobs were in jeopardy unless clients insist on using American-based workers due to confidentiality and national security implications.

Miami-Dade Beacon Council President Frank Nero predicted the area's skilled and multilingual workforce would keep jobs in his area. Unfortunately, his was a losing battle.

A competitor of The Answer Group stated: "Today many companies are looking with increasing interest at relocating part or their entire global contact center to offshore markets in order to benefit from cost savings through economies of scale or local competitive advantages. As the availability of offshore alternatives increases, many companies have already found cross-boundary solutions and the associated cost benefits extremely successful."

U.S. call centers will fall the way dinosaurs did unless current operational dynamics are altered by "Call in America" stipulations or requirement for security guarantees.

Some industry leaders have complained that giving foreign nationals access to customers' personal information, and transaction data and commercial processes of a corporation in a time when terrorists are looking to gain better intelligence to hurt the U.S. is akin to asking for a punch in the nose. But these voices are in the minority: the majority of practitioners are unapologetic.

Companies like GE, Oracle, Conseco, IBM, McKinsey, Ford, Citigroup and Microsoft are outsourcing thousands of U.S. jobs to India. Delta Airlines will outsource some of its reservations services to a company in India. The relocation of these jobs will reportedly save Delta $12 million to $15 million annually.

Wave Technologies, Inc. is one of the few firms playing the security angle to strengthen its call center operations. It opened a call center at Lumberton, North Carolina in a Native American community. Vertical integration allowed Wave to offer a competitive contact customer service with security guarantees, a package that attracted business from U.S. government agencies and the intelligence community.

However, Wave's vertically integrated system is a niche market opportunity, hard to duplicate by many operators. Moreover, the possibility of service disruption in the wake of a potential 9/11 event seems lost on many clients of offshore call service providers.

Because of the labor-intensive nature of the customer contact service industry, relocation overseas can be devastating to entire communities. According to Data-monitor, 200,000 jobs have been lost to India alone in recent years from the United States, with thousands more moved to other offshore locations. The hemorrhaging of jobs continues unabated.

Taking advantage of lower salaries for specialists, a new set of call centers is being set up to offer more value-added services. The objective is differentiation from the so-called "bottom feeders" by carving out niche areas like technical assistance, research and information analysis.

In addition to e-mail interactivity, in which electronic queries are answered from offshore, firms perform what is called "Knowledge Acquisition." Under this mode of operation, the company provides consulting services in areas like biotechnology and medical feedback. To undertake the project, one offshore company hired scientists holding PhDs in molecular biology and genomics to help scientists around the globe collect and analyze data, establish quality control procedures, and set up information management systems in their area of expertise.

Research projects require extensive literature search to identify work previously done and methodologies used. Even in the age of the Internet research is time-consuming. The offshore firm offers research service, while maintaining interaction with the research manager.

IDC, a Framingham, MA research house estimated the worldwide customer-care services market, consisting of customer-service outsourcing and customer-resource management services, was $34.9 billion in 2001, with upward potential of $90.3 billion in 2006. In 2002, customers seeking information on products and services made 10 billion contacts with companies by phone and e-mail. That number is projected to grow by fifteen percent a year within the next four years.

A market this size is like a bleeding carcass on the open plains of the Serengeti: it attracts top predators from many miles away. So the IT industry heavyweights have either attacked the call center industry or are contemplating doing so. As best practices and workout solutions are applied, the customer service industry as a whole, not just call centers, will be decimated in the U.S. as never before.

Convergys, an Ohio-based company, bills itself as the global leader in customer care services. It employs 48,000 workers at 48 contact centers around the globe including the US, Philippines, Malaysia and Australia. It signed a five-year contract with Office Depot to "provide outsourced health and welfare benefits and leave of absence administration services" to the company's employees. It also inked another deal with the United States Postal Service (USPS). The contract with the USPS will be carried out from Convergys' facility in Denver. But, in effect, unless a client stipulates center of service, Convergys may carry out the contract from any location overseas.

Convergys, Truedial, Teletech and other major contact center operators are moving part of their operations to an even lower cost base, India. The net result is loss of thousands of jobs in the United States.

When the new welfare laws were promulgated in the United States in the nineties limiting the duration of welfare eligibility, thousands of females were retrained and employed at call centers. They were offered an opportunity to be productive, while improving their self-esteem. Now many of these females face the risk of being dumped back into the same morass from which they worked hard to escape, or going to work at McDonalds and Burger King at reduced benefits.

"One of the fundamental facts about business in a free market economy is that production travels based on the principle of lowest cost. This dynamic, which has played itself out in the manufacturing sector, will now get repeated in the services sector," says Matthew Halle, VP at QCSI, a healthcare solutions provider.

Nothing could be more blunt: What was done to Pittsburgh and all the other great American manufacturing cities is being repeated in the "services sector" across the entire length and breadth of the U.S. Cities will be winnowed out, reducing massive office buildings to empty shinning hulks. Owners of real estate will foreclose on their properties; banks holding the mortgages will go into a tailspin, reminiscent of the Savings and Loans debacle in the eighties. Demand for electricity will decrease as computers are shuttered, leaving utilities holding the bag for investments made to forestall blackouts.

The healthcare industry in the U.S. is a complicated beast. There are producers (employers), providers (doctors and hospitals) and payers (health plan, managed care company or insurance carrier). Then there are health management organizations (HMO), Preferred Provider Organizations (PPO), and many more names and acronyms to confuse a thesaurus. But even more daunting is the huge amount of paper generated and the high cost associated with processing it.

Health care in the U.S. is a paper-generating machine of gargantuan proportions, and the main reason is the relatively large number of stakeholders (participants) involved in the process. An employer, hospital and or a doctor, insurance company, Medicare (for the elderly) and Medicaid (public assistance) may all be in line to receive processed paper from just one patient.

Paper flow is meant to determine a patient's entitlement, payment responsibilities, schedule of payments, etc. The system provides a conflict resolution mechanism, which can turn around the entire process of verification.

As to be expected, the processing of paper is labor intensive, requiring thousands of workers to complete all the transactions promptly and accurately. The 25 billion or so health care administrative transactions are said to cost about $250 billion. Medical claims filed by physicians' on standard paper cost about $10 each to process. This includes forms, postage, handling and repeated billings.

With health care costs expected to increase beyond today's already high rate as boomers head into retirement, the drive is on to examine every cost component in order to extract as much savings as possible before the system collapses under excessive load of paper.

Many payers have outsourced paper handling to an external service representative that translates raw data into processes leading to payment or denial of payment. Until recently, the ESPs have been U.S.-based companies operating in less populated areas. The use of optical character recognition (OCR) and other electronic data capture and filing technologies are becoming commonplace as well.

Adopting electronic filing in a web-based architecture provides all parties with data simultaneously in order to understand the reasons for claims denials, eliminate unnecessary re-billing, and provide a means to reconcile claims for proper payment. According to MedSynergies Inc. CEO John Thomas, "Electronic verification of patient insurance coverage could reduce the total cost of claim processing by over 5 percent alone."

Potential savings for stakeholders are significant. Thomas summarized findings from a benefits consultant who reported "electronic claims submission…would result in decreases of 35-50 percent in billing and transaction costs for providers." A separate study "found that medical groups could save up to 37 percent in bad debt and postage and some 50 percent in overall administration costs by automating these types of transactions."

Web-based electronic data interchange (EDI) further reduces the cost of processing claims by slashing volume of paper handled, minimizing the need for mailing, providing a "print-as-needed" capability and marginalizing the cost of software. Web EDI provides accessibility of information from any computer terminal with Internet access.

Perot Systems of Plano, Texas, describes the activities of its healthcare subsidiary, Perot Systems Healthcare, as follows:

"Perot Systems Healthcare is one of the largest providers of full service IT operations in the hospital industry, managing significant relationships with four of the top 20 U.S. health systems. More than 4,000 employees from the Health-care industry Group serve both the for-profit and not-for-profit healthcare marketplace, providing integrated end-to-end technical and business solution services. Perot Systems healthcare clients represent more than 300 healthcare providers, thousands of caregivers, 200 health insurance organizations, as well as leading biopharmaceutical and healthcare supply chain companies."

Perot Systems reported 2002 revenue of $1.3 billion. The company employs 10,000 "associates" located in North America, Europe, and Asia. A bulletin posted at the company's website on August 8, 2003 contained the following: "Perot Systems Corporation today announced that it completed the acquisition of Vision Healthsource India Private Limited and Vision Healthsource, Inc—collectively known as "Vision"—a leading provider of billing and claims solutions for healthcare service providers in the United States.

With this acquisition, Perot Systems establishes a healthcare processing capability in India as part of the company's healthcare transformation strategy and global service delivery model, to be followed by weapons of human destruction as thousands of American workers are furloughed.

Offshore processing has become one of the key strategies American companies are using to reduce costs of processing health care claims. According to all stakeholders in this process, "Offshore BPO has just begun and it is apparent that it is here to stay. What we have seen so far is not even the tip of the iceberg with the best yet to come. The benefits are far too compelling to prevent rapid growth."

And what an iceberg did to the "unsinkable" Titanic is well known. Offshore processing of healthcare claims will slam shut the hopes of many looking to the service industry to become an engine of growth. There is going to be gnashing and grinding of teeth. And like the victims of the Titanic, many will find themselves trapped in the middle of the ocean without lifeboats. Arms flailing, screams unanswered, many will simply sink to the bottom of the ocean.

Perot Systems is only one of many external service providers and payers who have set up or acquired operations overseas to handle processing of health care claims of American patients. Aetna Inc of Hartford, CT moved their claims adjudication process to India, and their apparent success has many other organizations literally foaming at the mouth to move overseas. Wellcare out of Florida is in India. Wellpoint, Coventry Health, United Healthcare, Horizon BCBS, and BCBS of Michigan are all in India or are contemplating doing so in the near term.

Aetna's move to India will traumatize claims processing employees on a scale far greater than the hurt dished out by the automobile and steel industries, because Aetna is a Goliath in the healthcare industry in the U.S.

Based out of Hartford, CT, Aetna is one of the nation's leading providers of health care, dental, pharmacy, group life, disability and long-term care products, serving more than 13.0 million medical members, 11.3 million dental members and 11.7 million group insurance customers as of June 30, 2003. The company says it has more than "579,000 health care service providers, including nearly 349,000 primary care and specialist physicians and 3,589 hospitals."

Aetna says it "provides these benefits to employer and plan sponsor customers in all 50 states, ranging from large multisite national accounts to middle-market and small-employer groups." The company claims it serves "more Fortune 1000 customers" than any of its competitors. Aetna's products include "the full range of health insurance, including dental and pharmacy benefits, from HMO and POS to PPO and indemnity, as well as group insurance products such as life, disability and long term care insurance."

In the past insurance companies played the role of pure claims payers: hospitals and physicians submitted claims for approved services to patients, and the insurance company paid the bill. Faced with increased costs from hospitals and physicians, insurance companies decided to play a role in the delivery of medical services in order to contain costs. Thus was born health management organizations or HMO's.

At their core, HMO's make arrangements with selected providers to furnish a defined set of health care services to members, set standards for the selection of health care providers, and make available financial incentives for members to use providers and procedures associated with the health plan. At the core of the program is the dreaded primary care physician (PCP), who, like a doorman, evaluates services required by members before directing further services provided by only approved specialists. No deviation is allowed, and the member assumes full cost of using services of a provider outside of the HMO network.

At its functional best, HMO's provide quality care, while containing costs of healthcare delivery. At its worst, cost containment overrides quality care by restricting access to specialists who may not necessarily be at the top of their game. Pharmaceutical procedures could also limit members to drugs that may not be considered by some experts to be the most effective.

Within the HMO are different models such as staff and group models. The staff model involves physicians who are salaried employees of the HMO. The physicians provide services exclusively to HMO members, and the HMO shoulders the entire cost of healthcare services rendered to its members. In a group model HMO, the HMO secures a contract with a group of physicians to provide services in internal medicine, gynecology, cardiology, etc. The HMO pays the group via a monthly capitation check, a lump sum negotiated with the group based on the number of physicians in the group and services to be rendered. Members pay a co-payment, and are responsible for full payment of services not covered under the agreement. There are variations of the staff and group models within the HMO concept.

Faced with mounting frustrations about the strict constraints imposed by HMO's, different managed care programs like preferred provider organizations (PPO's) and point of service (POS) have popped up. Under POP, which is gaining increasing popularity, there is no PCP. A member can choose from physicians and hospitals in a network or from physicians and hospitals outside the network upon satisfaction of a deductible and co-payment. POS requires a PCP who refers members to providers on an approved network, but members may use out of network providers upon satisfaction of a deductible and co-payment.

Aetna, a provider of HMO, PPO, POS, and basic life insurance products, therefore handles an exceptionally large volume of claims, requiring thousands of employees. Aetna in India is therefore a terrible development for the many Americans suffering from the pain of unemployment.

Females dominate the handling and processing of claims. So the move of claims processing offshore will bludgeon wives, sisters, mothers and daughters in the same manner that husbands, brothers, fathers and sons were decapitated by an earlier generation of managers.

The move offshore by Perot Systems, CSC, EDS, ACS and other external service providers, who collectively cover an even wider range of customers, will scorch America as never before and females in particular will be hurt as never before.

And unlike automobile plants or steel complexes with their noisy machines out in the open, the wreckage of moving claims processing overseas will happen in the sanitized environment of an office with no union to attempt to come to their rescue and no protesters shouting outside the gates.

And unlike a product with a "Made in China" tag, there is no label on the performer of IT-enabled service. There is no fingerprint or DNA marked "Made in India." So to the customer the service may as well have originated in the U.S.

The type of services being performed initially by offshore processing is the lower end known as "bottom feeding." These include enrollment of new members, eligibility verification, claims data entry, claims re-pricing and scanning of documents. But when a company like Perot becomes more comfortable with the initial phase, it is bound to move up the value chain to balancing suspense accounts, policy changes and risk assessments.

Under previous offshore models, independently owned offshore companies performed these "bottom entry" services for American-based companies for a fee. This arrangement was not considered to be conducive to handling sensitive integrated data, or performing predictive analysis considered too sensitive for "foreign" eyes. But any such apprehension disappears under the Perot strategy, thereby opening the door for development of total service packages from offshore facility.

Many in the healthcare industry require data to assist them in making informed decisions, but are overwhelmed with the data collected. Knowledge discovery in databases (KDD) can help organizations turn raw data into useful information. KDD is the process of finding patterns and relationships in the mountains of data collected, and an army of consultants and workers is employed by the healthcare industry in the US to perform these tasks. With complete ownership of offshore data processing facilities and availability of enabling technologies, sooner or later these functions will be moved overseas as well, jeorpadizing the careers of thousands of professionals.

Providers have a vast quantity of data such as charges, claims, frequency of service utilization, lab test, radiology procedures, medication, etc. in their archives. Organizations are taking advantage of KDD techniques to dig through the data, which is called data mining, to unearth potential fraud, extract information for marketing and design strategies for customer retention.

Stakeholders, including governments and advocacy groups, are placing demands on payers, providers and employers to provide information used to drive public policy. Manipulation of data in order to provide requested information occupies the attention of many industry professionals. As offshore outsourcing companies move up the value chain, the careers of these professionals will be placed in jeopardy.

Horizons Consulting, a healthcare BPO consulting company, analyzed differences in labor cost between India and the U.S. for claims examiner, health coder, data entry operator, enrollment specialist, etc. The study found that workers performing these tasks were paid $24,000 to $40,000 in the U.S. versus $1,200 to $3,600 in India. Workers in India, on the average, put in 400 hours more than their U.S. counterparts.

As firms move billing and analytical operations offshore, U.S. operations will be scaled down to only front office-liaison with the medical profession. Automatic data entry systems will render even optical scanning redundant.

American firms are in the process of moving whole offices overseas. Customer service, accounting, data processing, data analysis and entire back office operations are moving offshore in droves. The huge morning commute from New Jersey across the Hudson River to the skyscrapers in New York will tail off, with those who sent American jobs overseas celebrating the reduced traffic congestion. The huge amount of equity built into shiny office buildings will collapse.

What is the cost of exposing the entire medical and financial information of a country to foreigners? What if the processing of America's information is interrupted? What if sensitive information falls into the hands of Al-Qaida? Remember nobody conceived of the possibility of terrorists learning to fly on American soil and using American planes to murder Americans. The terrorists have sworn to damage America and will probe to unearth any vulnerability.

Under no circumstance will Germany or Japan or China or even India, the largest foreign operator, allow medical and financial information of their citizens to be handled by foreigners in the callous manner being done by some Americans. Never. But some Americans choose to give this critical information away, voluntarily.

Wages in the United States are as they are because of relatively high cost of living. A worker earning $50,000 in the Unites States may be comfortable, but being well off is not an applicable description. Tuition, housing, medicines, food and many other items of necessity are far more expensive in the United States than in many developing countries. But neo-employers consider $50,000 employees too much of a hassle; they are too expensive. They must be cut. They must be terminated in enough numbers to cause these United States to experience pain. And the pain will not stop even when workers are sprawled helpless on the wasteland of unemployment. "It's not personal...It's strictly business."

The last office worker leaving the last desolate skyscraper in the United States, please turn the lights off.

8

OFFSHORE OUTSOURCING IN PROFESSIONAL OCCUPATIONS

An excerpt from a World Development Report released in 1999 read, "For countries in the vanguard of the world economy, the balance between knowledge and resources has shifted so far towards the former that knowledge has become perhaps the most important factor determining the standard of living—more than land, than tools, than labor. Today's most advanced economies are truly knowledge-based."

For the past two hundred years, conventional economic theory labeled capital and labor the two most important factors of production contributing to the standard of living of a country. Knowledge, education, and intellectual capital were considered important but not critical. Then in 1969, Peter Drucker perceived the arrival of knowledge workers as an important factor in the deterministic characteristics of economies. But it was Stanford economist Paul Romer who popularized the so-called "third factor of production" in his New Growth Theory in 1986.

Romer and others considered knowledge a basic form of capital, suggesting that its accumulation engendered technological breakthroughs, which then became new platforms for more innovations. Therefore with knowledge as a driver of economic growth, countries with a high composition of "knowledge workers," or intellectual capital, can invest in technology to create higher-valued products and processes in order to sustain growth ahead of countries with unlimited labor and capital.

Knowledge workers or "symbolic analysts" applied to workers who manipulated symbols rather than machines. These included teachers, pharmaceutical researchers, architects, bank workers, financial analysts, stock brokers, or policy analysts. With sixty percent of its workforce falling into this category, the underlying unmentioned thesis was that the United States would be able to stay ahead of developing countries by transforming to a "knowledge-driven" economy in which a strong relationship between intellectual capital and technological developments underpinned permanent growth. This so-called virtuous circle was supposed to remove growth and recession cycles prevalent in traditional economic domains.

When the theory of the "knowledge-driven" economy was being enunciated, the full impact of the Internet had not yet been recognized. As such, information communication technologies were considered to be "facilitators of knowledge creation in innovative societies," but not as agents for transformations in society (OECD, 1996).

Communication was deemed, initially, only as an enabler of change within discrete entities and boundaries. The Digital Revolution, pioneered by Microsoft, increased internal productivities, without affecting efficiency of interactions between discrete entities. The ubiquitous fax machine enabled information to be transmitted between entities, but its linear effect prevented achievement of dynamic advantages.

The most momentous change arrived with the extrapolation of information made possible by the interconnectivity of computers and other communication devices through the Internet. The combination of knowledge-driven factors and interconnectivity led to the creation of the Network Economy, the preferred terminology of Wired Magazine, which stressed the predominance of the network above all other components. The Network Economy unleashed a set of forces that maximized the power of knowledge and innovation beyond discrete boundaries.

The force unleashed by the new mechanism is illustrated by the mathematical fact that the sum of a network increases as the square of the number of members. In other words, the value of the network increases exponentially even as the sum of its members increases arithmetically. Therefore, the value of the Internet skyrocketed as the number of nodes expanded beyond the initial research community to the rest of the United States, and finally to the global community.

However, unlike the linear effect generated by connecting fax machines, the exponential effect of the Network Economy can lead to totally unpredictable consequences. Indeed, one of the safest ways to harness the power of the Network Economy is to assume that forces within the system can disintegrate any present-day activity. This phenomenon has been compared to biological systems, where a subset can diverge and grow separately from a main organism, and then explode after a critical mass has coalesced. But how or when this explosion occurs is unknown, not even to the host body.

When the theory of the Knowledge Economy was first promulgated, it was embraced by policymakers in developed countries as a protective armor against the onslaught of cheap goods imported from less developed countries. Policymakers in developed countries anticipated maintaining the relatively high standards of living in their domains through a continuous process of learning, innovation and new product development. Wealth creation by individuals, firms and countries was said to be in proportion to their capacity to learn and share innovation (Foray and Lundvall, 1996).

However, the assumptions of policymakers contained two fatal flaws. The first was a fundamental misjudgment of the behavior of multinational corporations. The second was to assume that old rules of predictability applied to the medium in which network supremacy over knowledge factors had obliterated conventional thinking.

Multinational corporations sit at the intersection of production, international trade, and cross-border investment. A multinational corporation engages in direct investment and owns or controls value-adding activities in more than one country. They have four characteristics.

First, multinational corporations coordinate economic production among a number of different enterprises and internalize this coordination within a single organization. Second, a significant portion of the economic transactions connected with this coordinated activity takes place across national borders. Third, multinational corporations like General Electric, IBM, General Motors or Ford Motor Company bear no allegiance to any one country: GE is a global company that happens to have a head office in the United States, but its policies do not necessarily have to favor Americans. And the fourth reason is that, just as they operate across national boundaries, their ownership is drawn from a global base of shareholders. With multinational corporations involved directly or indirectly in two-thirds of global trade in goods and services, their policies and actions take precedence over those in many countries.

Rules drawn up by the World Trade Organization or International Monetary Fund enable multinational corporations of today to operate under the assumption that states have withered away. This gives them the freedom to make cross-border investments to improve efficiency of their operations by rationalizing production and trying to exploit economies of specialization and scope. In the past, only cross-border investment in manufacturing fit into this category, but with the advent of the Network Economy, the same rules are increasingly being applied as well to the execution of services.

In electronics and computers as well as in the auto industry, firms allocated different elements of the production process to different parts of the world. In computers, electronics, and electrical equipment, for example, it used to be that the human and physical capital-intensive stages of production were performed in developed countries, while the more labor-intensive assembly stages of production were performed in developing countries. However, with the advent of China as a center of high-quality manufacturing, that country is witnessing more vertical manufacturing.

Therefore, with multinational corporations eschewing the demarcation imposed by borders, a product researched and developed in the United States does not have to be manufactured in that country. The benefits of investing and building human capital, sometimes with assistance from state and federal governments, do not therefore always accrue internally. With the emergence of advanced manufacturing centers at lower cost in developing countries, the hypothesis that a knowledge-driven economy would be a driver for internal growth to maintain or even improve standard of living in developed countries is not supported by emerging facts in today's corporate environment. It is conceivable, and increasingly likely, for the people in a country with a relatively small number of knowledge workers to consume the fruits of the labor of knowledge workers in another country, with a multinational corporation striding the middle to maximize profit.

Therefore, under the new economic dispensation where labor cost differential exerts a significant gravitational force, the old rule of investing in people, research and product development for the purpose of improving standard of living may not always apply. The stark reality is that, without a radical change in the cost component of factors of production and/or restricted plant locations, a government in a developed country may not realize any returns on its investment in people and processes.

While knowledge in the Network Economy is crucial, developed countries, contrary to popular opinion, do not have a monopoly on intellectual capital. Many in developed countries assume the bitter poverty in Calcutta that Mother Theresa tried to alleviate through her herculean efforts somehow meant a dearth of intellectual capital in India. Or that the excruciating poverty in the slums of Manila implied an inferior education system in the Philippines. Or that Soweto,

Alexandria and the other slums ringing Johannesburg are testimony to a failed educational system in all of South Africa unable to produce top caliber graduates. Nothing could be farther from the truth. Very few in developed countries are aware that products from local universities were instrumental in developing nuclear weapons in both South Africa and India, while those in the Philippines are renowned computer hackers. While most of the consuming world is being ravaged by higher and higher oil prices, very few are aware that South Africa is reaping the fruits of being the only country in the world to have mastered the efficient extraction of oil from coal.

While reasons for low standard of living in developing countries abound, intellectual capital has never been in short supply. But until the advent of the Network Economy, this resource was boxed, isolated, localized and exposed only to those with the means to import a fraction for their own use. Now, as a result of the interconnectivity of the Network Economy, this competitive resource has been made available almost overnight at the click of a mouse. And as predicted by the rules of the Network Economy summarized by Kevin Kelly in 1997, the law of inverse pricing, which says the very best gets cheaper each year, is in full effect: the comparably educated citizens from developing countries are plentiful and cheap. And with their arrival comes the disappearance of another tenet of the original Knowledge Economy, which assumed that developed countries would maintain a lead on intellectual capital.

The power of multinational companies to transcend borders, coupled with exposure of lower cost intellectual capital in certain developing countries by the Internet, opened the door to offshore outsourcing of professional jobs like financial analysis, accounting, research and development, radiology and engineering from the United States. And with the door wide open, other companies and organizations are driving through with more jobs headed to offshore destinations.

Therefore, the U.S. will not be able to count on the supposedly resilient service sector to hold the line against unemployment, that is if offshore outsourcing continues on its current trend.

In the field of accounting, India has many experts conversant in U.S. GAAP accounting practices. A New York-based company took advantage of this expertise to open a 10,000 square foot office in India to handle accounting for New York companies. The company hired 125 accounting professionals with the objective of moving to Web-enabled accounting, so clients in the U.S. could obtain real-time information about their finances. The COO of the company claimed the reason for their move to India was due to shortage of accountants in the U.S. But when questioned further he conceded that the fact an accountant in

India gets one-fifth the salary of a U.S. counterpart was a nice bonus. The company planned to move eighty percent of its back-office accounting practice to India.

Most Indian-based companies start with routine functions in order to build confidence and establish credibility. Once those goals are achieved, they are used as case histories to perform more complicated assignments. For example, a company in India started by dealing with routine inquiries on debit cards for a large financial institution. Now the company handles claims investigations, which requires accounting skills and extensive knowledge of financial systems, all for a fraction of the cost to deliver this service in the U.S. In another expression of the value-added service, another company developed software to provide information to customers regarding ATM locations.

Companies are letting foreign operations handle internal finances. Procter & Gamble Co. maintains an office in Manila staffed by 650 employees, many with business and finance degrees. They assist with preparation of P&G's tax returns around the world. According to the local manager, "All the processing can be done here, with just the final submission done to local authorities" in the U.S. and elsewhere. According to Business Week, the Philippines has an oversupply of accountants trained in U.S. accounting standards.

JP Morgan Chase & Co. outsourced some of its stock market research to Bombay, confirming the trend predicted by BPO companies overseas. Brokerages like Lehman Brothers Inc. and Bear, Stearns & Co. are starting to use Indian financial analysts for number-crunching work.

Business consulting firm A.T. Kearney released a survey recently of 100 major American banks, brokerage houses and insurance companies, indicating 500,000 financial services jobs, or eight percent of total employment in the sector, will be shifted overseas between 2003 and 2008. This number may be conservative, given daily improvements in efficiency of offshore outsourcing models.

"The relocations will involve a wider range of high-end internal functions than have typically been slated for overseas transfers, including financial analysis, research, regulatory reporting, accounting, human resources and graphic design. Until recently, offshore job transfers have primarily focused on back office functions such as data entry, transaction processing and account reconciliation. The relocations are expected to reduce annual operating costs by more than $30 billion," the A.T. Kearney study reported.

The study was conducted with financial services firms in banking, brokerage and insurance sectors, and reflected the "opinions of respondents including CEOs, CFOs, chief administrative officers and executives."

"Any function that does not require face-to-face contact is now perceived as a candidate for offshore relocation," said Andrea Bierce, an authority on offshore relocations and the A.T. Kearney managing director who oversaw the study. "The debate at major financial services companies today is no longer whether to relocate some business functions, but rather which ones and where," she concluded.

Geopolitical tension is not even considered enough of a deterrent. The report found "one major financial services company...decided to move several jobs to India at the height of tensions between that country and Pakistan."

And while India is cheaper today, the groundwork is apparently already being laid for a move to even cheaper China: "Although India will likely maintain its lead for the next several years, China is expected to become an increasingly popular location once U.S. financial services firms have the necessary confidence that their intellectual property rights will be safeguarded," concluded the Kearney report.

A.T. Kearney found that "64 percent of the financial services firms surveyed had already begun to implement offshore business process initiatives, and 57 percent have already engaged or intend to engage outside assistance with these increasingly complex initiatives."

And in a message sure to chill financial services professionals in the U.S., A.T. Kearney vice president Bart Kocha concluded, "Because offshore activity is evolving to include not only traditional back-office functions but also more complex, analytical activities with higher value-added, we are now beginning to see aggressive efforts to capitalize this trend."

In a soft economic climate, not all the highly skilled displaced professionals will find work at equivalent salaries. There is therefore a distinct possibility that gains in corporate efficiency resulting from offshore outsourcing would be overshadowed by the debilitating effect of lost jobs and reduced salaries of a highly salaried professional class on local, state and federal tax revenues. The effects of such a massive job loss on New York City would be devastating. Assuming an MBA beginner's salary of $100,000, the half a million lost jobs would result in the disappearance of $50 billion in wages, not counting benefits and the economic impact of these wages on other sectors of the economy like real estate, consumer goods and entertainment.

American Express employs 650 accountants and data processors in India, while American Annuity Group has 120 employees in Bangalore to process insurance claims. Standard Chartered Bank has moved all their U.S. and European back office functions to a facility in India expected to employ 1,400 workers.

Accenture plans to employ 2,000 workers in the Philippines for accounting, software development and back-office work. Charles Schwab, Citibank, HSBC, and many other financial institutions have operations in India and elsewhere handling financial transactions on behalf of U.S. clients.

So salaries, bank and brokerage statements, credit card information, and anything else submitted as part of a tax return could be going to companies abroad without the knowledge of a client. An accounting industry consultant estimated that between 25,000 and 45,000 returns were processed in India during the 2003 tax preparation season. This number will explode over the coming years, and the accounting profession in the United States will take the brunt of this development.

Processing insurance claims, selling stocks, analyzing companies, equity analysis, industry reports, summaries of financial disclosures, conducting credit checks, and many other jobs that were exclusively for U.S. workers are being moved offshore at a furious pace. McKinsey, the world's largest management consulting firm, operates a research center in India staffed by librarians and computer experts who serve the company's worldwide operations.

Robert Z. Lawrence, a prominent Harvard free-trade advocate, was quoted as saying, "If foreign countries specialize in high-skilled areas where we have an advantage, we could be worse off." But then he added, "I still have faith that globalization will make us better off, but it's no more than faith." The evidence suggests Mr. Lawrence's faith to be misplaced.

To establish a beachhead in a new discipline known as bioinformatics, an Indian company has hired over one hundred biologists with Ph.D.s to analyze biological information. Before bioinformatics, development of drugs was largely an expensive trial and error process defined more by failure than success. The antiquated process started with a large amount of molecules extracted from natural proteins. These were isolated and tested sequentially to determine the most promising leads.

Bioinformatics is a discipline that employs computers and the Internet to mine through the vast amounts of data buried in tons of research publications and biological databases. This more rational approach calls for an understanding of molecular structures, biological mechanisms and the effects of interactions between different structures. With the decoding of the human genome, this sort of analysis is critical as it holds the possibility for groundbreaking discoveries of linkage between genes and diseases. Drugs can then be formulated to terminate the linkage.

In just the recent past, only the United States and a few other countries in the developed world were equipped to tackle bioinformatics. Now that is changing, because the process of analysis, even in the age of computers, is time consuming and expensive. Large drug companies have been on the prowl seeking destinations where they can outsource such work cheaply, and India is welcoming them with open arms.

India is marrying its software expertise and available talent pool of biologists to penetrate the huge bioinformatics market. The Indian companies are unfazed by the huge databases loaded with information of mind-boggling detail and complexity, because the strategic approach is an extrapolation of data mining techniques familiar to software engineers working in the healthcare industry.

One Indian company employs five people in bioinformatics, twelve molecular biologists and sixty chemists. The bioinformatics team works mainly for an American company, Camitro Corporation. The team uses molecular modeling and other computer-based tools in an attempt to predict the physical and chemical properties of molecules. This saves up on the expensive process of extracting such information in a laboratory. By using special software, the company can predict the toxicity of a molecule, which will cut down on the number of animals used for such studies.

The demand for such predictive analysis is huge, because drug companies uncover about 100,000 lead molecules, each of which has to be tested for toxicity. The utilization of software to pre-screen these molecules reduces the time to conduct trials significantly, while saving the lives of millions of animals.

Another company in India is working with Surromed Corporation of California to gather and document precise clinical data. Every prescription and procedure performed by physicians in the U.S, together with outcomes, is documented in order to determine efficiencies of various drugs and medications in relation to gender and racial groups. Pharmaceutical companies, hospitals and governments have an acute interest in this information, which can be used as the basis for prescriptions for other patients, and as research material for development of new drugs and processes. By working with Surromed the Indian company is aiming to establish leadership in analytical software for data mining in the biological industry.

While the U.S. has a large lead in computing technology, the power of supercomputers can be linked through the Internet to allow offshore partners to gain access for development of software and other products. With an estimated market of $30 billion in information technology products from life sciences, offshore outsourcing could erode the lead established by the U.S. in this crucial market with enormous growth potential.

The belief that the United States leads the world in intellectual capital is a fallacy. What is correct is that, because of open access, availability of affordable capital, advanced technology and abundance of opportunity, the U.S. has in the past been a leader in importing intellectual capital from many parts of the world where these opportunities were lacking. For example, foreigners comprise about half the student populations in science and engineering graduate schools at many U.S. colleges. Now with the advent of the Network Economy, many of these students are either staying in their native countries or shuffling back home upon graduation. The foreign talent pool previously deployed in the U.S. is now assisting the same U.S. companies, but from the native land of the foreigners.

With the starting point of any research being accumulation and analysis of past body of work in the field, researchers and other professionals spend an inordinate amount of time searching for information related to particular subjects. Following Einstein's assertion that he succeeded by identifying several paths of failure, it is imperative for any researcher to identify past successes and failures, methodologies and technologies.

Lucent Technologies has built its largest worldwide center in India to develop the next-generation of integrated network management solution framework for its global customers. Even as it cuts back on employment in the U.S., Lucent has hired 500 engineers in India as part of its global plans.

Adobe Systems' only research and development center outside of the U.S. is found in India, where it concentrates on new technologies and new product ideas. The Adobe PageMaker version 7.0 was developed entirely in India. The first palm-top Adobe Acrobat Reader was also developed in India.

Bechtel Group, the large construction-engineering firm, employs over 400 engineers in India. The group handles projects from all over the world. Design work is also going global. Fluor Corp. of California employs 1,200 engineers and draftsmen in the Philippines, Poland and India to convert layouts of budding industrial plants into detailed specifications and blueprints. When employees asked him about this, Fluor CEO Alan Boeckman apparently made no apologies: "We have developed this into a core competitive advantage."

Meanwhile, employment for electrical engineers has not recovered from the troughs of 2003. According to the Institute of Electrical and Electronics Engineers: "We knew anecdotally that things were bad for many in engineering and computer fields, and these statistics confirm our concerns for engineering employment." He added, "While we realize the sluggish U.S. economy is responsible for much of the unemployment, we can't discount the role played by off-shore outsourcing."

The key to success in these fields for the offshore external service representative is industry-based expertise. Every industry from airlines, to healthcare, to banking, has its own unique characteristics. Seeking to land planes in the most convenient time frame, an airline may require software to assist in determining frequency of plane landings and the factors that would lead to the achievement of the desired result. Such software requires knowledge of industry wide systems, practices, technologies and language. Offshore companies are developing top-to-bottom expertise in specific industries, or "domain expertise in distinct verticals," in order to communicate with US based managers in their own language. Consulting contracts, marketing and field studies then become an opportunity for offshore companies to pounce. Industry experts believe an estimate of $1 billion annual revenue for this type of service is underestimated.

Most jobs are advertised on websites, where applicants fill and forward an application to a human resources manager. Unbeknown to most people, the application does not go directly to the intended recipient. Rather, a data extractor, whose job is to draw out the critical information relevant to the position e.g. education, employment history, etc., intercepts it. From available public databases, the extractor verifies the contents of most of the information provided. In the end, the extractor winnows the list down to the number required by the human resources manager. Many companies are increasingly using offshore companies to sift through the many applications received by managers.

Carnegie Mellon University (CMU) has developed an eServices Capability Model aimed at providing external service providers the tools to identify industry standards. It provides the means to measure and evaluate service delivery in order to enhance productivity, reduce delivery cycles, and reduce cost. Most offshore companies are gearing up to be certified under this model to obtain a label for marketing purposes. It is expected that the model, known as Capability Maturity Model (CMM), will accelerate offshore outsourcing even further. Its impact is predicted to be on the same scale as the International Standard Organization (ISO) quality control series, where a certificate is akin to a global stamp of approval, allowing an offshore company an opportunity to brand itself versus its competitors.

A huge cottage industry has been built on contracts from international organizations like the UN, UNESCO and FAO. These organizations are magnets for data acquisition, analysis, formatting and presentation. Hitherto, companies in the west have feasted on these contracts. Now, many in India and elsewhere are gearing up to claim a piece of this pie. And the CMU model allows certification to international standards.

IBM Global Services, the IT services arm of IBM, accounts for about a third of the sales of the parent company. It is also the most profitable division of IBM. In addition to computer and software integration operations, the company performs complete top-to-bottom analysis of companies across all industrial sectors. From data collected, the company is able to recommend strategies to maximize efficiencies and increase profitability. Usually, one or more arms of the services division can implement the solutions recommended by the review team.

IBM Global Services maintains a fully functional division in India performing the same services as its parent company. It came as no surprise, therefore, that the Indian division entered BPO and human capital solutions in 2004. According to a senior executive, "With the rise in BPO call centers business in India, human capital solutions is assuming increasing significance and offers a major area of growth."

This was an ominous announcement, for thousands of IBM techies in the U.S. perform call service technical functions across all product lines of the company. Setting up a BPO division within its division in India, which was already the fifth largest foreign employer in India, could only imply a platform to shift more jobs and responsibilities offshore. In this case, the technical support staff, not the lower end of the call center spectrum, would be blunted.

According to the New York Times, "If you lose your luggage on British Airways, the techies who track it down are here in India. If your Dell computer has a problem, the techie who walks you through it is in Bangalore, India's Silicon Valley. Indian software giants...now manage back-room operations—accounting, inventory management, billing, accounts receivable, payrolls, credit card approvals—for global firms like Nortel Networks, Reebock, Sony, American Express, HSBC and GE Capital."

Global chipmaker Intel invested in a BPO company based in India. The company provides "processing services in the fields of human resource, finance & accounting, customer contact (including voice, mail and chat), insurance, healthcare, banking and financial services, among others." The same report also contained the announcement that Citigroup had bought a stake in another Indian company for $20 million.

The involvement of IBM, Intel, Citigroup and many other blue chip companies in the BPO market in India and other offshore locations is a sure sign of a major move to offshore centers offering technical assistance in India and elsewhere. And to make sure the message was crystal clear, IBM said it intended to increase its labor force in India from 4,500 to 10,000 within a year, likely to result in major job losses in the United States.

EDS of Plano, Texas is a global giant in business process outsourcing. The company had 138,000 employees around the globe, with 64,000 of these in nearly all 50 US states. The company is involved in all facets of the outsourcing industry: systems integration, human resources, data processing and supply chain management. But it was the company's activities in India that generated headlines.

Established in 1996 as a full-fledged subsidiary, EDS India underwent rapid expansion to increase revenues in systems development, management, support and integration and network management. According to EDS: "EDS-India strives to play a dual role of a virtual, 24-hour office providing cost-effective services to EDS' global accounts by leveraging the local pool of high-quality IT professionals and the availability of high-speed data communication links to beat time-zone difference."

Computer Sciences Corporation (CSC) based in El Segundo, CA is a classic American success story. Roy Nutt and Fletcher Jones formed the company in 1959 with $100 and a contract from Honeywell to develop a business language called FACT. Nutt had built his reputation by developing the first widely accepted assembly program, called SAP.

In 2002 CSC generated annual revenues in excess of $12 billion from a diversified business base, including global business process outsourcing. CSC, like its major competitors IBM and EDS, is also in India in a major way, and is ramping up to shift more of its global processing activities there.

The irony is that, with fundamental software research increasingly being done in India, the next Nutts will not be American.

GE Capital had 10,000 employees at four centers in India delivering services such as processing of mortgage loans, insurance claims and payroll and credit card collections. Until now, GE Capital serviced its own customer base. All that changed when GE Capital agreed to extend its service to third parties, causing the company to double its staff in India involved in customer services by the end of 2003.

Information Technology Association of America (ITAA)—a trade association representing 400 U.S. IT firms—issued a paper on August 6, 2003 declaring its support for offshore outsourcing for competitiveness of the industry. The paper from ITAA also "asked foreign governments to widen up the market and encourage globalization by reducing trade barriers."

Microsoft, ICS, Oracle, Dell and every major name in the computer industry has already outsourced some or all of their technical support functions overseas. Sprint Corp. of Missouri sent hundreds of technology jobs overseas at the expense of American professionals.

Car manufacturer General Motors announced plans to spend over $60 million in its technical center in India over a period of three years. "We will spend over $20 million per year over the next three years in technical infrastructure, manpower and facilities for the technical center," said a company spokesperson. The company planned to hire 160 engineers for the center.

Engineering functions like designing, specifications and scale ups are being done with software packaging systems. As such, engineering teams in an office in India or elsewhere are able to execute a project with available process variables. Many drafting and design projects are being done overseas. But as proven in other disciplines, the offshore professionals move quickly up the value chain once they demonstrate their capabilities in entry-level vocations.

DaimlerChrysler outsourced maintenance for 150 core applications that support its engineering, manufacturing and sales activities to India. The move allowed the company to terminate "high-priced" consultants in favor of other staffers. Ford Motor Company established a significant presence in Chennai, India to support its back office operations. AltaVista outsourced about eighty five percent of its e-mail based customer support to an overseas vendor.

"Blue-collar workers who lost their jobs typically faced a lower standard of living, and the same fate could face programmers and others," according to Josh Bivens, an economist at the EPI. Terminated professionals are turning to restaurant management and the police force for alternative employment. When the tax base shrinks severely enough, patronage at restaurants would decline and the police force would shrink.

Potential loss of intellectual property and business process secrets make companies outsourcing offshore vulnerable to copying and resale of the same outsourced products. Where there is demand, there is supply: the offshore group would bypass the contractor and head straight to the heart of its customer base. Accenture, McKinsey and the other management-consulting firms operating offshore today are in fact assisting in the establishment and development of their less-expensive competitors tomorrow.

Another generation of Americans was counseled to "think not what your country can do for you, but what you can do for your country." Today's offshore outsourcing practitioners follow another creed: "Think not what your country can do to you, but what you can do to your country."

9

OFFSHORE OUTSOURCING IN INFORMATION TECHNOLOGIES

The sermon preached by inventors of dotcoms in the early 1990s promised to divert traffic and sales through the newly constructed information superhighway at the expense of traditional brick and mortar stores. The new business model predicted that customers would trade the feng shui of shopping centers for steep discounts made possible by stale Internet shopping, thereby rendering multiple stores and the employees that come with them redundant. Investors, dazzled by the specter of relatively negligible infrastructure costs, boosted stock prices of dotcoms through the stratosphere. And nobody benefited more from the acceptance of this illusion than the high priest of dotcoms, Jeffrey Bezos, founder of Amazon.com.

Founded in 1994, Amazon.com turbo-charged along the information superhighway in a mad dash to obliterate several brick and mortar players. So diversifying from its rudimentary base of books, videos and compact disks, the company plunged into consumer electronics, kitchenware, tools and hardware leading to spectacular growth. Cumulative customer accounts grew from 180,000 in 1996 to over 1.5 million mouse clickers in 1997, with sales skyrocketing from $15.7 million to $147.8 million within the same time frame. Following these trends, the share price of Amazon.com accelerated until it hit an eye-popping $400 in 1998.

Financial market success of Amazon.com engendered a stampede of human and financial resources into Silicon Valley, dotcom's technology base, at an unprecedented rate. Not since the migration of the forty niners, motivated by the gold nugget discovered by James Wilson Marshall on January 24, 1848, had the geographical area attracted so much attention.

Every conceivable variation of the Amazon.com model was devoured with the same eagerness as a pack of lions tearing into a prey at Kruger National Park. Furniture.com, Pets.com, eToys.com all found eager suitors in short order. Eve.com offered even an ancient product like perfume, used to devastating effect by Cleopatra, and over which consumers fuss incessantly before making a purchase, as a model.

In the sign of the times, Idealab founder Bill Gross apparently listened to Eve.com's sales pitch for only 90 minutes before deciding to invest. After making Eve.com an offer, Bill Gross proffered this anti-conventional business theory: "After a few years in this business, I've learned that making instinctive decisions is the best way to make an investment." Eve.com raised a total of $3.2 million based on projected sales of $1 billion by 2003. "There's money in them makeup" was absorbed by the investment community wily nilly.

An eager investment community convinced the Internet had changed the rules of business, and that napkins could serve a dual purpose as parents of business plans as well as orphans in garbage cans, swallowed initial public offerings for all manner of companies. Paper billionaires cashed in the same day of the offerings, threatening Bill Gates' status as the wealthiest person in the world.

The litany of start up companies hired battalions of computer scientists to construct ramps to the information superhighway. Then with the Y2K phenomenon threatening to paralyze water supply, electricity, and everything else in sight, the demand for computer scientists exploded in 1999, opening the floodgates for foreigners to enter the US under special permits to bridge the gulf in supply of technical experts.

With demand outstripping supply, many computer scientists made fortunes, sometimes performing mundane tasks like installing Windows software, or educating consumers to refrain from wiping video screens to erase mistakes. The wealth displayed by computer scientists attracted many more thousands to the profession.

But when profit expectations were not met, investors suddenly discovered valuations of dotcoms were unrealistic, and they bailed out in a hurry. E-grocer Webvan.com crashed and share price of Amazon.com went into a tailspin until it bottomed out at $6.96 on November 1, 2001.

Collapse of the dotcoms hit computer scientists the hardest. Thousands were furloughed after the geese that laid the golden eggs were put out to pasture. Suddenly, the profession that was the envy of many had been pummeled into submission. The employment status of a good portion of the displaced workers was worsened by the fact that many had entered the marketing and sales sectors of the profession, forsaking the unglamorous programming sector. The foreigners who had been hired under special dispensation exploited the opportunity to prove their mettle in programming, laying the foundation for the coming exodus of jobs overseas.

While the dotcoms were bingeing on the vast amounts of capital infused into the industry, the brick and mortars were transforming into lean and mean models of efficiency. Grizzled in business, they knew the dotcom model was bogus because wives would never forsake the one opportunity—shopping—they had all week to drag their complaining husbands away from watching sports on television.

Wal-Mart introduced enterprise resource management (ERM) software across its company platform, allowing suppliers to track movement of goods through their stores for automatic replenishment. This ensured that fast-moving goods were always on the shelf or isles. ERM could spot an item moving quickly at one store, while it lagged at another, enabling Wal-Mart to implement the successful model at all stores. Meanwhile, pioneering companies like Siebel and JD Edwards introduced customer relationship management software that made customer/company interactions more productive. On the employee side of the ledger, Peoplesoft introduced software to improve human relationships within companies. Within the same time frame, Oracle introduced entity relationship modeling, a new program to handle larger databases.

So when the dotcoms collapsed like a deck of cards, the derided bricks and mortar players were still standing, citadels of efficiency requiring more of the software that had helped make them more efficient: the froth had been removed from the computer industry but the demand for productivity-enhancing software still raged.

Meanwhile, the computer industry had discovered that the foreigners who had arrived to assist in rewriting code for COBOL, the language embedded in older computers, were also very proficient in writing code for the new software. Not only that but new technologies had made it unnecessary to bring them to the U.S: they could work and communicate just as efficiently from their native countries, saving the companies the $15,000 or so it took to sponsor a foreigner to work in the U.S. Human resource managers everywhere could choose from a global base of computer programmers, and quite a few abandoned U.S. citizens in favor of less expensive foreigners. American computer programmers were about to be thrust into turbulence without the protection of seat belts.

Newsweek documented his story. He was a 54-year-old computer programmer who lost his $50,000 job in 2001. He went to a job fair held by the California Employment Development office for eighteen positions, but he arrived too late behind seven hundred people, some of whom showed up as early as 6:30 a.m. Dejected, he returned to his part time work as a gas reader, a position he secured ahead of three hundred other applicants. And the reason for not arriving as early as he had wanted was because he had to go home and change into regular clothes. "I stopped at home because I didn't want to show up in my gas uniform," he said.

This was one of the people who did the grunt work that led to the creation of UNIX and the Internet. The information highway was supposed to be the new road to the middle class for such qualified people. But the information highway is carrying their jobs away instead, and at supersonic speed.

Of the 2.7 million jobs lost between March 2001 and July 2003, more than half a million—or one in five—were in programming, Internet publishing, computer systems design telecommunications and data processing. The UNIX, Internet, and all the wonderful zip and zap technologies created by America and given free of charge to the world to improve communications are being used to legally bludgeon Americans.

In a paper disseminated among its clients, IBM called offshore outsourcing a "compelling alternative." The paper warned "firms lingering with a domestic model will see their competitiveness erode rapidly if they do not make the leap to global outsourcing." It predicted that, "Dramatic structural changes...will ensue, as the magnitude of cost savings for those adopting offshore strategies will swamp those who dither." Then the paper lowered the boom, "In five years or less, this gap will become unbridgeable."

To encourage companies with cold feet, the IBM paper offered not only a reassurance but it threw in a bonus as well: "Concurrently, developments in many of these [centers] over the last five years have lowered the risk profile for undertaking such ventures—and provided some unexpected benefits that are enabling companies to develop new business models with much bolder long-term ambitions." It compared offshore outsourcing to the well-trodden path followed by manufacturing: "For some time, the manufacturing sector has effectively deployed the massive labor-cost differential, by utilizing global resources. Now...countries are taking on service-sector work."

And many companies are following the offshore outsourcing recommendation to the letter. The departed CEO of General Electric, Jack Welch, issued a 70:70:70 rule: 70 percent of GE's work would be outsourced. Of this, 70 percent would be done from offshore development centers. And of this, about 70 percent would be done in India. This ultimately boils down to about 35 percent of all of GE's work being done in India.

The 70:70:70 rule is already in full swing. General Electric uses four major Indian partners with dedicated facilities that employ 3,200 people who develop and maintain GE's systems. For customer service, GE Capital has a 10,000-strong workforce in India offering accounting, claims processing, credit evaluation services to 80 branches General Electric Co around the world. GE Capital was said to be in the process of doubling this facility.

Policymakers everywhere predicted the disappearance of manufacturing jobs was inconsequential because these would be replaced by higher-paying, cleaner jobs in the information technology and other service industries. The mantra was that displaced manufacturing workers would be retrained to occupy jobs in the "burgeoning" service industry. Unfortunately, both manufacturing and high quality service jobs are fleeing—the former via the Pacific Ocean, the latter via the Information highway—to overseas destinations.

Back in the midst of the Cold War, Soviet Premier Nikita Khrushchev sneered at Americans: "We will hang you...And you will sell us the rope." Now the rope is not even being sold; it is being given away free of charge. For never in the annals of history has the world witnessed the voluntary transfer of jobs and assets to other countries on the scale being perpetrated by the United States.

And the nonchalance with which many of the practitioners of offshore outsourcing execute their duties is stupefying. According to Ann Livermore, head of services at Hewlett Packard Co., "A basic business tenet is that things go to the areas where there is the best cost of production. Now you're going to see the same trends in service that happened in manufacturing." Hewlett Packard operates a center in India staffed by 3,300 software engineers.

And they are mocking you: "America has long relied on cheap immigrant labour, filling jobs US workers find unappealing. Consumers have grudgingly accepted even sending factory jobs to Asia or Mexico as the best way to satisfy their appetite for inexpensive clothing and electronics. But with businesses now shipping white-collar service and high-tech jobs overseas to cut costs, a whole new sector and class of workers is feeling the pain."

And the fire continues to rage daily. When an uninhabited forest in Arizona burned, America gathered its bravest to wage war against it. Huge tankers loaded with foam battled relentlessly until the fire was extinguished. But nobody lifts a finger while America's children are engulfed in flames.

"Bill Gates says India is IT superpower: strikes strategic alliances with...to develop applications on the .Net platform."

"Sun Microsystems has decided to outsource most of the development for its new and upcoming J2ME platform to its center in Bangalore, India."

Offshore outsourcing has consolidated its penetration in U.S. by moving up the value chain. The fundamental basis for business growth—to develop new products—is being shipped overseas. Eventually, only face-to-face salesmen would be left in the U.S. Even sales presentations would be coordinated from offshore.

"BellSouth Corp. may save as much as $275 million in IT costs over five years as the result of a plan to move its application development and maintenance work offshore." A spokesperson was quoted as saying: "Our current business case suggests moving a third to half of our IT application work offshore. This equates to 600-900 positions over the next four years."

BellSouth's plan was not unique. Gartner Inc. predicted 10 percent of the positions at IT vendors and technology services firms and one out of every 20 corporate IT jobs would migrate overseas by the end of 2004. And that could be only the beginning. Gartner predicts the pace of offshore outsourcing will accelerate in three to four year's time.

Many more corporations are planning to follow the path contemplated by BellSouth either on their own or through benchmarking specialists like IBM, EDS, CSC or Hewlett Packard. With no constraints on where functions should be carried out, many outsourcing contracts will migrate overseas. Already, IBM Global Services maintains a huge offshore facility in India.

Rapidigm, a corporate superstar in the IT industry in Pittsburgh, started operations in India in 2000 with a core group of four technocrats and a team of twenty. The Indian staff grew to 100 and 350 in 2003 and 2005, respectively. And now, according to a posting at its website, Rapidigm planned to increase the staff at just one of its Indian locations to 1,200 in the near term.

According to Rapidigm, its staff in India added valued services in SAP, Oracle, Peoplesoft, and e-business solutions. Operating on a 24-hour business cycle allowed the company to coordinate the activities of its many U.S. locations and India seamlessly and effectively.

While part of the growth of Rapidigm in India is due to local demand, the most significant growth factor is undoubtedly due to customer demands in the U.S. The undeniable fact therefore is that Rapidigm, one of the stars of the new economy in Pittsburgh, is hiring staff in India at the expense of Americans, and this trend is being duplicated across many corporate platforms in the United States.

Many computer science graduates are emerging from their cocoons on college campuses in the U.S. to the realization that their careers have been yanked from under their feet while they were busy studying. As companies in the U.S. ramp up offshore outsourcing options across several professions, the threat to America's workforce will cut a much wider swath.

A thirty-year old man scoured the Employment Development Department in Pleasant Hill, CA, hoping to find clerical or any kind of work. He had dreamt of finding a nice girl, marrying, settling down and sowing his genes, but his circumstances changed drastically. A member of the once highflying information technology occupation, he lost his job, and moved back under his parents' umbrella, dreams shattered. He said many more like him had come to the painful realization that their jobs were gone forever. He said he would like to try another profession, but jobs in those areas had disappeared, too.

He'd worked twenty-four years at the Bank of America branch at Concord, CA. One day, without warning, he was given a pink slip because his job had been moved overseas. He took it on the chin, resigned to his fate. But not everyone had the stomach to handle such a severe rejection. Another employee at the same bank shot himself in the head in the parking lot when informed of his termination. His father confirmed his son's death was the result of the bank sending his work overseas. A company spokesperson sent condolences to his family, colleagues and friends.

Opportunities for a whole generation of professionals are being eliminated. Computer science professionals are taking the brunt today, but engineers, financial analysts and scientists are getting squeezed as well. And the pain in America will worsen.

He is 27 years old, and his cry was heard on the Internet. Saddled with loans after four years of computer science education at an Ivy school, he was laid off after five years with a company. His questions were: "Is my career over at 27? How am I going to pay off my student loans?"

"When all the Microsoft, Oracle and IBM software production has been shipped offshore, and when all Intel factories are completely automated, and when all Home Depot stores have self-check-out counters…my question is: Who in America will be able to afford the food that the McDonalds' robots cook?

"I am struggling with what to suggest to my children for a course of study at college. It is becoming more and more difficult for college grads to find employment. Now with outsourcing rampant, they need something stable for their career opportunities. A small town dentist, doctor or lawyer might be appropriate."

"I am truly frightened after our experience. I am scared to buy another house (we had to sell ours for his new job). I am scared to have a baby. We can't afford to save for retirement. Pensions are a thing of the past."

"If we can't bring ourselves to do the hard thing and stop this mad export of our tax-sponsored genius, then we all deserve what comes. So, go out and study the convenience store business and the movie rental business—because we have worked and lobbied intensely hard to make this the future employment of majority of U.S. citizens."

Bank of America Corp. cut technology and operations jobs through the end of 2003 and, in the process, replaced some employees with lower-cost labor overseas. The bank was set to open a 1000-person facility of its own in India staffed with computer programmers and other support staff. Goodbye American staff!

As if being terminated is not cruel enough, some American computer programmers are subjected to further abuse by being coerced to train their replacements. According to the Charlotte Observer, "Laid-off employees said they have been asked to sign two sets of papers: One states that the employee will receive two weeks' severance for every year he or she worked for the bank. The other says severance will be cancelled if the employees talk to the media or quit before a certain date. They've also been asked to help train their India counterparts before their final day."

On April 19, 2002, Siemens ICN told employees it was going to outsource its IT department and that they would be laid off once the transition was completed. The employees weren't particularly perturbed, figuring they would be recipients of some of those outsourced jobs. Unbeknown to the employees, not only was outsourcing of the offshore variety, but they were also required to train their Indian replacements as part of their settlement.

Microsoft executives routinely implore their underlings to think about "offshoring" something to India every day. According to a company executive, "Two heads for the price of one" should be a fundamental thought process. Following through on this thinking, Microsoft set up a development center in India, and also outsourced some work to other Indian firms. The company Chairman visited India in November 2002, and said the following, "A couple of years ago, the biggest American corporations would have considered it risky to outsource mission-critical work to India, but it is now becoming a common sense proposition."

Unfortunately for Mr. Gates and the rest of America, the risk factor has not been mitigated by time; it has in fact been aggravated. The experience of 9/11 should teach that terrorists would go to any extent to harm America. Terrorists do not predicate their actions based on time: they will lie fallow, probing for paths of least resistance, before striking at the time of their choosing. And development of application software overseas increases the chance for insertion of a Trojan horse into core processes for subsequent exploitation.

The network of computer scientists overseas has the ability to hide source code for the products developed for Microsoft and Intel. According to Ken O'Neill, a Long Island computer programmer, "Anyone that tells you that 'offshoring' does not put the infrastructure at risk is lying." Mr. O'Neill talked about the "sleeper bugs that could be set to go off at a later date, or back doors that would let intruders in to shuttle money around, steal fractions of a penny from millions of transactions or shut down the system entirely. They warn of risks from political instability, organized crime and terror cells, and even from governments that might demand the ability to spy."

The American programmers also said that reviews of computer code drafted by foreigners weren't as complete as corporations claimed. O'Neill was quoted as saying: "If code runs, I assure you, nobody looks at it," comparing a line-by-line review of computer code with the likelihood that an electrician would tear into a wall to check wiring when the lights were working. "It never gets done in practice," was the conclusion the programmer offered to the Times.

The financial services industry is hemorrhaging information technology jobs to offshore operators. The TowerGroup, a research and advisory firm for the financial services industry, estimated North American brokerage firms would increase their budgets for offshore outsourcing from $417 million in 2002 to $1.31 billion in 2005, a compounded annual rate of 46.4 percent. The report cited a deal between Lehman Brothers and an offshore outfit with offices in the U.S., and Merrill Lynch's expanding offshore activities as examples of a growing trend.

The rush to offshore outsourcing in the financial services industry is proceeding apace despite the possibility of transactions being interrupted by regional conflicts. The protagonists have also turned a blind eye to critical issues such as confidentiality, misinterpretation of data and domain legal responsibilities.

Computer programmers regard the science of writing code as the ultimate test of individualism. As such, the profession regards unions and collective bargaining as symbols of failure. However, as the sword of offshore outsourcing cuts across the industry, many are finding that there is, indeed, strength in numbers. Once unfathomable, labor protests are sprouting up across the U.S. For example, displaced information technology workers from insurance and financial services companies in Connecticut formed The Organization for the Rights of American Workers (Toraw). In June 2002, Toraw and similar groups from around the country mounted a vociferous demonstration at the Waldorf Astoria hotel in New York City, where a Strategic Outsourcing Conference was being held. In the same month, other displaced workers demonstrated outside an outsourcing conference at the Hynes Convention Center in Boston.

However, unlike traditional labor unions that generate publicity from sympathetic ears in government and media, the cries of the wounded information technology workers are being smothered. United Technologies, Procter and Gamble, Prudential, DaimlerChrysler, Cigna, ING, Northeastern Utilities are all sending information technology jobs out of the U.S. at a rate much faster than manufacturing ever did. According to one observer, "[IT work] will move faster because it's easier to ship work across phone lines and put consultants on airplanes than it is to ship bulky raw materials across borders and build factories and deal with tariffs and transportation."

Offshore outsourcing has skewed productivity calculations. Wall Street rejoices when productivity increase is reported, but this could be attributable to foreign workers removed from the calculations. An available large labor pool also prevents U.S. wages from increasing in an offshore outsourcing environment, a trend confirmed by data from the Economic Policy Institute showing wages for new college graduates had declined over the past three four years.

According to the CIO Magazine, "Until now, offshore outsourcing has been mostly limited to large companies that have big chunks of work to send off-shore...But as the offshore outsourced companies have matured, so have their processes." The paper quoted a global outsourcing company executive as saying his clients were starting projects with only five people. Large or small, most companies have set their sights on reducing cost by moving jobs overseas.

The dominant perception is that offshore outsourcing affects only entry-level occupations in the information technology industry. This is no longer true. A CIO survey found that "eleven percent of the companies had outsourced system and architectural planning, and fourteen percent had outsourced research and development." These were two categories most experts assumed were immune to the offshore outsourcing phenomenon.

Swifter decapitation tools available to employers mean workers in information technologies could suffer more devastating fates than workers in the steel industry, where it took a "leisurely" twenty years for employment to be slashed by eighty percent. With labor savings far more dramatic and easier to achieve, employment in the information technology industry could be eviscerated within ten years or less.

But many of America's brightest are not waiting: they are jumping to relatively safer professions like medicine before they are pushed. And just like manufacturing, the consequences of a brain drain from the information technology industry would have far reaching repercussions on innovation and product development across the U.S., for it is far easier to destroy than to build.

The peoples America is feeding with its inordinate resources are ancient, and patient. They are lying in watch as America gradually discourages its young, knowing very well that replenishment of American talent will be impossible sometime in the near, say, 20 years. Then as demand catches up with supply, the price of overseas labor will increase proportionately and the tables will turn. By then, the generation that destroyed the gift bequeathed to them will be long gone, leaving their children and grandchildren to wonder at the sheer stupidity of the whole enterprise of offshore outsourcing.

Instead of speeding jobs to offshore destinations, the United States should be taking measures to nurture and develop more people like William Joy and James Gosling. Joy was a brilliant software designer at the University of California at Berkeley in the 70s and 80s when UNIX was selected as one of the candidates for integration into the Internet framework. Working with uncommon wisdom and resolute determination, William Joy debugged the Internet communications protocols, TCP/IP, and incorporated them into the UNIX at Berkley, making it feasible for the protocols to become the standard transmission mechanisms for the Internet.

Not satiated by his transcendental achievement, William Joy, together with others, went on to found Sun Microsystems, the company whose workstations formed the backbone of local area networks and wide area networks that allowed the Internet to be extrapolated to consumers and corporations alike. William Joy resigned from all his corporate responsibilities to pursue, in his words, "the joy of writing code alone." Only a "geeky" genius will describe working alone as a "joy."

Like many of his predecessors, James Gosling of Sun Microsystems is a radical who refused to accept the limitations of programming languages prevalent at the time. Also like his mentors, he simplified programming by breaking codes into smaller pieces. Then championed by William Joy, Gosling used this approach to develop JAVA, an object-oriented programming language in 1991. Today, JAVA has become the de-facto Internet programming language, and has been adopted in large computers, as well as cell phones, smart cards and personal digital assistants. Sun's licensing revenue from JAVA runs to at least $100 million annually.

A policy expert observed, "Technology has been the driver of economic growth and change, and if you are not on the cutting edge, if you don't have a large number of people working on technology, you have to wonder about your military capability going forward."

Americans have maintained a high standard of living by leading the world in innovation. Storied names like Andrew Carnegie, Henry Ford, Thomas Edison, Steve Jobs, and Bill Gates, to name a few, are synonymous with millions of high paying jobs born out of their ingenuity. But the rampant pace at which offshore outsourcing is proceeding in all areas of computer software engineering could result in the next JAVA being born somewhere across the oceans. When that happens the United States could be at the mercy of vendors who may demand a pound of flesh in return for their products. Worse than price, the software that runs missiles, frigates, fighter jets and other elements of America's defense system could be encoded with hostile bugs pre-programmed to precipitate failure upon start up, thereby jeopardizing the security of all Americans.

While workers in electronic manufacturing in the U.S. are going home, their counterparts in India are going to work. According to Intel India President Ketan Sampat, a "Made in India" Intel chip is scheduled for release by 2006. "We are in a three year development phase. So a 'Made in India' chip is likely to be released in the year 2005-2006." He added that the design center in India was developing a high-end 32-bit computing Xeon chip processor, which would be the first of its kind from the Intel Indian team.

Every technology company of consequence in the U.S. operates a sophisticated design and product development center in India. This includes IBM, Intel, Oracle, Sun Microsystems, Microsoft, Adaptec, Cadence and Synopsys.

Internal corporate software development is a support function without much external ramifications. Consulting in software applications is also bread and butter service. But research and development is at the heart of not just the well being of the company, but of the host country as well. So no matter how much protection is offered in other countries, uprooting research and development is not dissimilar to ripping out the future of the United States, loading it on a plane and speeding it elsewhere.

Dominance of U.S. military is due in no small part to U.S. leadership in advanced technology. So the U.S. stands to lose more than currency as some corporate leaders trade its technological leadership for a plate of lentils.

Ironically, the U.S. Air Force funded the Internet during the Cold War as a mechanism to prevent America's defense structure from being decapitated by a Soviet preemptive attack. Today, that preventative mechanism is yielding to a process with the potential to breach the defenses of the defender. By any definition, this act is potentially suicidal, but it is the path the United States of America is following with unbridled offshore outsourcing.

The long-term implications of offshore outsourcing on U.S. information technology industry are being recognized by a perceptible few. The CIO Magazine has commented: "As the bulk of technology work moves offshore, the deep, experiential knowledge that comes from coding applications and solving technology problems—the soil of technology innovation—could move offshore with it."

A concerned information technology expert remarked: "Can a company afford to completely divest itself of in-house IT skills? After all, business code is an extension...or expression...of business knowledge. I see anything that threatens business knowledge continuity as a very shortsighted approach. If the immediate bottom line is the only factor being considered in business planning, then what provision do we have for the future? The question 'Who will provide the innovation for the future?' Shortsightedness has never been associated with long-term business success. So do we recycle our companies too?"

Some propagators of offshore outsourcing are also beginning to doubt the wisdom of their own actions. An information technology executive heavily engaged in offshore outsourcing questioned, "We haven't eliminated all our developer jobs, but a good portion is gone. So where do you look for that superstar who is doing a great job and has a rapport with the customer and understands your business?" Another executive was reported by CIO to be having recurring nightmares about his own actions. He worried that it was too easy for "companies like his to outsource overseas today." And in a tone apparently wracked with guilt, the executive lamented, "I don't want to wake up one day and find that American IT has disappeared."

Quantitative proof of the shrinking middle class in the information technology industry is being catalogued, and the picture being painted is grim. According to the outplacement firm Challenger, Gray & Christmas, nearly 700,000 information technology job cuts, more than a third of total payroll reductions proposed by U.S. firms, were announced in 2001. In 2002, thirty three percent of all proposed job reductions were in the information technology industry.

The meager up tick in employment prospects for information technology workers in recent months is illusory. It was caused by an unsustainable combination of consumer and government spending, the former due to home refinancing, the latter due to military hardware. Even then, Americans are nowhere close to deriving the optimum benefit from the increased expenditures: enough quality jobs are created overseas at the expense of Americans to question who is the primary beneficiary. What good does it do America if funds from home refinancing create far more jobs for overseas manufacturers of cars, televisions, computers, digital cameras, digital video recorders, stereos, clothing, furniture, toys and shoes? And what is the sense in the phenomenon where America's currency puts more food on the plates of software developers overseas than on plates in American homes of their American counterparts?

Excruciating pain will be inflicted when binge spending grinds to a halt. Then the tears will turn into a torrent.

Americans will do well to keep an eye on Connecticut, for that is where the pain will be felt the most as information technology is uprooted from the U.S. Dubbed a "perfect model" because of the depth of insurance, information technology and other high quality service jobs, the export of these jobs will do to Connecticut what steel did to Pittsburgh, and will be just as ugly.

Many people believe Mark Twain was looking out at the Mississippi River as he wrote many of his popular books. In fact, the Park River in Hartford, Connecticut was the object of his affection. Hartland in the Northwest, Enfield in the Northeast, Marlborough in the Southeast and Southington in the Southwest define the rectangular boundary of Hartford County, with the city of Hartford stationed almost in the middle. Many who may not know it was home to Mark Twain are aware of its moniker as "The Insurance Capitol of the World." For this stretch of land serves as head office for venerable insurance titans such as AETNA, Cigna, Hartford Insurance Group, Phoenix Mutual, St. Paul-Travelers and Hartford Steam & Insurance. Firms such as Blue Cross & Blue Shield, Met Life and New York Life whose head offices are out of state are still heavily represented in this quadrant.

Hartford may one day wear another championship belt known as the "Offshore Outsourcing Capitol of the U.S." For on top of every offshore outsourcing list sits the same insurance titans of Hartford. Phoenix Mutual has since sold its offshore outsourcing unit to an Indian firm, but this has by no means put an end to offshore outsourcing of internal business processes. AETNA, Cigna and hundreds of small, medium and large insurance firms in Hartford County are all heavily engaged in the practice.

According to CIO of The Hartford Dave Annis, "There is a great opportunity and we are going to start a few small pilots in India to test the waters." This was back in May 2001. Today, the systems are primed for full scale up, and the insurance professionals and support teams in Hartford are caught in the cross hairs. The data entry teams were the first to be hit, but now the move up the food chain is complete. Their Indian replacements have become just as conversant in the algorithms and terminologies of the industry, and the offshore outsourcing perpetrators are licking their lips at the significantly larger labor cost differential to be exacted by the replacement of higher paid U.S. professionals. Hartford is about to be turned into the Pittsburgh of the eighties. Pittsburgh lived by steel and died by steel. Hartford has lived by insurance since the industry mushroomed in the mid-19th century. Now it is about to be gorged by insurance.

According to a study published in April 2003 by the Connecticut Technology Council, each information technology job added another 2.3 jobs to the state economy. Therefore, job deterioration in the information technology and related sectors will set in motion a ripple effect that will scorch an already shrinking middle class in other employment sectors.

The shrinking middle class in the information technology industry is bereft with qualitative problems as well. Many displaced workers lucky to find new employment are discovering that wages and compensation such as medical insurance and 401K contributions have dropped dramatically. The Economic Policy Institute showed wages had declined by 15 percent to 25 percent, traceable directly to globalization. What was true of manufacturing is now true of the information technology sector: when supply of a product of equivalent value increases, price falls. As for stock options, once the seductive juice in the industry, they were uprooted long ago by the storm of 2001.

Rapid incorporation of information technology systems into every facet of U.S. society has enhanced the importance of workers in the industry to national competitiveness and wealth creation. Therefore, the erosion of this asset created largely by Americans, and the resultant debilitating effect on the middle class ought to be matters of the utmost concern to policymakers, educators and ordinary citizens everywhere.

"Offshoring contributes to high unemployment levels among U.S. technologists, and poses a serious, long-term challenge to the nation's technological and innovative leadership, its economic vitality and its military and homeland security," according to a position paper developed by IEEE-USA.

History is a great teacher. In its heyday during World War II, the Sparrows Point, Maryland plant owned by Bethlehem Steel employed 45,000 middle class workers. This juggernaut was the centerpiece of a sprawling enterprise that manufactured steel, iron rods, and many other units used for the construction of mammoth ships emblazoned with "Made in America" tags. As incompetence and overseas competitors gutted the American showpiece, policymakers and the popular press provided assurances that the displaced workers would be retrained for a brighter future in a New Economy based on high technology. As of May 2003, only 2,800 workers remained at this plant that was once the envy of the world, and the promise extended to the displaced workers turned out to be as solid as a mirage.

A policy expert of Indian extraction made this comment: "The United States does have a vested interest in seeing other countries grow and seeing other people get good jobs. But we cannot abandon people here."

10

GLOBALIZATION AND THE SHRINKAGE OF THE AMERICAN MIDDLE CLASS

Business Week dated the arrival of the New Economy to the mid-1990s, and classified it as a fusion of globalization of business and revolution in information technology. Globalization was defined as introduction of market forces, freer trade and deregulation around the world, while information technology was characterized by digitization of words, pictures or data.

Globalization was sold to Americans in two parts. As a mechanism to contain prices and enhance purchasing power, the first part promoted manufacture of "low-tech" goods such as toys, shoes and clothing—"Old Economy" goods—in lower wage developing countries. To reassure Americans, the second part claimed Americans would gain higher paying jobs by exporting services and "high-tech" goods—"New Economy" products—to those newly opened markets. According to this composite logic, goods and services from the U.S. would become more affordable to consumers in the developing world as they manufactured more "Old Economy" products. Displaced "Old Economy" workers in the U.S. would be retrained for employment in the higher-paying "New Economy," with concurrent increase in the standard of living of workers in developing countries such as China and India. To rephrase the words in the old song, nobody should worry because everybody was going to be happy. These arguments have turned out to be loads of baloney.

The evidentiary record suggests indisputably that the reality of globalization is starkly different from what it advocates had promised. What has transpired instead is a classic Faustian bargain in which promised lower prices have materialized, but in exchange for jobs. The great new jobs offered in reassurance in the

U.S. are not only nowhere to be found, they are being offered at reduced rates to the same crowd, or similar ones, manufacturing the products from the "Old Economy." So the developing countries are double winners, and the United States is a double loser. The promised win-win scenario has turned into win-lose reality.

Promised service jobs included software development and financial analysts, while robotics, disc drives and memory chips were offered as more satisfying manufacturing employment in "clean" environments. Wages in all industries were predicted to rise as productivity increased with deeper penetration of information technologies. "These trends can combine in powerful ways to raise Americans' standard of living, create jobs, spur entrepreneurial effort—and do all this without boosting inflation," purred Business Week.

Citizens in low wage countries producing cheaper goods were promised improved living standards as a result of better paying jobs created by the increase in demand from developed countries. It was assumed that companies moving to low wage countries would offer better wages and benefits than native manufacturers by passing on some of the savings of relocation. "Forget hopelessness in the developing world," proclaimed Business Week. "We are talking about raising living standards in India and Brazil." Some of this has happened.

Promising a perpetual stream of lower inflation, higher economic growth, reduced unemployment and higher wages for all citizens of Mother Earth, the slogan used to sell globalization could have easily read, "Globalization and prosperity for all, pain and suffering for none."

When a skeptical Robert Samuelson, renowned columnist for The Washington Post, wrote in 1997, "We have not created permanent economic bliss," Business Week referred to him as the "normally astute," meaning he had taken leave of his senses with regards to the utopia promised by the New Economy. Business Week, the self-proclaimed mouthpiece for the New Economy, branded it nonsensical when The Economist said the new thinking in America verged on "claptrap."

Then with U.S. unemployment at 4 percent in 1999, consumer inflation at its lowest in 34 years and economic growth of 4 percent for six successive years, seeming evidence of the wonders of the New Economy caused the mouthpiece to go ballistic in January 2000 with the headline: "The New Economy—It works in America. Will it go global?" "It seems almost too good to be true," said Business Week prophetically. "This spectacular boom was not built on smoke and mirrors."

It was, indeed, too good to be true, and while not built on smoke and mirrors, neither was it built on a foundation of steel and concrete. Globalization's creaky foundation was evident in the fact that core economic principles had to be violated for the benefits promised by its advocates to reach all citizens. Some of its tenets like mobility of capital, entrepreneurship and information could be applied to the fullest extent possible through multinational agreements, while others like mobility of technology and labor content and the powers of supply and demand had to be applied selectively, if at all. Since these contradictions are irreconcilable, it is obvious that globalization was a fraud peddled mostly by some multinational corporations to their benefit.

In this contradictory context, the presumed relative immobility of technology and high-skill labor content would have allowed high-tech manufacturing and high-skilled services to remain the preserve of advanced countries. These restraints were prerequisites for displaced workers in the Old Economy to be retrained for a smooth transition to jobs in the New Economy, and for high-skilled service providers in advanced countries to increase their numbers and suffer no degradation in wages even as less expensive competitors in developing countries became available.

The sacrosanct principle of the effect of supply of a commodity (labor) on price (wage) would have to be completely nullified for there not to have been any deleterious effect on wages in advanced countries of coupling several hundred million much lower paid workers in developing countries, as globalization was intending to do, to millions of higher paid workers in developed countries. The laws of gravity and thermodynamics had to be violated for globalization to work as its advocates promised

That the American public has largely accepted that globalization, despite the enumerated implausibilities, is a beneficial, and risk free, phenomenon is testament to the propaganda coup scored by its advocates in public service, academia and the mainstream press, those, unsurprisingly, who are immunized from its poisons. Because the evidence is indisputable that under globalization, mobility of technology and skills has enabled corporations to reap huge financial rewards at the expense of workers in both the Old and New Economies by shifting production of toys, textiles, computers, flat screens, memory chips and other goods from developed to developing countries. Therefore, not only have American workers been booted out of low-tech industries, they will, for the most part, not reach the oasis of high-tech jobs. Furthermore, there is incontrovertible evidence that globalization has caused wages and benefits of remaining American workers to diminish. And to add insult to injury, the service jobs created by the information technology boom in advanced countries are also being atrophied by globalization.

The Scriptures warned that, "Those that have, more shall be given to them and those that have not, the little they have shall be taken away and given to those that have." This admonition seemed implausible until the emergence of multinational corporations. For what the world is witnessing is that multinational corporations—the undisputed heavyweight winners of globalization—are stuffing their bank accounts with more cash as the deprived middle class gasps for air.

The first stop of multinational corporations was Mexico, which they deserted for Thailand and the Philippines as soon as those meager wages began to increase. And when China—the mother of all low wages—opened up, desertions from all parts of the world turned into a stampede.

To the American middle class, globalization has turned out to be a Faustian bargain, and no amount of band-aid provided by safely ensconced tenured apologists in academia and the media will stem the blood pouring from the wounds it is continuing to inflict. What doth it profit the American middle class to gain lower prices for shoes, electronics and clothing from Wal-Mart but lose its livelihood to China and India?

Unfortunately for the American middle class, advocates of globalization in academia and the mainstream media continue to deny its debilitating effects on employment and wages, thereby strangling an honest debate on actions needed to stanch the bleeding.

Using a Poisson process to replicate transitions from one job to another, many apologists build empirical models that confirm predisposed positions, conveniently neglecting the irrefutable phenomenon of capital replacing higher priced labor in the U.S. with lower priced labor overseas. For example, Davidson and Matusz advised, "Rather than focussing on the well-understood benefits of liberalization, some policy makers and editorialists tend to focus on the potentially costly aspects of resource allocation." Then they issued this wisdom which flies in the face of perpetual unemployment among some workers: "Most workers who lose their jobs due to liberalization will find new employment opportunities, but there is typically a period of active search before such opportunities are found." The empirical model built by Davidson and Matusz and many other advocates seem to always produce a positive effect of globalization on employment because it is predicated on the discredited foundation "that labor released from a contracting sector would be absorbed into an expanding sector," except of course if the expanding sector was meant to be at Wal-Mart and McDonalds.

Many economists have been blindfolded by history into adopting the optimistic view that technological change, by increasing productivity, would add to employment and incomes in the long term. Going back in history, economic transformation from agriculture to manufacturing increased employment by several orders of magnitude. Within industrialization, compounded components of the automobile led to a quantum leap in employment when it replaced stagecoaches. In the field of communication, ancillary requirements for the computer caused employment to explode when it supplanted typewriters and fax machines in the 1990s. More recently, the preeminence of service—as it covered computer technology—over manufacturing caused employment to skyrocket. But the assumption by many economists that this process will continue to march on inexorably is false, leading to erroneous conclusions of the positive effect of globalization on employment.

The full effects of four dramatic developments have not yet been properly injected into economic analysis. The first is availability of skilled labor in Asia, now only being discovered due to liberalization of previously shuttered economies. The second is the mobility of technology, spurred by mobility of capital and availability of skilled labor in Asia. The third is standardization of management, quality control and productivity, especially by multinational corporations. The last, but certainly not the least, is the Internet. These developments explain why, contrary to conventional wisdom, job destruction, rather than job creation, is parallel with increase in productivity in the United States.

Proponents of globalization emphasize the importance of education, training and acquisition of skills by the workforce as the key contributors to maintaining, or even improving, standard of living. Policymakers have embraced this dictum by providing funds for retraining at employment development centers in order to transform the workforce into one capable of dealing with rapid technological changes. Close collaboration between labor market and industry development plans has been said to be a fundamental tenet of the New Economy. According to Lester Thurow of MIT, the future of advanced capitalist economies depends on it. In his book, Comparative Advantage of Nations, Harvard economist Michael Porter cited human capital factor as indispensable to the creation of comparative advantage by countries lacking natural resources and large populations. Leo Reddy, president of the National Coalition for Advanced Manufacturing made a similar point: "Global competitiveness and growing exports exert added pressures on the U.S. workforce. The only way in which our workforce can withstand these pressures is to continuously improve the skills it needs to produce globally competitive products."

But by constantly referring to labor in advanced countries as highly educated, highly skilled and easily trainable, proponents of globalization indirectly convey the impression that labor in developing countries is neither of these. The supposed 'human capital' advantage of developed countries contains an outdated imperial image of superiority over hewers of wood and drawers of water in developing countries. But conveniently forgotten is the fact that "Comparative Advantage of Nations" has been translated into many languages, and its message is as clear to the policymakers in Beijing as it is to those in Washington, which is, perhaps, why the United States has, in fact, fallen behind Asia in the development of crucial science and engineering graduates. The following is an excerpt from a report prepared by Morgan Stanley dated October 15, 2002:

"The developing world—notably Asia—is increasingly expanding its share of the world's skilled human capital. Developing Asia is generating scientific and engineering talent faster than any other region, a trend evident from recent figures from the US National Science Foundation. In 1999, universities in Asia produced more graduates with engineering degrees (322,100) than the US, Japan, and the European Union combined. For every engineering graduate in the US in 1999, Asia produced over five graduates. China, home to the region's largest pool of graduating engineers, produced nearly 200,000 engineering graduates in 1999, over three times the level of the US, nearly double Japan's engineering output, and 45% higher than Europe. Against this backdrop, is it any wonder that the world's leading manufacturers and service companies are flocking to China?

At 147,000 India ranks as the nation with one of the largest pool of graduates with a bachelor's degree in science. The US produced nearly as many science graduates (144,441) as India in 1999, although we note that around 10% of US graduates in science and engineering in 1999 were foreign-born students, many of whom were from China and India. Combined, India and China produced nearly 23% of the global total of graduates in science in 1999 and nearly 26% of the world's newly minted engineers. These figures no doubt reflect the massive absolute size of each nation's population. However, in contrast to the US, where overall science and engineering degrees awarded represented roughly one-third of the total number of bachelor's degrees in 1999, the ratio in many Asian nations was substantially higher. In China, for instance, science and engineering degrees accounted for a staggering 73% of total bachelor's degrees in 1999; in South Korea, the percentage was 45% and in Taiwan, 40%."

Another misconception that needs to be debunked is that cheap labor available in Developing Asia—China and India—at a fraction of the cost of that in the U.S. would be employed to manufacture only toys and other low-tech commodities in order to preserve high-tech manufacturing jobs for U.S. workers. This is the fallacy propagated by advocates of globalization. The reality is that, with the skill level in Developing Asia comparable to that in developed countries, any product can be manufactured overseas. Extracts from the Morgan Stanley report are:

"It's this emphasis on science and engineering that has begun to attract the capital and attention of leading multinationals, since a high ratio of college-aged students earning science/engineering degrees correlates with the rising technical skill level of the given workforce. Importantly, as the knowledge-based workforce expands in Asia, it is poised to decline in the developed nations. According to the National Science Foundation, the total number of US graduates with science and engineering degrees expected to retire is set to increase sharply over the next two decades. The same is true for Europe and Japan."

"Over the past quarter-century, the rising share of Developing Asia's technology exports has been stunning. In 1980, Developing Asia accounted for only 12.1% of total world exports of office machinery and telecom equipment, compared to Japan's 21.2% share and America's 19.5% share. In the ensuing decade, though, Developing Asia's global share of office machinery/telecom exports soared to 21.5%, roughly in line with Japan's (22.4%) and greater than America's (17.3%). By the end of the decade [1990s], though, the race was largely over. Developing Asia emerged as the undisputed champion of tech exports, with the region's share soaring by over 10 percentage points to 31.9% between 1990 and 2001. Meanwhile Japan's global share of office/telecom exports plunged by over 10 percentage points over the last decade, dropping to 10% by 2001. America's export share dipped as well, but not by nearly as much as Japan's, from 17.3% in 1990 to 15.3% a decade later."

"The technological capabilities of leading multinationals and the cheap, skilled labor of Asia are being fused into a dynamic, competitive force. The global IT production base is shifting to China and India, home to a growing pool of knowledge-based, skilled workers. This process has only begun as the world's leading multinationals begin to leverage China not only as a large domestic market, but also as an export base."

In a conclusion that must put a lie to the assurances provided by proponents of globalization, and, more importantly, frighten every manufacturing worker in the U.S., Morgan Stanley stated, chillingly:

"At this juncture, very few investors truly understand the seismic shift the world's knowledge-based work force is undergoing; even fewer have begun to contemplate the consequences of such a shift."

Before the downturn of 2001, high-tech companies boasted 2 million manufacturing jobs in the U.S., more than any other industry, according to the AeA, an industry group formerly known as the American Electronics Association. By the end of 2002, companies like IBM, Hewlett Packard and Intel had shed 435,000 jobs or about 20 percent of the total workforce. High-tech manufacturing jobs dwindled every month of 2002. While slowdown in the economy is assumed to be largely responsible for this attrition, it has not escaped attention that these same companies have ramped up their manufacturing facilities in China and other low-wage countries in recent years. There should be no doubt that a significant amount of these high-paying high-tech jobs has been moved to China at the expense of American workers, causing the American middle class to shrink. According to Economy.com, forty percent of the 900,000 high-tech jobs lost between 2001 and 2004 in the U.S. were transferred overseas.

And still some analysts pretend not to understand the new phenomenon. According to Newsweek, "America's strengths—innovation and entrepreneurship—remain formidable and should keep its middle class relatively prosperous, despite gains being made by other nations. When Japanese and South Korean companies began to dominate the low-end memory-chip market in late 1980s, U.S. competitors like Intel and Motorola shifted gears and began to specialize in the production of more sophisticated, higher margin semiconductors. That same process of climbing the value-added product ladder will have to continue."

Newsweek was locked in the thinking of the eighties, because Intel's innovation, unlike the days of semiconductors, is no longer exclusively American. Indeed, at the pace at which research and development is being carried out overseas, Intel's innovation is more likely to come from an overseas source.

And anybody who has visited Bangalore or Shanghai—or studied a bit of history—will testify to the fact America does not have a monopoly on entrepreneurship. It is even debatable whether such a monopoly ever existed. What America had far more than any other country was capital and the unique ability to use it to nurture talent. NASDAQ, the catalyst for Microsoft, Intel, Oracle and the darlings of the "New Economy", followed the New York Stock Exchange, the greatest source of capital for old and mature industries. But, now, some Americans are using its greatest advantage to buy cheaper labor in other countries. In effect, other Americans are negating America's greatest advantage because capital from NYSE and NASDAQ, courtesy of multinational-instigated multilateral agreements, is no longer wearing Old Glory: it is clothed from head to toe in the stateless garb of the globe.

Multinational corporations, owners of massive amounts of capital, are keenly aware of capital's status as a consumer. And having used multilateral agreements to break down barriers between nations, capital—just like any consumer—is now buying the cheapest product that meets quality specifications. Indeed, some have said that quality of the cheapest product is even superior, an unbeatable combination, since workers in China and elsewhere in the developing world are non-union and more pliable.

Between 1979 and 1999, headline stories in manufacturing were related mostly to shrinkage of the steel industry, closures of automobile assembly plants, and transformation of the industrial belt into the so-called "Rust Belt." During this period a total of 2.4 million manufacturing jobs disappeared from the United States. Between March 2001 and September 2003, without any fanfare and reference to any particular industry, the United States witnessed the disappearance of 2.3 million manufacturing jobs. In effect the United States lost almost the same amount of manufacturing jobs in 30 months as it had over a 240-month period. There should be no doubt that globalization was responsible for sending a great portion of these jobs overseas at the expense of American workers, causing the American middle class to wither.

And some cling to the discredited notion that the benefits of offshoring will outweigh the costs. According to Newsweek, "Globalization keeps consumer prices low, raises corporate productivity and frees up money for further investment in new technologies and industries." Missing from this deduction is that any money freed up from corporate productivity is more likely to be pulled in the direction of the gravitational force exerted by labor cost differential.

The reality is that a more massive wave of offshore outsourcing is at hand. The first round was used mainly as a test run to squeeze any bugs from the system and build up models for different industrial sectors. Now a new wave is about to hit the well-educated middle to upper income workers in financial and risk management, accounting, healthcare and information technology. According to McKinsey Group, the shift will likely involve "hundreds of billions of dollars" from the developed world to emerging developing countries.

Advocates of globalization contend that management, quality control and "labor productivity" in the developing world are not up to developed world standards, hindering relocation of factories from the United States. But this is another misconception, fostered by the antiquated image of the Chinese peasant farmer drawing water from a pool with buckets hanging from a pole slung across his shoulder. The 60,000 multinational corporations who control 50 percent of global trade in goods and services install the same bottom-line managers, while maintaining identical quality control methods whether a plant is located in Shanghai or Charlotte. The only difference is that the training manual in Shanghai would be written in Mandarin, while that in Charlotte would be in English. With regards to productivity, attributes like "dedicated," "work-ethic," and "hard-working" have typically been ascribed to workers in developed countries, while "laziness" and "absenteeism" typified those in developing countries. Today "labor productivity," especially in Developing Asia, increasingly the foreign destination of choice for relocated industries, is organizational not national.

The Internet, the most powerful tool for supervision, has reduced the risk of locating plants overseas by enabling managers to obtain real time information on any plant regardless of location. At almost negligible cost, a manager in the United States is able to log onto the Internet to inspect a plant in operation in China, obtain staff, sales, production, inventory, quality control, maintenance, and other critical data, and hold a videoconference with local management. At the click of a button, the manager is able to extract comparative global costs of operations and potential profits to assist decisions related to location of new plants.

Business Week magazine estimated the cost of Chinese factory labor to be 64 cents an hour, compared with the U.S. rate of about $22.00. Therefore, a company employing 1000 workers divided into two 10-hour shifts for a 250-day work year will spend about $53.4 million less on labor in China than in the U.S. This amount, known as labor-cost differential, is the driving force behind globalization. If the number of employees is extrapolated to 10,000 for a multinational corporation like Dell Corporation, the labor-cost differential balloons to $534 million per year, not counting additional savings accrued from negligible benefits in most of China. Labor-cost differential, also known as the bottom line, is the only driving force behind globalization, not workers, not technology transfer, and definitely not the environment. The fact that the process hurts a large number of American workers is completely irrelevant. For when all is said and done, the bottom line is the only line of consequence.

Therefore, with the benefit of labor-cost differential provided by the developing world, Bruce Sundquist of Penn State concluded: "One might imagine an eventual steady-state global economy composed of the developing world producing all of the world's transportable goods and services, with multinational corporations providing all the financial capital for facilities in the developing world that produce transportable goods and services for export, and with the developed world exporting some [of] its food and natural resources to the developing world. This is the direction in which the world is headed."

The scenario described by Sundquist is one in which traditional tables would be reversed. The developing world would manufacture advanced products traditionally associated with the developed world, while the advanced world would manufacture products that have traditionally emanated from the developing world. A review of the products currently being traded between China and the United States shows that this scenario has become a reality perhaps much quicker than even Sundquist imagined.

As Karl Marx predicted, the state has indeed began to whither away, but not in the manner that he envisaged. He said the existence of the state would suppress freedom, so it had to wither away for people to act according to their needs. Today, because of trade agreements like NAFTA and GATT, and the besmirched organization WTO, multinational corporations are the only "people" with the freedom to operate in a manner commensurate with the withering away of the state. Onerous shackles have been placed on states, making national laws subservient to international agreements that favor multinational corporations.

IBM, Dell, General Electric, Intel and other preeminent companies were born and nurtured in America. But having grown into adults, they brand themselves American only when it serves to secure U.S. government contracts and other benefits. In reality, they roam the globe in a stateless robe, rationalizing and apportioning financial, human and other factors of production in a manner designed to maximize profits. With their head offices in the U.S. only accidents of history, when American employees fall victim to the axe of corporate efficiency, even sympathies need not be extended, for the contract between employee and employer is not indefinite. The message these corporations in effect transmit to workers in the U.S. is, "sorry, you have to compete with workers in poorer countries for jobs and wages—the fact that we are citizens of the same country creates no obligations on our part to look after your welfare."

In the past, because of high tariffs, American companies such as General Motors, Ford and General Electric invested overseas to produce goods for local markets. Even countries in close proximity, such as France and England, had their own General Motors or Ford plants. This policy of no-displacement without replacement spurred enormous economic development across Europe, allowing even smaller countries like Belgium and Denmark to afford elaborate social programs for their citizens. But replicating capital in several countries causes diffusion, which negates the benefits of economies of scale arising from concentrating capital in fewer locations.

By aggregating into a continuous landmass with no borders and no tariffs, the United States of America demonstrated the benefits of economies of scale when smaller companies grew quickly by servicing a larger population base more efficiently. Not wanting to lose this crucial advantage was one of the main reasons Confederate forces marshaled maximum resources to win the Civil War. Similar economies of scale objectives were behind the formation of the European Common Market, as it was initially known, after World War II.

In 1950 France, fearing a repetition of the ban imposed on importation of coke from Germany during the war, persuaded a suspicious Germany to band together to mutually abrogate tariffs on steel and inputs between the two countries. Joined later by five other nations, and protected by a high tariff wall against non-member countries, the steel industry in the Common Market grew by about 80 percent within three years. European-based American companies like DuPont, Caterpillar, General Motors and Ford also tasted the fruits of protection-engineered economies of scale when the arrangement was extended to other industries in the budding Common Market.

Europeans were able to parlay benefits of protection-engineered growth in productivity and massive exports to colonies in Asia and Africa into wages that quickly equaled those in the United States. Achieving wage parity and thereby negating labor-cost differential restricted trade between the Common Market and the United States to products where each had a clear advantage derived through cost, patents or superior quality. Machinery, chemicals, textiles and drugs were traded between the two groups based on earned advantage, or comparative advantage, to use classical economic terminology. There was no advantage to relocating plants from the United States to the Common Market, or vice versa, with the sole purpose of exporting goods from the plants back to the United States: companies in each market had to build on innovation to either reduce cost or invent a new product in order to penetrate the other market.

So despite protective tariffs for some industries, trading between the United States and the Common Market was, for the most part, between equals: it was fair trade and, as predicted by David Ricardo, the father of comparative advantage, it benefited peoples in both markets. The key lesson here was that the relative inefficiency of capital allocation was a common denominator for all participants in the market. But the participants were not happy, and rapidly changing global conditions would cause them to vent their frustration.

The period after World War II was marked by a raging Cold War in which the United States and the Soviet Union fought through proxies to influence governments in the developing world. It was also a period of great risk for capital, as governments and ideologies were violently overthrown, causing assets of foreign companies in developing countries to be nationalized. Infused with distaste for their ex-while colonial masters and seduced by flowering rhetoric such as "Workers have nothing to lose but their chains," many governments in developing countries embraced socialism, and its accompanying waste and capital shortage. China remained embalmed under Mao Zedong, India wasted away under Indira Ghandi, Latin America was stomped on the head by soldiers, and Africa rotted under corruption.

But four tectonic events were to transform the global economic landscape. The first was the rise of Deng Xiaoping to the leadership of the Communist Party of China in 1980, at which time he started full implementation of his "Four Modernizations" of agriculture, industry, science and technology and the military. Under this regime, which was a latent admission of the failure of communism, special economic zones, such as Shenzhen and Xiamen, were established to encourage foreign investment.

The second was when Deng Xiaoping, officially out of power but increasingly disturbed by the slow pace of reforms, adopted an old trick used by Chinese Emperors to express displeasure by touring Shenzhen in November 1992. From then on, disguises used to cover capitalist transformation were stripped away, launching the ongoing boom in China.

The third was the official dissolution of the Soviet Union on December 5, 1995, bringing with it the end of the Cold War and indisputable ascendancy of free markets, a development that caused a "thousand capitalist flowers" to bloom. When Mikhail Gorbachev launched perestroika at the 27th Party Congress in 1986, his program of economic, political and social engineering became the unintended catalyst for dismantling the Marxist-Leninist dictatorship built over three-quarters of a century. As the developing world witnessed in disbelief for the first time the wrenching poverty, hunger, filth and desolation inside the Soviet Union, conditions worse than in some developing nations, it became apparent that the system that had also built fearsome nuclear weapons and was the first to send a man into space was not one to emulate. Almost all developing nations, some grudgingly, beat a retreat from socialism into the welcoming arms of the "exploitative bourgeoisies."

The fourth was the increasing influence of the Bharatiya Janata Party (BJP) or Indian People's Party in India, culminating in the election of its leader, Atal Behari Vajpayee, as Prime Minister in 1998. The BJP was an unvarnished capitalist party that discarded in short order the socialist policies of the Congress Party, led at one time by the first Iron Lady, Indira Gandhi. Making its intentions unambiguous, the BJP dismantled barriers to foreign ownership in key industries such as energy, transportation and heavy industry, and dared Indians to unfurl their mercantile heritage. Buoyed by their Prime Minister, Indians answered the clarion call for action, especially in intellectual entrepreneurship, with vengeance.

So for the first time in recorded history, with the exception of the bearded one in Cuba and the pariahs of North Korea, capitalism—the worst economic system ever created, except there is none better—reigned supreme around the globe. With this consensus in place, rules and responsibilities were promulgated through agreements to provide maximum insurance for global capital. Doors were also opened in China and India to reveal educational institutions and graduates of the highest order, and about 1.2 billion hard working people paid only a fraction of what workers in developed countries earned.

The confluence of all these factors unleashed multinational corporations from their cages, leading to the creation of the phenomenon now known as globalization. But before leaping into China, the mother of all globalization potentials, the multinational corporations needed a laboratory in which to test the tenets of this newly minted principle. Fortuitously, they found one in an old stomping ground called Mexico, which is how the North America Free Trade Agreement (NAFTA) between the United States, Canada and Mexico came into being on January 1, 1994.

Before NAFTA, however, there was the Free Trade Agreement (FTA) between the US and Canada. Trade between the two countries was dominated by automobiles and related parts, with the sixty percent Canadian content for vehicles sold in Canada mandated by the Canada-US Auto Pact of 1965 compelling GM and other companies to duplicate plants in both countries. The need to rationalize the automobile industry across the two countries was the primary motivating factor for the FTA, part of which replaced the sixty percent Canadian content with a North American (Canada and US) content of fifty percent.

The battle for the FTA was waged ferociously in Canada, with the opposition Liberal Party and unions, especially the Canadian Auto Workers union, fearing rationalization would favor the larger American market, while businesses eyed the amalgamation of an approximately 300 million strong market with glee. The Conservative Party of Canada led by Prime Minister Brian Mulroney fought a gallant electoral battle over the FTA, with the Liberal Party leader Jean Chretien branding the prime minister a traitor. In the end, though it won the electoral battle, the Conservative Party eventually lost the war of public opinion when the Canadian electorate rewarded the party by blowing it into smithereens after introducing another item the opposition besmirched with filth.

But when the FTA was implemented, both Canada and the United States ended up winners. As firms consolidated operations due to their comparative advantage, the trade deficit between the U.S. and Canada increased only slightly from about $12 billion to about $18 billion between 1989 and 1993, while overall trade between the two countries increased to about $198 billion from about $152 billion, a vivid demonstration of the powerful effects of free trade conducted between countries with roughly equivalent economic and social infrastructures. Today, even those who opposed the accord applaud Brian Mulroney—a close friend of his fellow Irishman Ronald Reagan—for sacrificing his political future for an instrument permitting Canada to ride a wave of relative economic prosperity.

When NAFTA was enacted, the North American content of vehicles sold in the trade area was increased from 50 percent to 62.5 percent, but the caveat was that the definition of North America was altered to include Mexico. With wages in Mexico averaging about $1.25 an hour compared to $15 an hour in the U.S., the picture that emerged for the U.S. was dark and stark. Between 1983 and 2000 the U.S. trade deficit with Mexico increased from a relatively miniscule $1.5 billion to a whopping $36 billion. General Motors increased its Mexican workforce from 7,000 in 1981 to 75,000 in 1996 in 54 facilities.

Before NAFTA was enacted, employment in the maquiladoras, special manufacturing zones set up across the U.S. border to export goods northwards, increased by 60,000 each year. Between 1995 and 1997, maquiladora job growth accelerated by 150,000 positions each year. In 2000 employment in maquiladora had reached 1.3 million positions, concentrated mostly in electrical and electronic products, auto parts, and apparel and textiles (Table 10a).

Table 10a	
Employment in Selected Maquiladora Activities in 2000	
Industry	Employment
Electric and electronic parts and components	335,668
Apparel and textiles	281,866
Transportation equipment and parts	237,004
Electric and electronic apparatus and appliances	104,262
Other manufacturing activities	142,805
Authors from Economic Policy Institute	

From analysis of data provided by the Bureau of Labor Statistics, the Economic Policy Institute (EPI) estimated that NAFTA destroyed about 766,000 jobs in the U.S. between 1993 and 2000, with the hardest hit states (Table 10b) being those with industries that had moved to Mexico (such as motor vehicles, auto parts, electrical appliances, computers, textiles and apparel) and Canada (motor vehicles and auto parts). A typical example is DaimlerChrysler's consolidation of parts purchases with Magna International of Aurora, Canada, a diversified auto parts manufacturer with $11 billion in annual sales. Magna was founded by Frank Stronach, who immigrated to Canada from Austria at the age of 22 with only a suitcase and a few dollars in his pocket.

NAFTA produced clearly identifiable winners and losers. The biggest winners were corporations that secured labor-cost differential by relocating plants from Canada and the United States to Mexico. And despite arguments to the contrary, workers in Canada and Mexico have also been net winners under NAFTA.

Table 10b NAFTA-related Job Losses (1993 – 2000)	
State	Net NAFTA Job Loss
California	82,354
Michigan	46,817
New York	46,210
Texas	41,067
Ohio	37,694
Illinois	37422
Pennsylvania	35,262
North Carolina	31,909
Indiana	31,110
Florida	27,631
Tennessee	25,419
Georgia	22,918
Authors from Economic Policy Institute	

In Canada, while the Big Three UAW have shed jobs, Honda, Toyota, Magna International and others have furnished jobs at a respectable clip. An example is the Honda Canada plant at Alliston, Ontario, where Honda Civic, Acura 1.6 EL, Honda Minivan and Honda SUV are assembled. Set up in 1986, the Alliston plant assembles about 400,000 vehicles annually with 3,500 "associates," more than four times the initial number employed. Considered one of the most productive Honda plants anywhere in the world, it exports about 80 percent of its vehicles to the United States. The growth of this plant has indisputably been facilitated by NAFTA.

In Mexico, employment in the maquiladora increased by 800,000 between 1993 and 2000, while NAFTA was credited with 1.7 million new jobs across Mexico between 1995 and 2000. And while outsiders might sneer at the wages paid in the maquiladora, Mexicans employed in the economic zone are considered fortunate by their peers. Overall, the quick recovery of the devalued peso after December 1994, due in part to NAFTA-engineered economic integration, also benefited the average Mexican worker.

The incontrovertible losers from NAFTA have been workers in the United States displaced by relocation of plants in Mexico and Canada. True, many of the displaced found employment in other sectors, but a significant percentage ended up in the service sector where they suffered an average 34 percent reduction in wages and limited benefits. Moreover, as the EPI presciently pointed out in 2001, "Trade-displaced workers will not be so lucky during the next economic downturn. If unemployment begins to rise in the U.S., then those who lose their jobs due to globalization and growing deficits could face longer unemployment spells, and they will find it much more difficult to get new jobs." The 2.7 million jobs hemorrhaged between March 2001 and September 2003 and the lengthened period for reemployment of the American worker have made prophets out of the prognosticators at EPI.

Even before results of the Mexican experiment had been fully assimilated, multinational corporations had seen enough in the early years to seek out other countries with more advantageous labor—cost differentials. The Philippines, Thailand and Indonesia beckoned until China opened its doors wide open. With over 1.25 billion people and daily wages as low as a dollar in some areas, China proved irresistible for the world's multinational corporations. The country began to vacuum manufacturing of low cost items such as toys, apparel, textiles and kitchenware from the rest of the world, and then moved up the value chain to computers, circuit boards, memory chips, foundry products, brake systems, agricultural equipment, and networking equipment.

Whole industries were uprooted from North America for relocation in China, leaving behind skeletal remains of shoe firms, apparel and toy companies. "Mexico is seeing the flight of whole industries to the mainland," reported Business Week. In the maquiladros, 3700 plants closed between 2001 and 2003, putting 218,000 people out of work. Only auto-related plants run at close to full capacity; all others stripped bare, including textiles and electronics. Meanwhile, in just a matter of five years, with exports growing at twenty percent a year, China supplanted Mexico to become America's second largest trading partner, next only to Canada. In the process, China recorded a $103 billion trade surplus against the U.S. in 2002, $124 billion in 2003 and a staggering $162 billion in 2004.

Not surprisingly, manufacturing employment dropped by 71,000 in the U.S. in July 2003, the largest for any sector. According to the Bureau of Labor Statistics, the losses were widespread, covering both durables (e.g., metals, computers, machinery) and nondurables (apparel and textiles). Since the economy grew at a rate of between 2.0 to 3.0 percent, the loss of 700,000 manufacturing payrolls from January 2003 to July 2003 meant increased demands for goods had been supplied disproportionately from countries other than the United States.

Overall, manufacturing payrolls in the U.S. declined by 2.7 million, or 16 percent, for a record 37 straight month from June 2000 to July 2003, causing manufacturing's share of total employment to decline from 13 percent to 11 percent, a shocking shift in composition in a relatively short period of time. Indeed, at 14.1 million in April 2005, the number of manufacturing jobs in the U.S. was almost the same as that in 1945, except then the share of employment was 35 percent.

And to perpetuate its cost advantage over the U.S. as a manufacturing center, China maintains a fixed exchange rate of its currency to the dollar. Therefore, appreciation of the Yen and Euro against the dollar failed to boost manufacturing in the U.S., as China continued to record stiff trade surpluses. Quietly licking their chops on the sidelines have been multinational corporations, besides China, the next biggest beneficiary of the "do not disturb exports" fixed exchange policy.

All the while, growth of the Chinese economy outpaced the rest of the world until in 2004 its Gross Domestic Product reached $1.65 trillion, an increase of about twenty seven percent over just a two-year period, after attracting foreign direct investment of $60 billion in 2003, the largest in the world. Business Week reported, "Chinese factories are flooding the world with cheap goods, everything from televisions and DVD players to bicycles and children's pajamas." According to Morgan Stanley, "China's prices are becoming global prices." With China decimating industries in several countries, factories there are becoming production centers for the entire globe. This is the undeniable ugly consequence of globalization.

Michael Porter, Lester Thurow and other economists initially argued that the United States and other developed countries should become more "clever" in order to counteract disappearance of so-called low-skill jobs through creation of new jobs around new products and technologies. The U.S. was advised to boost education and training efforts so that their workers acquire the "skill premium" they will need to get or stay ahead.

These economists have not uttered public pronouncements in a while due, perhaps, to the realization that with multinationals in the breach, there is no guarantee that a product will be developed and manufactured in the United States. Because of mobility of technology and standardization of manufacturing and quality control methods, it is conceivable for a country that does not participate in research and development to consume the fruits of others by manufacturing products developed in a "clever country."

The globalization era enables a multinational corporation to act inimically to the state that fosters the development of a product through education and training of its workforce, grants for research and development and stimulation of early demand. The country that implements the key strategies enumerated by Michael Porter secures comparative advantage only on paper. In the new globalization dispensation, a country may propose, but a multinational corporation disposes. With the interests of the state and a multinational corporation not necessarily coincidental, the interrelationships in the diamond structured by Michael Porter may produce an outcome not beneficial to the state. In practical terms, all the brainpower, government support, patents and research and development could lead to products of the enterprise being manufactured outside the "clever country" by a multinational corporation.

And there are two countries in particular—U.S. and England—where multinational corporations are apt to give their governments and peoples a collective mooning by shifting manufacture of a product developed through state sponsored research and development overseas.

In Japan Tokyo University produces most of the elite, who then spread out to form a close-knit group in government, industry and finance, cross-linked by the Keiretsu system of corporate ownership. This group fiercely guards the interests of Japan Inc. through formal meetings coordinated by the Ministry of Finance, and informally through memberships in exclusive golf clubs. It is inconceivable for a Japanese company to locate manufacture of a product overseas against the interests of the collective. Television sets, electronics, compact disks and other commodity products may be manufactured overseas, but no Japanese company will subcontract the development of potentially groundbreaking technology like software overseas. Even when a Japanese company establishes a manufacturing plant overseas, Japanese management closely guards process secrets. This is evidenced by the very visible presence of Japanese upper management at any Toyota, Nissan or Honda plant.

In France most of the elite in government, business and academia attend Ecole Nationale d'Administration. This network, including members of the ruling government and opposition, guards the interests of France Inc with resolute vigilance. Germany, Italy and the "Tiger" nations of South Korea, Taiwan, Singapore and Malaysia all have formal and informal associations of business and government leaders looking out for the interests of their respective countries. The same is true of emerging China and India.

In the United States and England, business leaders are more likely to lobby their governments to act for the benefit of their corporations alone. Injury to the health of workers and the country as a whole is irrelevant to these greeds at the trough.

Some conventional economic hypotheses have been rendered ineffective in the era of globalization. For example, the orthodox strategy of pursuing faster growth as a means of generating more jobs and incomes collides with globalization's counter principle of meeting demand with products from any part of the world. Because economic structures in developed countries are geared to capital accumulation and investment, cutting taxes, deregulating capital and labor markets as panaceas to overcoming unemployment have obvious appeal. But countercurrent to this strategy is globalization-engendered mobility, whereby capital accumulated in the United States is more likely to be spent in China, where return on capital is higher due to advantages of labor-cost differential. Therefore, tax cuts in the United States create more employment in China, not the United States. An extreme example is what happened in Spain in the 1990s. Though GNP in Spain doubled over a 20-year period, unemployment actually increased to over 20 percent: the growth was consumed by imports.

In the globalization era, the only strategy with the potential to convince a multinational corporation to locate in a high wage country is one drastic enough to negate the disadvantage of higher wages. Genuine policymakers intent on achieving meaningful change need to understand this simple fact: patriotic appeals are meaningless because an American-branded company is American in name only. To paraphrase the Godfather, the only offer a multinational corporation will bow to is one they can't refuse.

"If a foreign country can supply us with a commodity cheaper than we ourselves can make it, better buy it of them *with some part of the produce of our own industry, employed in a way in which we have some advantage*" (Adam Smith, Wealth of Nations, Book IV, Section ii, 12). The use of the subjective "we" is an indication Adam Smith viewed trade through the prism of nations. If that were to be true today, the United States would trump, as it has done since the end of World War II, every other nation in job creation. But multinational corporations have obliterated the scenario envisioned by Smith, so that labor-cost differential reigns supreme over "part of the produce of our own industry, employed in a way in which we have some advantage." If the rules of free trade were as imagined by Smith, the United States would not have incurred a trade deficit of $162 billion against China in 2004, abetted by "our own industry" in the United States.

Globalization as practiced today is not free trade; it is one-way trade, with labor-cost differential pointing the direction of traffic.

To support globalization, others quote extensively from "On the Principles of Political Economy and Taxation" published in 1821 by David Ricardo, the first economist to summarize the theories of comparative advantage. Assuming that productivity of labor varied between industries and across countries, and that one country, Portugal, was more productive in both wine and cloth than England, Ricardo proved that, *if an appropriate terms of trade were chosen,* both countries could be beneficiaries of free trade if Portugal manufactured wine in which it had the most advantage, and delegated England to manufacture cloth in which it was least-disadvantaged. Because Portugal could produce wine at a lower opportunity cost than England, it was said to have a comparative advantage in wine. And because England could produce cloth at a lower opportunity cost than Portugal, it was said to have a comparative advantage in cloth. A pertinent fact, conveniently omitted by globalization advocates, is that the use of the phrase "if appropriate terms of trade were chosen" implies the conduct of managed, not free, trade.

In today's context, without transfer of capital and technology, the United States would be more productive in the manufacture of computers as well as toys vis-à-vis China. But the United States would hold a greater advantage in computers because of the demand for higher technology, and China would be least disadvantaged in toys because its proliferate labor would narrow the gap in this low-tech, labor-intensive arena. Therefore, according to Ricardo, since the United States and China have comparative advantages in computers and toys, respectively, the United States should negotiate with China to relinquish manufacture of toys, while retaining manufacture of computers. The efficiencies created by this arrangement will boost manufacture of computers by the United States for the Chinese market, while making available more toys for the American market from China. American workers displaced from manufacture of toys will be reemployed in the higher paying computer industry, while more Chinese workers will be employed to manufacture toys. Managed trade, not free trade, therefore produces winners in both the United States and China. This is how the thesis propounded by globalization's ardent supporters is supposed to function.

But Ricardo never contemplated that not only would this trade-off not be negotiated to the benefit of firms, consumers and workers in both nations, but that one country, China, without any technology and capital of its own, would manufacture both products to the disadvantage of workers in the more productive nation. Because of the behavior of some multinational corporations, using Ricardo's theory to support globalization is disingenuous, and should be a source of discomfort to its eminent propagators. Those who persist in citing Ricardo as the reason for supporting globalization even in the face of the pernicious behavior of some multinational corporations discredit only themselves.

Restoration of trade relations between China and U.S. in 1980 after a 29-year hiatus was conditioned upon annual verification of free speech, emigration and other policies of the mainland government. From then on, conferring nondiscriminatory tariff, or most-favored-nation, status on China became a fierce battle between free trade advocates who contended lifting the restriction would open a huge market for U.S. exports, and opponents who argued, among other reasons, that cheap labor in China would cause massive translocation of industry from the U.S. to China. Proponents of free trade—read, multinational corporations and their academic bedmates—emerged victorious when yearly review was cancelled in 2000, with trade normalization effective upon China's accession to the World Trade Organization in 2005.

The outcome of trade liberalization with China has been documented, and not only does it paint a sordid picture, it strips the cover from the covert planks used to promote the deed. U.S. exports to China rose from over $8 billion to only $34.72 billion (Table 10c) between 1993 and 2004, but imports from China exploded from about $31 billion to $196.70 billion.

Table 10c U.S. Trade with China, 1993 – 2003 ($Billion)					
Year	Exports	Imports	Total Trade	Deficit	Imports' Share in Total Trade
1993	8.76	31.54	40.3	22.78	78.3%
1994	9.28	38.79	48.07	29.51	80.7%
1995	11.75	45.54	57.29	33.79	79.5%
1996	11.99	51.51	63.50	39.52	81.1%
1997	12.86	62.56	75.42	49.70	83.0%
1998	14.24	71.17	85.41	56.93	83.3%
1999	13.11	81.79	94.90	68.68	86.2%
2000	16.19	100.02	116.21	83.83	86.0%
2001	19.18	102.28	121.46	83.10	84.2%
2002	22.13	125.19	147.32	103.06	85.0%
2003	26.1	151.7	177.8	125.6	85.3%
2004	34.72	196.70	231.42	161.98	86.9%
Authors from US Bureau of Census					

Clearly, predictions by proponents of free trade that "opening" China's market would be a bonanza for U.S. exports have proved to be false. Instead, China has strengthened its advantage, controlling about 87 percent of the trade between the two countries, and opened a gaping $162 billion surplus over the United States in 2004, with the trend worsening in 2005. The U.S. trade deficit with China for the first three months of 2004 was $30.2 billion, while comparable data for 2005 was $41.02 billion, an indication the trade deficit with China had turned into an avalanche.

By May 2005, the trade deficit with China, especially relating to textiles, had supposedly become a source of concern for U.S. government authorities. So in a rather feeble and comical attempt to express its displeasure, the U.S. in May 2005 limited growth of selected Chinese textile exports to 7.5 percent a year. This meaningless "restriction" applied to cotton trousers, cotton knit shirts and underwear, men's and boy's cotton and man-made fiber shirts, man-made trousers, man-made fiber knit shirts and blouses, and combed cotton yarn. All countries on which restrictions are imposed should be so lucky to enjoy annual growth of "only" 7.5 percent.

Then in an obviously orchestrated ploy to throw dust into the eyes of those concerned, China responded in kind by claiming to have imposed undisclosed tariffs on selected textile products. An official from the Chinese Commerce Ministry claimed, laughably, that the country had agreed to make "sacrifices" to diffuse trade tensions, but was still planning to appeal any "limits" to the World Trade Organization, the veranda boy of multinational corporations. And even though the magnitude of the Chinese tax remained purposely vague, the representative of U.S. multinational corporations in China Charles M. Martin chimed it was going to have "a real impact" of 7.5 percent growth.

But not even a week had lapsed when China announced it was rescinding the "sacrifices" it had promised. And the reason China felt emboldened in its behavior was the knowledge by all parties that the real culprit was not China, but multinational corporations.

The real reason for lack of a meaningful response to the galloping Chinese textile exports was that most of the textile manufacturers of note in China were of American origin, a group whose interests supersede all others under the new globalization dispensation. Multinational corporations are the new states before whom all must bow. This is the "New World."

The economic dispensation under which capital and technology are transferred by firms in a higher-wage country for the production of goods in a lower-wage country for the sole of purpose of export to the higher-wage country does not qualify as free or fair trade: it is rampaging trade of the highest proportion.

For the most part, trade between Canada and the U.S. (Table 10d) is the sort of free and fair exchange of goods envisaged by Adam Smith and David Ricardo in which comparative advantage yields benefits for both nations. Between 1993 and 2002, total trade (Table 10d) between the two countries jumped from over $211 billion to about $370.0, an increase of close to 76 percent.

Interestingly, though the U.S. trade deficit increased from $10.78 billion to $48.17 billion, Canada's share of total trade increased only marginally from 52.5 percent to 56.5 percent. Therefore, liberalization of trade between two nations with similar economic, social and political infrastructures yielded only a marginal advantage for one nation.

Table 10d U.S. Trade with Canada, 1993 – 2002 ($ billion)					
Year	Exports	Imports	Total Trade	Deficit	Share of Imports in Total Trade
1993	100.44	111.22	211.66	10.78	52.5%
1994	114.44	128.41	242.85	13.97	53.0%
1995	127.23	144.37	271.60	17.14	53.1%
1996	134.21	155.89	290.10	21.68	53.8%
1997	151.77	167.23	319.00	15.46	52.4%
1998	156.60	173.26	329.86	16.66	52.4%
1999	166.60	198.71	365.31	32.11	54.5%
2000	178.94	230.84	409.78	51.90	56.2%
2001	163.42	216.27	379.69	52.85	57.0%
2002	160.92	209.09	370.01	48.17	56.5%
Authors from U.S. Bureau of Census					

A summary of the products traded between Canada and U.S. (Table 10e) captures some essence of comparative advantage. Because of economies of scale, the U.S. has absolute advantage in manufacture of industrial supplies, while resource-rich Canada is blessed with absolute advantages in fuel and lumber.

In a perfect demonstration of comparative advantage, the U.S. provides Canada with industrial supplies required to extract resources, which are then exported to the U.S. to power industries and build houses.

In a demonstration of technology-based absolute advantage, manufacture of luxury civilian aircraft tilted in favor of Canada when Quebec-based Bombardier invented customized manufacturing processes. Meanwhile, U.S. utilized economies of scale to lead computer manufacturing.

However, Canada's lead in automobiles and parts is due predominantly to significantly lower health care benefit cost, as opposed to technological superiority.

Canada's lead in the lucrative automobile and parts market is driven primarily by lower health care cost.

Table 10e U.S. Trade with Canada by Product, 2002 ($ billions)		
Product	Exports	Imports
Agriculture	11.5	12
Fuel	3.0	29
Metals	10	14
Pulp, Newsprint, Logs, etc.	5.5	19
Plastic, Chemicals	12	11
Industrial Supplies, including machines, Cloths, engines	32	21
Computers	15	7.5
Aircraft, plus parts	4.5	7.5
Automobiles, including parts	45	60
Household goods, including toys, pharmaceuticals	22.5	28
	161	209
Authors from U.S. Bureau of Census		

Similarity of economic and other determinant infrastructures provides two telling lessons. First, the dynamics of trade between Canada and the U.S. provide confirmation of Michael Porter's thesis that a nation can secure comparative advantage by building human capital through education, training and skills-enhancement in order to spur technology development. Second, trade between nations can be more balanced in the absence of wage-induced incentive to trans-locate firms from one nation to another. But even so, Canada's advantage in the automobile and parts market illustrates yet again how cost skews comparative advantage to diverge from predictive analysis.

But in contrast to the relatively balanced trade between Canada and the U.S., a snapshot of goods traded in 2002 (Table 10f) between the U.S. and China, two countries with a steep wage gradient, reveals the extent to which China's industrial development is maturing at the expense of the United States.

Some multinational corporations have crippled the United States to such an extent that the once proud industrial giant is advantageous only in the production of food, chemicals and aircraft. So without aircraft, the U.S. would be reduced in its trade relations with China to the status of a developing country: food and chemicals to China, computers, industrial machinery and everything else from China.

The U.S. holds a distinct advantage over China in export of rubbish, another product previously classified as a "third world" product. According to a report in the New York Times, U.S. exports of "scrap and waste" surged thirty one percent in 2004. China is said to be a huge market for American scrap steel.

According to a report by Michael Hennigan in the Ireland Business News, U.S. exports of advanced technology were down twenty one percent between 1999 and 2004, but those of scrap and waste were up by 135 percent to a cumulative advantage of $8.4 billion in the same period. So the U.S. holds a comparative advantage over China in garbage, a stunning development that will bring discomfort to even the most ardent supporters of free trade. Or would it?

Table 10f U.S. Trade with China by Product, 2002 ($Billions)		
Products	Exports	Imports
Computers and related products	3.9	18.4
Furniture and household goods	1.2	28.6
Industrial Machinery, including pumps, machine tools	4.0	10.0
Chemicals and related products	2.6	1.5
Engines, including parts for aircraft	1.2	2.2
Cement, plywood and shingles	-	1.8
Aircraft	3.2	-
Metals and fuels	1.4	3.5
Agriculture, including wheat, cotton and meat	2.3	1.8
Industrial and general supplies, business machines	1.2	3.0
Pulp and Paper, cloths	1.0	1.2
Toys	-	15.0
Televisions, stereos and tapes	-	10.5
Apparel	-	13.5
Footwear	-	7.5
Sporting and camping equipment, including shoes	-	3.5
Jewelry and antiques	-	3.0
TOTAL	22	125
Authors from U.S. Bureau of Census		

Domination of the U.S. in traditionally classified developing country products, save for Boeing's aircrafts, while China dominates in traditional developed country products is confirmation of Bruce Sundquist's prediction that under globalization previous hewers of wood and drawers of water shall drink the water and obtain the wood from the developed country. Perhaps propagandists for globalization will interpret this scenario as appropriate confirmation of comparative advantage in which China needs wood, scrap metal and garbage from the U.S. to fire its industries in exchange for manufactured goods.

In 2000, Senator Ernest Hollings and Professor Charles McMillion raised an alarm in an opinion paper when data showed development of a technological trade deficit with China: "The US faces sharply worsening deficits with China in the trade of crucial advanced technology products." The paper warned, "Quite simply, China is developing its own export driven high-tech industry with U.S. assistance," it stated bluntly. Multinational corporation interests at General Electric's NBC ensured this warning fell on deaf years as the drumbeat for "friends" saturated U.S. airwaves.

A comprehensive study by The Economic Policy Institute concluded the "rise in the United States' trade deficit with China between 1989 and 2003 caused the displacement of production that supported 1.5 million US jobs." The high-wage, high-benefit American manufacturing middle class was found to have been at the receiving end of these job losses. And in a devastating indictment of multinational corporations and their apologists, the study found the fastest job losses to be occurring in "highly skilled and advanced technology areas once considered relatively immune, such as electronics, computers, and communications equipment." This should not have come as a surprise, because it is in the higher wage higher technology industries that job relocation garners the highest labor cost bottom line.

The harm inflicted on the industrial, economic and social landscape of Rockford, Illinois when jobs were moved to low wage countries is being repeated across America. According to analysis of Department of Labor data by MBG Information Services, the Rockford area lost more than 20 percent of its manufacturing jobs—about 10,000—between May 2000 and 2003. Most of the jobs lost were in machine tooling, the foundation of America's manufacturing industry, which traditionally employs the most skilled workers. Ingersoll International—the crown jewel of Rockford machine tooling—declared bankruptcy, discharging 300 employees. At Greenlee/Textron, which makes drill bits and tools for electrical contractors, only 180 out of 900 employees were left. The Goodyear tire plant shipped about 900 out of 1,650 jobs to Asia. At Rockford and other centers of industrial expertise, workers watch helplessly as the foundation of American industry is smashed to smithereens.

"The lesson of Rockford," said Jeff Faux, founding President of the Economic Policy Institute, "is it disproves the free traders' argument that America could afford to lose manufacturing jobs in areas like textiles and steel because we would ultimately triumph in global competition by making the things hardest to make. In fact those things are machine tools—and we're losing them."

Free traders argued that China's domination of major sectors of the American economy was inconsequential because displaced workers would be trained for new and higher paying jobs in the services sector. The refrain (is?) was, "China's peasants are tomorrow's factory workers, and today's American factory workers are tomorrow's service and information workers." Others, like Federal Reserve Board Chairman Alan Greenspan, go even further to suggest that manufacturing, as a business activity, is no longer critical to the economic health of the U.S. "Ideas," not physical goods, "are becoming increasingly the predominant means by which we create wealth," Mr. Greenspan said. "I think that's good, not bad, for the economy as a whole." Others will beg to differ with this assessment, because some of the skills being lost have a direct bearing on America's capability to sustain critical high technology industries necessary for defense and other industries.

Proponents of free trade have turned a blind eye to the service and information technology jobs beating the same path as manufacturing jobs out of the United States. As for "ideas," with farming of research and development in software, bioinformetrics, aeronautics, miniaturization, and other advanced technologies to overseas "knowledge workers," there is no assurance that the U.S. will continue to generate the lion's share of new ideas.

In April 2003, The New Haven Register ran a three-part series on U.S. companies sending white-collar jobs overseas: Below is a sampling of the response from readers:

"I am an MIT-educated software engineer with more than 10 years of experience who has been unemployed for more than 18 months, and I know 10 others in my situation."

"I want you to know that I have been terribly affected by this cancer. I have built a career in software consulting and seen it go down the drain in a very short time. There should be a sense of outrage for what is going on…I think it is a crime. I am a Vietnam veteran who feels the politicians are giving away my livelihood."

"Who will be contributing to the unemployment fund that will be needed to pay all of our unemployed workers? This is an insult to Americans. If these companies cannot afford to pay American wages, the solution would be that they move their businesses to that particular foreign country!"

Employment decline in service producing industries combined with decline in manufacturing produces a combustible unsustainable mixture to accelerate the destruction of the American middle class, the engine that powers the global economy.

Sprint Corporation of Overland, MO was supposed to have been the great hope for the future when it relocated to the Kansas City area. A symbol of the much sought after new company at the cutting edge of technology, Sprint inspired community leaders to build a 17-building corporate campus on a 200-acre leafy enclave. The campus was soon filled with thousands of people working for Sprint and ancillary companies. It was fulfillment of the new employment vision: clean, high-tech, high-paying companies. Unfortunately, the euphoric dream proved to be short-lived.

Caught in a glut of surplus goods, Sprint started to slash its workforce so furiously that it shed 18,000 employees between October 2001 and July 2003. The Kansas City area took the brunt, with the elimination of over 10,000 jobs. Needless to say, business leaders and policymakers alike were stunned by what came to be known as the "Sprint issue," because the core of the new employment theory, according to which displaced workers would be retrained, laid in tatters.

Governments everywhere made retraining "blue-collar" workers for the "New Economy" a priority. But this time around, overwhelming majority of the unemployed were the highly educated, high-tech workers of the new economy. These highly trained workers are retraining for transportation, distribution and retail industries for which multiple vacancies exist at reduced salaries and benefits.

Retail and logistics will create groundbreaking technologies to sustain America's middle class? Good luck, America. The multinational corporations have moved on, with securing property and intellectual rights for products developed by their new "Knowledge Workers" in India and China as their next objective.

In all 44,000 workers in the Kansas City metropolitan area, or about five percent of the total workforce, lost their jobs, substantially greater than the two percent national average.

The light of opportunity is dimming for both high-tech workers and so-called "blue collar workers" in equal measure. The door of hope is being slammed in the faces of many, with comfort nowhere in sight. Like manufacturing employees in heavy industry before them, professionals are now in tears all over the land.

Basheer Jangua, CEO of Integnology and a naturalized U.S. citizen of Indian extraction, decided to attempt to reverse the offshore outsourcing trend after witnessing firsthand its devastating effects. Applicants, some without jobs after almost eleven months, would break down in tears in his office. He posed the question, "When you have a 6-foot-tall U.S. grad sitting in your office and literally breaking down into tears because he can't find a job in eleven months, what are you going to do?'

Stanford MBA graduates sent Mr. Jangua 150 resumes in one year. Overall he was receiving 70 resumes a day. One case in particular nearly broke his heart. An engineer, a former U.S. Air Force pilot, who was without a job one year after starting his search, contacted him. According to background information supplied through the grapevine, somebody from the pilot's church had to give him $50 to buy cake for his daughter's birthday.

"If more companies-and more service providers such as Jangua-took the initiative to lay out the substantial benefits of domestic IT resources to their clients, a movement could be born," implored eNews. An expectant eNews wrote: "Between efforts such as Jangua's and initiatives in states where lawmakers are struggling to pass new legislation aimed at curbing the loss of jobs, the tide can be turned." Finally, eNews moaned in pain, "The U.S. high-tech work force has suffered more than enough."

Comparative advantage was supposed to be between countries with similar economic infrastructures. When practiced the way it was first designed, similar in most parts to trade between Canada and the U.S., it is mutually beneficial. Any advantage was supposed to be earned by production advantage, not based solely on wages.

Trade between the United States and emerging developing countries like China and India is not, according to renowned conservative commentator Paul Craig Roberts, "a manifestation of the beneficial workings of free trade and comparative advantage." It is a manifestation of absolute advantage, with China and India the absolute winners and the United States the absolute loser.

And, unfortunately, America's children will not stop bleeding any time soon, if current indifference continues.

11

EMPLOYMENT PROJECTIONS

Increased productivity and loss of export markets have contributed to job losses in manufacturing and business processing sectors of the U.S. economy. But translocations of manufacturing plants and business processes to overseas destinations point to a devastating effect of offshore outsourcing on jobs in the U.S. in automobile, automobile parts, computers, electronics, call centers, data processing, computer programming, software development, engineering and many other sectors of the U.S. economy.

This would not normally be worrisome since the U.S. economy is a dynamic machine that consistently destroys and creates jobs with the development and implementation of new technologies. The advent of computers, for example, caused job losses at typewriter and ribbon manufacturers, but the economy was replenished by many more computer programmers and employees of manufacturers of microprocessors and circuit boards. Millions terminated from heavy manufacturing found lifeboats in the emerging information technology industry. The resulting increased demand for workers caused employers to pass along part of productivity savings to workers in the form of higher wages.

But the current job destruction phenomena are markedly different from earlier technological innovations. American firms set up branches overseas to manufacture products for those markets after the Second World War. Inputs to these overseas firms from the US and repatriation of profits provided a boon to the U.S. economy and workers. Employment increased in both the U.S. and overseas markets in a classic win-win scenario.

But current translocation of manufacturing plants is motivated almost exclusively by significantly lower labor costs overseas, with the products manufactured in China, for example, beyond the economic capability of most of the working population. The result is a Faustian bargain in which the U.S. trades good paying manufacturing jobs for lower prices and lower paying jobs in distribution and retail.

This process in which savings generated from one imported product are used to purchase another imported product creates a vicious circle, leading to swelling trade deficits and erosion of employment and wages in the U.S. Unlike the increased productivity of bygone eras caused mostly by technological innovation, this era's increased productivity is not engendered by new technology around which new labor grows. On the contrary, labor takes the brunt as it is continuously replaced by less expensive alternatives.

Substitution of higher paying jobs with lower paying alternatives has serious ramifications for the U.S. economy. At some point, absent development of a new job-generation technology, the decline in purchasing power of a lesser-paid working populace will lead to decline in demand, causing the U.S. economy to sink into a prolonged downturn.

And the advent of overseas outsourcing of business processes threatens to cause exponential damage. While translocation of manufacturing was slow and laborious, outsourcing of business processing jobs happens at a click of a mouse, affecting thousands of workers instantaneously.

Massive stimulus of home-refinanced consumer spending and government outlays for the military and entitlements broke the U.S. recession, which began in March 2001. But private sector jobs lost during the recession had barely been recovered as of April 2005; a full 41 months after the recovery began in November 2001. If historical trends had persisted, over 7 million private sector jobs would have been created.

Though reduction in business activity in 2001 has continued to exert a downward pressure on wages, the lack of a bounce in professional wages in particular during the period of the recovery up to May 2005 suggests that virtual linkage of employment markets has depressed wages as well. Salaries for information system managers, the highest in the computer industry, had declined to about $100,000 from $130,000 by the first quarter 2003, while those for entry-level computer technicians had declined from $50,000 to $35,000, both a reflection of the reduced demand for U.S. labor.

While the historic struggle to close the gap between male and female wages is noble, the expectation had always been that this would be achieved through a faster increase in wages for women. This cherished objective had also been convoluted. Instead of women's wages increasing, the historic gap had been closed to 81.3 per cent in July 2003, the lowest since data collection began in 1979, through shrinkage in men's wages and stagnation in female wages, a scenario that not even the most pessimistic could have anticipated.

Translocation of manufacturing plants and business processes to overseas locations therefore have a deleterious effect on wages and the number and quality of jobs created in the United States, contradicting employment projections issued by the US Bureau of Labor Statistics (BLS).

On December 3, 2001, the BLS released its employment projections for 2000-2010. Then on March 3, 2003 the Connecticut Department of Labor released an updated version of its occupational forecast for 2010. Both forecasts were obsolete from the day of publication.

Data provided by Connecticut Department of Labor (CTDOL) (Table 11a) showed the projected ten fastest growing occupations for the state by percent change between 2000 and 2010. The top seven positions were occupied by computer-related occupations, with customer support specialists ranked first in terms of percent net change.

Table 11a Projected Employment Change for Connecticut				
JOB TITLE	2000	2010	Net Change	Percent Change
Computer Support Specialists	7,720	12,980	5,260	68.1%
Computer Software Engineers, Systems Software	2,430	3,920	1,490	61.4%
Network and Computer Systems Administrator	3,460	5,450	2,000	57.8%
Computer Software Engineers, Applications	6,720	10,560	3,850	57.3%
Database Administrators	1,930	2,910	980	51.0%
Network Systems and Data Communications Analysts	2,290	3,440	1,160	50.5%
Computer Specialists, All Other	2,040	3,030	990	48.8%
Medical Assistants	3,890	5,640	1,750	44.9%
Physician Assistants	800	1,110	340	42.1%
Personal Financial Advisors	2,230	3,150	920	41.3%
Authors from Connecticut Department of Labor				

But some of the most intensive offshore outsourcing programs have been executed in the computer support arena, with Dell, Hewlett Packard, IBM, EDS and others delegating to their own offshore branches or to offshore firms owned by foreigners. Traditionally high demand for computer support specialists convinced the CTDOL to rank this profession highest in job generation. But that this demand would be met by an increasing foreign component was unanticipated.

Of the other computer related professions targeted for rapid growth, computer software engineers (systems software and applications) are also easily replaced by overseas experts. However, network and database administration are considered sensitive assignments and are therefore not easily delegated to offshore outfits.

So, of the total projected increase of 15,600 computer-related jobs between 2000 and 2010 for Connecticut, a full 10,600 or two-thirds of these are easily replaced by less expensive professionals overseas. The evidence suggests that this is happening on a massive scale: the savings in wages and benefits are proving to be simply irresistible.

A sample of projected job increases and accompanying salaries for Connecticut are provided in Table 11b. It shows anticipated increase of 5,620 and 4,920 for customer service representatives and specialists, respectively. These professionals execute their functions by telephone and/or computers. But these are the very assignments being farmed out on a massive scale to overseas locations. With overseas counterparts earning an average annual salary of $7,000, customer service representatives and customer support specialists earning average annual salaries of $31,794 and $45,796, respectively, in Connecticut are subject to massive layoffs. The pain has only just begun to be inflicted.

Table 11b				
Wages for Professionals Subject to Outsourcing				
JOB TITLE	2000	2010	Net Change	Average Salary
Customer Service Representatives	27,850	33,470	5,620	$31,794
Customer Support Specialists	7,720	12,980	4,960	$45,796
Computer Software Engineers, Applications	6,720	10,560	3,850	$76,431
Computer Systems Analysts	8,970	12,300	3,330	$66,923
Authors from Connecticut Department of Labor				

Most of the software engineers earning an average annual salary of $76,431 stand no chance. Most of the computer systems analysts earning $66,923 better start looking for employment elsewhere, if they can find one.

And this is just the beginning. Connecticut is a microcosm of the wave of decapitations happening in the United States. And it has only just begun. The U.S. has only seen the tip of the iceberg. When the full force strikes many, like the unfortunate victims of the "unsinkable" Titanic, will not know what hit them. The offshore outsourcing systems have only just been debugged. Trial runs have only just been completed. Quality certificates have only just been obtained from Carnegie Mellon, and blood will ooze across these United States.

It is called Capability Maturity Model (CMM), similar to the certificate awarded by International Standards Organization (ISO) for manufacturing plants. The highest is a Level 5. A firm with CMM Level 5 certification is committed at the highest level to "best software engineering practices throughout the organization." American firms are outsourcing business process systems to overseas firms with CMM certification without any hesitation, which will cause floodgates to open.

According to the Bureau of Labor Statistics (BLS), "The 10-year projections of employment by industry and occupation, labor force, and economic growth are widely used in career guidance, in planning education and training programs, and in studying long-range employment trends." The BLS predicted, "Total employment is projected to increase by 15 percent, slightly less than the previous decade, 1990-2000."

According to the BLS' industrial employment scenario, "The service-producing sector will continue to be the dominant employment generator in the economy, adding 20.5 million jobs by 2010…Manufacturing will return to its 1990 employment level of 19.1 million, but its share of total jobs is expected to decline from 13 percent in 2000 to 11 percent in 2010."

The BLS' crystal ball on occupational employment was that "Professional and related occupations and service occupations are projected to increase the fastest and to add the most jobs—7.0 million and 5.1 million, respectively. These two groups—on opposite ends of the educational attainment and earnings spectrum—are expected to provide more than half of total job growth over the 2000-2010 period." The BLS concluded, "Eight of the 10 fastest growing occupations are computer-related, commonly referred to as information technology occupations." Wrong on all counts!

According to the EPI, manufacturing's share of total jobs had reached 11 percent by July 2003, a level projected by the BLS to be reached only by the end of 2010. With factory closures in textiles, furniture and other industries continuing unabated, jobs in the manufacturing sector will continue to deteriorate, weakening its share of the labor market even more, and upsetting BLS conservative projections for the sector. Continuing deindustrialization of the American economy, and the shrinkage of a core productive sector, will deprive the economy of resources from one of its pillars, therefore contributing to decline in standard of living of Americans.

The BLS reported in its April 2005 "Industrial Payroll Employment" that "Employment in manufacturing was little changed in April at 14.3 million....Long term employment decline continued in furniture and related products and in textile mills." Employment numbers will therefore under no circumstance "return to its 1990 employment level of 19.1 million," predicted by the same BLS for 2010.

It is obvious the BLS did not anticipate offshore outsourcing would be so pervasive across many industrial sectors in the United States. They were not alone.

The BLS was also not unduly concerned by the stagnation in manufacturing jobs, predicting that growth in demand for jobs would be absorbed by enhancement in the services sector. But a declining manufacturing sector, coupled with a less than stellar growth in the "quality" services sector, will upset economic indicators even further, resulting in a deteriorating jobs outlook. However, simultaneous decline in manufacturing and the "quality" services will spell economic disaster, impacting negatively on standard of living of Americans.

The BLS assumed that call center activities would grow as more companies tried to deepen interaction with their customers, a natural assumption based on desire of many companies to multi-target clients with different products. The BLS placed major emphasis on not only growth in employment in information technologies but in the higher salaries typical of that industry. However, as demonstrated previously, these occupations are the very ones under relentless assault from offshore operators.

Table 11c projects the ten fastest growing occupations by percent according to the BLS, showing information technology with projected employees of 3.912 million or 76.7 percent of projected total.

Table 11c				
Projected Fastest Growing Occupations (Thousands)				
Occupation	Employment		Change	
	2000	2010	Number	%
Computer software engineers, applications	380	760	380	100
Computer support specialists	506	996	490	97
Computer software engineers, systems software	317	601	284	90
Network and computer systems administrators	229	416	187	82
Network systems and data communications analysts	119	211	92	77
Desktop publishers	38	63	25	67
Database administrators	106	176	70	66
Personal and home care aides	414	672	258	62
Computer systems analysts	431	689	258	60
Medical assistants	329	516	187	57
Authors from US Bureau of Labor Statistics				

The BLS, just like CTDOL, assumed one of the fastest growing offshore out-sourcing segments—computer support specialists—would register the second highest growth potential in percent terms. However, the net change of 490,000 for this occupation was projected to be the fifth highest of all occupations in numerical terms (See Table 11d).

Though low in percent terms, it is noteworthy to mention that customer service representatives, generally those who provide information about a company's products, were ranked second only to food preparation and food servers in numerical terms. BLS projects an increase of 631,000 jobs by 2010 for this sector from a 2000 base of 1.946 million. This is another occupation attacked relentlessly by offshore operators.

Table 11d Projected Fastest Growing Occupations (thousands)				
Occupation	Employment		Change	
	2000	2010	Number	%
Combined food preparation and serving workers, including fast food	2,206	2,879	673	30
Customer Service Representative	1,946	2,577	631	32
Registered Nurses	2,194	2,755	561	26
Retail Salespersons	4,109	4,619	510	12
Computer Support Specialists	506	996	490	97
Cashiers, except gaming	3,325	3,799	474	14
Office Clerks, general	2,705	3,135	430	16
Security Guards	1,106	1,497	391	35
Computer Software Engineers, applications	380	760	380	100
Waiters and Waitresses	1,083	2,347	364	18
Authors from US Bureau of Labor Statistics				

Computer software engineers (applications and systems software) and computer systems analysis are all hemorrhaging jobs by the thousands to offshore locations. Therefore, unless there is a dramatic policy reversal, not only is it unlikely for information technology sector to create 1.786 million new jobs in the U.S. between 2000 and 2010, it is actually possible for jobs to contract below the lofty 2.126 million level of year 2000.

The information technology sector, more than any, had been specified by policymakers from local, state and federal governments as the engine of growth for the new economy, making even an anemic growth, let alone flat or negative growth, a nightmare of unimaginable proportions. On a national scale, adding the projected growth for the endangered customer service representative occupation to the growth projected for the threatened information technology sector means that a total of 2.417 million projected new jobs may not exist by 2010. Even more threatening, the 4.072 million combined jobs in information technologies and customer services in 2000 are in danger of being negatively affected.

The projected effect of information technology on the economy extends far beyond numerical factors. The BLS projected that not only would the information technology sector lead all groups in percent change in employment, but it would also register the highest annual wage increases. Therefore, the calculations by the BLS were considerate of reverberation of increased discretionary expenditures by the information sector on other sectors. Should the wage increase for the information sector not materialize as anticipated by the BLS, it is fair to assume that projected growth for many other sectors will not occur.

Pointedly, it seems the BLS underestimated employment growth in one sector: food services. The BLS predicted (Table 11d) a total job growth of 673,000 by 2010 for this sector. But the April 2005 BLS payroll employment report contained the following: "Since its most recent low in June 2002, employment in leisure and hospitality has expanded by 823,000, with four-fifths of the gain occurring in food services." In other words, projected growth for food services for the ten-year period has been achieved in just five.

Not even the Bureau of Labor Statistics anticipated that the U.S. would rapidly exchange jobs in manufacturing and information technologies for jobs at McDonalds and Burger King.

Forrester Research Inc. estimated in a November 2002 report that, 472,632 out of the 3.3 million jobs "white-collar" jobs expected to be lost to offshore outsourcing would be from the information technology and mathematics sectors. It expected $136 billion in lost wages to move offshore as a result. These estimated losses seem rather conservative in the face of accelerated pace of offshore outsourcing in information technologies, data processing and professional occupations.

Combination of job losses in the manufacturing sector and contraction of employment in the information technology sector would shrink two key pillars of the U.S. economy, depriving governments everywhere of the resources needed to fund mandated entitlements, pay police, firemen, nurses, etc., just as demand for these services is increasing. In the end, the per capita income of Americans would decline, hospitals would close, old age homes would be shuttered, classroom sizes would increase, and the overall standard of living would decline. This is the only possible conclusion from accumulating jobs data in the United States.

Despite significant tax cuts, massive government spending and heavy consumer spending engendered by home refinancing, the average annual increase in wages between 2001 and 2005 has been only 1.5 percent, compared to inflation rate of 2.5 percent. Meanwhile productivity gains averaged 4 percent, meaning, contrary to conventional economics, benefits are not being distributed. But if the wage of the average worker has deteriorated in the face of a three-pronged stimulus package, what would happen to wages when the catalysts for wage growth are removed?

And the major contributing factor would be offshore outsourcing of manufacturing and information technology assets of the United States by the United States and against the United States.

12

TWIN EVIL FORCES OF DEFICITS

The value of all goods and services (GDP) produced in the United States was $11.74 trillion in 2004. By comparison, the GDP of South Korea, a country with one-sixth the population of the US, was "only" $680 billion. How was it then that a comment by the central bank of South Korea on February 22, 2005 was enough to trigger a precipitous decline of the US dollar and a massive retreat on Wall Street?

It seems financial markets are sitting on needles and pins. Because a similar remark by People's Bank of China Policy Board member Yu Yongding on November 26, 2004 also caused tremors in financial markets, with the dollar tanking that time to four-year lows versus the euro and the yen.

Are financial markets sitting on tectonic economic fundamentals that are about to quake to unleash a destructive tsunami across the global economic system? Or is the nervousness much ado about nothing?

Not long after George W. Bush was elected president, the economy of the U.S. officially entered into a recession in March 2001. The U.S. Congress injected liquidity into the economy by enacting the Economic Growth and Tax Relief Reconciliation Act of 2001, otherwise known as Bush's tax cuts. Among measures enacted were reduction of marginal tax rates, increase in base deductions for married couples, increase in child tax credit from $500 to $1000, and expansion of the child and dependent care credit.

More liquidity was injected into the U.S. economy in 2002 with the passage of the Job Creation and Workers Assistance Act of 2002. The act provided for so-called "bonus depreciation"—a first-year deduction of thirty percent of the adjusted basis of qualified investments made by businesses after September 10, 2001, and before September 11, 2004. The Jobs and Growth Tax Relief and

Reconciliation Act of 2003 increased the bonus depreciation deduction to fifty percent and extended the expiration date to January 1, 2005.

All in all, the Tax Foundation estimates the three tax cuts injected a princely total of $188.1 billion into the US economy from 2001 to the end of 2003. This cash infusion helped stimulate consumer spending and the economy in the short run.

But the greatest stimulant to the U.S. economy from 2001 to 2003 was not provided by the Bush tax cuts, but by the Federal Reserve driving short term interest rates to as low as 1 percent in June 2003 from a high of 6.5 percent in January 2001 and by government outlays that grew from $1.79 trillion in 2000 to $2.16 trillion in 2003.

With interest rates at an all time low, it paid for everybody to borrow as much money as they could. This is how, according to the Federal Reserve, $700 billion in purchasing power was generated in 2002 alone through "cash outs" of home equity. According to the USA Today, "The refinancing boom helps explain the unusually persistent growth of consumer spending through the recession."

And the spending spree unleashed by the heavy wards of cash explains why the gross domestic product grew smartly from 1.9 percent to 3.0 percent and 4.4 percent in 2002, 2003 and 2004, respectively.

But tax cuts that played a relatively small part in economic growth are not free. The imperatives of the U.S. budget imply that tax cuts must be financed with increases in other taxes or reductions in government programs or combination of both. But the U.S. Congress has enacted no such financing mechanism, thereby adding to deterioration of the U.S. fiscal budget.

The U.S. recorded a budget surplus of $129 billion in fiscal 2001, the last year attributed to the Clinton Administration. From 2002 to 2003 and 2004, the U.S. recorded budget deficits of $159 billion, $377.14 billion and $412.55 billion, respectively. While contraction of tax collection due to collapse of the dotcom bubble and increased military and national security expenditures were major contributors, the Congressional Budget Office calculated the tax cuts contributed a hefty $200 billion to the U.S. budget deficit in 2003 alone.

As a percentage of gross domestic product, these deficits are not excessively high by historical standards. And this is one of the arguments used by proponents of tax cuts for doing nothing about the deficits. But the deficits are astronomical in absolute terms. And since savings rate in the U.S. is too low to allow domestic borrowing to cover the shortfall in the budget, foreigners have become lenders of last resort to the U.S. by purchasing Treasury Securities. Foreigners like the Japanese, Chinese and South Koreans.

As of December 2004, Treasury Securities held by foreigners had climbed to the princely sum of nearly $2 trillion. In plain language, this implies that every American household owes about $17,000 in Treasury Securities to foreigners!

The United States owed a relatively small amount of $69 billion, or 3.5 percent of the total, to South Korea and $193.8 billion, or 10 percent of the total, to China. At $711.8 billion, or about 37 percent of the total, Japan was the biggest lender by far to the United States. Table 12a provides a breakdown of who has loaned what to the United States.

| Table 12a
Major Foreign Holders of
US Treasury Securities (December 2004) ||
COUNTRY/GROUP	AMOUNT ($ Billions)
Japan	711.8
China	193.8
United Kingdom	163.0
Caribbean Banking	69.4
South Korea	69.0
OPEC	59.8
Taiwan	58.8
Germany	53.8
Hong Kong	52.7
Switzerland	51.1
Canada	41.2
Mexico	40.3
Others	370.6
TOTAL	**1935.3**
Authors U.S. Treasury Department	

The uncomfortable truth for America, therefore, is that part of the tax cuts used to stimulate the economy was borrowed from foreigners. And, eventually, they would want their money back, with interest. And just like a credit card, the longer payment is delayed, the greater the interest.

With an excellent credit rating and as one of the safest money stores around, the United States has no trouble finding buyers for its Treasury Securities, even though yields have been low by historical standards. But if demand slows, perhaps due to better yield elsewhere, then the U.S. has to raise interest rate to make the Securities more attractive. Raising interest rate sharply enough will cause the U.S. economy to wobble, with negative repercussions for U.S. workers and the global economy.

The stress imposed by the increasing U.S. budget deficit on global financial instruments is therefore one of the reasons why financial markets listen when foreigners speak. But this stress pales in comparison with that posed by an even more ominous factor: the United States current account deficit.

The balance of trade is a measurement of the difference between export and import of goods and services. The current account is a broader measurement encompassing the balance of trade as well as returns on investment and other assets in the U.S. versus the rest of the world.

In 2004, the U.S. current account was in deficit to the tune of a whopping $665.9 billion, compared to $530.7 billion in 2003. But the true story lies not in the current account deficit, but in deficit in goods.

Table 12b shows the U.S. trade deficit in goods has increased in tandem with increase in economic activity, and that the trade deficit in goods in 2004 ($665.5 billion) was almost eerily equal to the current account deficit ($665.9 billion). This illuminating information means that while the U.S. is holding its own in all other areas of economic activity, it is being taken to the cleaners when it comes to trading in goods. And the United States is being hammered in trading of goods principally due to the steep labor cost in favor of China in particular.

Table 12b U.S. Deficit in Goods	
YEAR	**US DEFICIT IN GOODS ($ Billions)**
2001	427.4
2002	484.2
2003	547.6
2004	665.5
Authors from U.S. Bureau of Economic Analysis	

Nouriel Roubini of New York University, Josh Bivens of the Economic Policy Institute, Governor Donald Kohn of the Federal Open Market Committee and many others have raised this alarm: "The large and growing discrepancy between what the United States spends and what it produces," coupled with the large and growing indebtedness of the United States, poses an unacceptable risk to the health of the economies of the United States and the world at large.

Whether through re-investment in the United States in the form of purchases of fixed assets, stocks, U.S. securities other than U.S. Treasury securities, or other financial instruments, the bottom line is that foreigners are lending $665 billion to the United States to cover the current account deficit. For example, net foreign purchases of U.S. securities other than U.S. Treasury securities jumped from $251 billion in 2003 to $414.1 billion in 2004; net financial inflows for foreign direct investment in the U.S. were $115.5 billion in 2004, up from $39.9 billion in 2003; foreign official assets in the U.S. increased $355.3 billion in 2004, following an increase of $248.6 billion in 2003; U.S. liabilities to foreigners reported by U.S. banks increased $338.2 billion in 2004, following an increase of $75.6 billion in 2003.

While there are outflows from the U.S. as well, the steep increases in foreign ownership of U.S. equity assets from 2003 to 2004 reflect the need to bridge the ever-exploding U.S. current account deficit. According to the BeA, "Net recorded financial inflows—net acquisitions by foreign residents of assets in the United States less net acquisitions by U.S. residents of assets abroad—were $615.5 billion in 2004, up from $545.8 billion in 2003," figures almost identical to the current deficits for 2004 and 2003, respectively. Early indicators for 2005 offer no comfort that the demand for foreign bridge financing will abate any time soon.

Economic instability normally associated with borrowing on such a massive scale has been subdued due to the low interest rate climate fostered by the Federal Reserve in order to spur economic growth. But not even the Federal Reserve can engender violation of one of the fundamental laws of economics: that price (interest rate) increases with increase in demand.

Since U.S. deficit in goods is now structural due primarily to continued relocation of manufacturing assets to China, the current account deficit is not about to shrink any time in the foreseeable future. Fundamental structural adjustment necessary to raise funds domestically is also not being contemplated. Demand for bridge financing from foreign sources will therefore not abate any time soon in the U.S. Therefore, the cost of borrowing—interest rate—will press upwards inexorably as the sheer size of the demand for foreign sources of finance increases.

But the question is this: will the rise in interest rate happen slowly or will it be forced upwards abruptly due to forces beyond the control of the United States? And this is where institutions like the relatively miniscule central bank of South Korea come into sharp focus.

According to summaries provided by the Economic Policy Institute, the external debt of the United States will rise from twenty four percent of GDP at the end of 2003 to sixty four percent of GDP by 2014, if there is no improvement in the current account deficit. The cost of servicing just the additional debt incurred from 2004 to 2014 will amount to a stunning $250 billion. Clearly, something needs to be done as quickly as possible, but the what and the how are not even being debated.

Former UN Ambassador to the United Nations Madeleine Albright once told Lieutenant Raoul Cedras, leader of the Haitian junta: "You have a choice. You can depart voluntarily and soon or you can depart involuntarily and soon."

In the same manner, the United States has a choice with regards to its current account deficit imbalance. The United States can fix its current account deficit problem voluntarily and soon or it will be fixed involuntarily and soon. Either way, it will be fixed. Why?

Due to depreciation of the U.S. dollar, Japan projects that unrealized losses in its foreign reserve holdings came to about $110 billion by March 31, 2005. If China accumulates reserves at the same rate as 2004 and maintains the same peg of its currency to the U.S. dollar for another three years, it will realize a loss of $300 billion, or sixteen percent of its projected GDP, if the dollar depreciates by thirty percent.

Some have argued that these losses are only on paper and therefore should not be a cause for concern. But in 2004, South Korea incurred a loss of $10 billion, or five percent of its stock of foreign reserves, due to purchases of dollars necessary to prevent its currency from appreciation too rapidly. It is this very real loss that prompted the central bank of South Korea to contemplate shifting more of its foreign currency holdings from the U.S. dollar to currencies of higher value like the yen and euro.

If South Korea decided to cut its losses by dumping a significant amount of dollars in favor of other currencies, other countries and institutions holding dollars will follow suit, thereby precipitating a free fall of the dollar. The U.S. would then have to increase interest rate dramatically and quickly in order to attract demand for the dollar.

A dramatically higher interest rate will cause the U.S. economy to grind to a screeching halt, with repercussions—business losses, unemployment, higher budget deficit—perhaps exceeding those caused by implosion of the dotcom bubble.

This involuntary rectification of the current account deficit is what pushed the dollar into free fall following the announced intention by the central bank of South Korea to diversify into other currencies and away from dollar-based assets.

Fortunately, financial Armageddon was averted this time when the South Koreans and other central banks in Asia, fearing lowering of the Sword of Damocles, disavowed any intention of shunning the dollar.

But as the New York Times warned in an editorial: "When a seemingly innocuous remark from the central bank of South Korea makes the dollar tank, all is not well with the United States' position in the world economy."

Dollar reserves held in developing countries have risen sharply in recent years. Up $292 billion in 2003, reserves rose a further $378 billion in 2004 as most countries increased their exports to a voracious United States, the economic Godfather to the world.

The World Bank has sent a chilling message about potential losses of these dollar denominated assets caused by depreciation of the dollar. In its 2005 Global Development Finance Report, the World Bank identified the "gravest risk" for emerging markets as deep and disorderly dollar decline that would create financial market volatility and push up interest rates. Because of the sheer size of global dollar denominated reserves, the bank predicted heavy capital losses in the event of even a modest decline in the dollar.

For the necessary rectification steps to be applied to forestall a meltdown of the global economic infrastructure, the causes of the U.S. current account deficit need not only be clearly identified, but false theories must be debunked as well.

One such false theory is that "The U.S. would rather consume, than save, while the rest of the world would rather do the opposite." This is incorrect, for consumption, as an isolated factor, did not cause the U.S. current account deficit. It is the source of the goods being consumed that has caused the current account deficit.

Why is the U.S. buying more overseas goods? Because, besides products from overseas like vehicles of clearly superior quality, many products previously manufactured in the United States have been shifted to countries like China and Mexico to take advantage of much lower labor cost inputs. The ever-increasing trade deficit with China is clearly illustrative of this fact. And the 2.8 million American manufacturing jobs lost since January 2001 bears testimony to this translocation of assets previously planted in these United States.

Not just toys, clothing, watches, and other products of relatively lower value, but several higher value added products like computers, capital equipment, and automobile parts that generate much higher labor cost advantage for investors are moving away from these United States.

Even an overall depreciation of the value of the dollar against major currencies in the past three years has not impacted on the trade deficit. This is due in part to the refusal of China, the country with which the U.S. has the largest deficit, to re-evaluate its currency. But even a re-evaluation will not stop—nor slow down—relocation of manufacturing assets overseas.

Japan, China and the other countries holding large amounts of dollars stand to lose just as much as the U.S. in the event of wild fluctuation in its value. They are therefore not likely to take any precipitous action that will cause sharp fluctuation of the dollar to ensue. But when vulnerability is at such an acute degree, a relatively minor act like a major corporation defaulting on its loan commitments could be the catalyst that plunges the world into financial crises, with negative consequences for the United States and the global economies.

Therefore, to forestall the possibility of a financial Armageddon, it is incumbent on the United States to take concrete actions in the near term to bring its current account deficit caused by the twin evil forces of exploding trade deficit and budget deficit into relative balance. And the only economic activity likely to generate a significant positive impact on the U.S. current account deficit is manufacturing of more goods in the United States.

13

COLLABORATION NOT CONFRONTATION

In 2003 the United Auto Workers Union (UAW) entered into wage and benefit negotiations with General Motors, Ford and Chrysler. The economy was mired in a jobless recovery, the market share of the Big 3 UAW had declined from 68.3 percent in 1999 to 59.3 percent in 2003, with employment by the group falling from 372,143 to 303,886 in the same time frame.

Despite the obvious deteriorating market position of the Big 3 UAW, the new agreement hammered between the union and the car companies called for the average wage and benefit package per worker to increase from $57.06 per hour in 2003 to $66.28 per hour in 2007. The wage component per production worker was scheduled to increase from $37.25 per hour to $41.65 per hour in the same time frame.

Meanwhile, a production worker at the Toyota Motor Manufacturing plant at Georgetown, Kentucky was paid an hourly rate of $22.03 per hour in 2003, but earned a bonus of $8,547, making the full average hourly wage higher than that at a Big 3 UAW plant.

The tale of two differing wage structures—one inflexible, the other flexible—portrays contrasting philosophies, which is one of the reasons for increasing sales of vehicles with Japanese nameplates versus declining sales of those with American nameplates.

The Toyota model—true of all Japanese companies—is collaborative, giving the company the flexibility to forego the bonus in years of low or negative earning and, thus, allowing for labor cost flexibility with the market. The Big 3 UAW model, on the other hand, is confrontational and unyielding.

The Big 3 UAW model assumes a fallacy, which is that the company will survive regardless of market conditions. The Toyota model, going by the motto "expect the best but plan for the worst," recognizes the inherent volatility of market conditions, and thus builds in necessary safeguards.

Reduction of GM and Ford corporate bonds to junk status on May 5, 2005 by Standards and Poor's was due to declining sales and lack of cost flexibility in their business models, which prevents the urgent financial surgery necessary to realign expenditures with income in the near to medium term from being done. The unhelpful announcement by the UAW of its refusal to reopen the labor agreements before 2007 only served to confirm the conviction of the markets that restructuring North American operations of GM and Ford would be a long, arduous process.

Labor cost flexibility would have enabled the $3000 per car cost disadvantage suffered by GM and Ford in comparison to Japanese nameplates to be dented. Instead, at precisely when cost reduction was most critical, GM and Ford had to contend with increased borrowing costs wrought by reduction of their bonds to junk status.

Contrasting fortunes of Japanese nameplates and the Big 3 UAW is not accidental, for Japanese collaborative relationship engenders maximum progress, while the opposite is true of the confrontational relationship at the latter. And while collaboration underpins everything Japanese, its application in American interrelationships has been nonuniform, which explains in part maximum progress in some corporate sectors in the U.S. and retardation at others.

As its Latin roots *com* and *laborare* suggest, collaboration in its most basic form means "to work together." However, the most powerful definition is, according Barbara Gray, "a process through which parties who see different aspects of a problem can constructively explore their differences and search for solutions that go beyond their own limited vision of what is possible." Another useful definition is that provided by David Chrislip and Carl Larson: "A mutually beneficial relationship between two or more parties who work toward common goals by sharing responsibility, authority, and accountability for achieving results."

Collaboration is therefore a consensual process filled with trust, patience, dialogue, respect, integrity, dignity, goodwill, compromise, unity of purpose and celebration, all of which are Confucian, the ideology underpinning the Japanese society. The strength of the family or team is not only sacrosanct, it is believed to be the foundation of all success.

Confrontation, derived from the Latin words *con* (against) and *front* (face), translates literally as challenging someone face to face. Interpreted by some as a small-scale cold war, a confrontational process is filled with rancor, selfishness, paralysis, anger, revenge and hostility. Bitterness is the residue of confrontation.

Shades of confrontation have colored many an American workplace for too long a time, with the resultant "we against them" attitude being one of the causes of the relatively unsatisfactory vehicle performance at the Big 3 UAW today.

On the roads of North America today, many a satisfied driver of a vehicle with Japanese nameplate can recite variations of cases of being burned by poor quality of a vehicle made by the Big 3 UAW. Even when the last American giant of the automobile industry, Lee Iococca, invented the minivan and the Sports Utility Vehicle, the lead of the inventors was short-lived as Siennas, Odysseys and Highlanders quickly replaced Caravans, Voyagers and Jeep Cherokees.

Poorly manufactured vehicles, plus failure to learn the fuel-efficient lessons of the seventies and the high cost of benefits, is one of the reasons GM and Ford, unlike the Japanese, lose money consistently on vehicles, pulling into the black only when offset by loans and leases. For example, had it not been for the $728 million profit registered by GM's GMAC finance arm, losses for the first quarter of 2005 would have been nearly $2 billion, instead of the $1.3 billion posted.

Quality of products manufactured by American companies must improve immeasurably for any cost reducing strategy to be effective. No matter how low the price, a product will rust in a warehouse or in a showroom if consumers perceive quality to be questionable. Many a salesperson has been told in the face that the joy of buying a product of poor quality lasts much shorter than the pain of living with the burdens of poor quality.

It is therefore imperative for manufacturers to demonstrate a quantum leap in the quality of products manufactured in the US. And for this to happen, the mentality in workplaces like GM and Ford must change from confrontational, or shades thereof, to total collaboration.

Even cooperation is not enough because, instead of being a decision by the whole team, which is collaboration, this implies a decision made by just one side with the others being convinced to go along.

With collaboration the only mode of operation in the workplace, the company manages systems, not people. The system is fine tuned to such perfection with participation by all members of the team that well trained workers anywhere are able to deliver impeccable results. This is the Japanese way. The Big 3 UAW way of the dinosaur era is to manage people, thereby subtracting resources that could otherwise be spent improving the system. This is one of the reasons why productivity at Japanese auto plants is still higher than at the Big 3 UAW.

The functionability of managing systems as opposed to people was brought into sharp focus when Toyota picked a Corolla at random from its many plants around the world for quality inspection in the nineties. Before then, the Big 3 UAW complained bitterly about the laziness and lack of dedication of North American workers. But when the Corollas were inspected, though it came as no surprise to the Japanese, the media was shocked to learn that a vehicle from the Cambridge, Ontario plant had the fewest defects.

Or perhaps the truth should finally be recognized: that the managements in place at GM and Ford are incapable of building vehicles of acceptable quality and ergonomics. Perhaps like the many hundreds of thousands of employees whose jobs have been transferred to other countries, current GM and Ford managements should be scrapped and replaced by others who understand the true essence of collaboration.

The American landscape is not all doom and gloom, however. Intel, Microsoft, Advanced Micro Devices and most leading companies of the information technology era are active practitioners of the collaborate mode of management. The CEO of Intel not cutting himself off from the rest of the workforce, but rather having his office in the same cubicle-style as other employees is evidence of collaborative style of management. Microsoft's leafy campus set-up, stock options and casual clothing for workers are all meant to foster collaborative participation. Writing code for the huge and complicated Windows and other programs necessitates a collaborative interaction between different teams, and Microsoft demands no less.

But even before the birth of Microsoft and Intel, Henry John Heinz defined the very essence of a collaborative relationship when he founded his company in 1869 on the philosophy of "heart power is better than horsepower." Conveying love, caring and sharing, nothing portrays collaboration better than the heart. H.J. Heinz believed that "kindly care and fair treatment" was the right and moral way to treat employees, which he demonstrated by providing free healthcare for his employees and treating his employees to rooftop gardens and lunchtime concerts, a far cry from the brutal and suffocating conditions under which most workers of that era labored.

That the H.J. Heinz Company is today one of the most successful and respected global enterprises descends directly from the care H.J. Heinz devoted to his products and the collaborative relationship he forged with his employees. These attributes not only have persisted till today, they have been cemented into the family philanthropy to "approach change broadly, encourage coalitions," and to bring change through "collaborative responses."

Collaborative interaction is demanded in all areas of society, not just in the corporate world. A true collaborative enterprise is the Bay Area Economic Forum, a public-private partnership of business, government, university, labor and community leaders that "develops analyses and implements programs to strengthen the region's competitive economy and quality of life."

With major manufacturing sectors in California threatened by inshore and offshore outsourcing, the Forum demonstrated fruits of collaboration by producing a document suggesting lower wages in Asia could be surmounted by exploiting proximity to sale advantage, lowering health care burdens and eradicating non-productive regulations. Collaborative participation paved the way for immediate dissemination of the proposals and implementation of some key aspects.

The education system in the United States is broken, and will short circuit any advantages garnered from implementing cost reduction strategies. Bill Gates minced no words when he told an audience of governors: "American high schools are obsolete. By obsolete, I don't mean that our high schools are broken, flawed and under funded....By obsolete, I mean that our high schools, even when they are working exactly as designed, cannot teach our kids what they need to know today." Like everything else of true import, the speech was given short rift by the "scandal-du-jour" media.

Like everything else, the education system was designed for the brick and mortar business era when human resource structures were stratified into discrete entities, with information passed vertically through the structure. Employee interactivity with this two-dimensional structure was limited to only those entities in direct contact; middle management reigned supreme, original thought was discouraged and basic processing of information was sufficient to ensure life-long employment. The priorities for this obsolete era were established as reading, 'riting and 'rithmetic, in that order. That arithmetic was at the bottom of the list was not by coincidence, for only rudimentary mathematics was required then.

Middle management, which acted as custodian of corporate culture and an unwitting impediment to progress in the obsolete era, has been obliterated. It has been replaced by a flattened structure in today's multidimensional world in which every employee is required to be a problem solver. The skills of the obsolete era do not therefore translate into the new era.

The new era requires collaborative interactivity, but high schools are still churning out graduates with the mindset of the obsolete era. The problem solving required of everyone in today's era demands standardized skills, with no weak links accepted. In this regard, math and science skills must not only be rigorous, they must be universal.

Having a week off for March break and another week off for spring break, coupled with "snow" days, summer vacation and Government-sanctioned holidays is defeatist. Having Grade 8 students take reading, social studies and English simultaneously is redundant. But not having computer intensive curriculum in early grades is unpardonable.

Grade school and K-12 curriculum must be radically transformed. Math and science must only be intensified, they must relate to solving practical problems in a collaborative environment. It requires a new breed of teachers and it must begin immediately, for time is running short for America's children.

Decision-making by political leaders must be radically transformed from high-wire zero-sum style of management to collaborative leadership. One of the most successful presidents of all time, Ronald Wilson Reagan, was an active practitioner of collaborative leadership. The story has been repeated many times of how he cut backroom deals with fellow Irishman House Speaker Tip O'Neill to resolve thorny issues of the day over whisky and a boatload of bawdy jokes. One of the greatest Conservative leaders of all time was not above raising taxes when that was precisely what was required to fix the deteriorating finances of the United States. For him, doing right by his beloved America trumped everything else.

The United States was forged through collaboration, with the interest of the Union paramount. John Hancock, Samuel Adams, Benjamin Franklin, Thomas Jefferson, and the other founding fathers that signed the Declaration of Independence were driven not by personal interest but by the demands of the Union. Alexander Hamilton, James Madison, George Washington, Abraham Baldwin and the other founding fathers that signed the United States Constitution were not motivated by their personal needs, and not even those of the Union alone, but by the needs of all mankind.

Strategies based not on collaboration but on offshore outsourcing, where employees know not whether the next phone call or meeting is to announce their jobs going overseas, demoralize and weaken not just a company or a people but a country. The wanton transfer of jobs and resources from the United States to other countries by profitable enterprises forcing others to follow in their wake is akin to a people cannibalizing their young, with no one left to tend the future.

If America remembers that winning is when every one wins and losing is when only one side wins, a new course will be charted blazing the way for a communal effort that will raise the United States and its peoples and the whole world to a level of unprecedented prosperity. And if there be any doubt, remember Henry John Heinz from Birmingham, Pennsylvania who built not just a successful company but a successful people by preaching on the philosophy "heart power is better than horsepower."

14

NEW BUSINESS IDEAS TO RETAIN JOBS IN AMERICA

The American Middle Class, built painstakingly through contributions by vision-aries such as Andrew Carnegie, Henry Ford and George Washington Carver, is in the most trouble it has ever been. It is being dismantled block-by-block, county-by-county and state-by-state across the entire United States. Plant relocation to serve previous export markets, currency appreciation and other contributing mar-ket forces are logical. Job losses due to substitution of technology are unfortunate but welcome. But cost of doing business, a key contributor to job losses, has assumed a whole new level of importance under the specter of globalization, and small to medium sized businesses in the U.S. are paying a heavy price.

Unlike the not too distant past, using financial stimulus to create high paying jobs in today's economic environment in the U.S. is not completely curative. The reason is that stimulus is causing more demand than usual—thus the widening trade deficit—for overseas goods. This causes the current account deficit to worsen, thus exerting upward pressure on interest rates, which then threatens to counteract the initial job growth objective. And one of the reasons for this vicious cycle is the cost of doing business in the United States.

"The evidence grows that our trade policies will put unremitting pressure on the dollar for many years to come," he commented in a letter released on March 5, 2005 to shareholders. He continued: "The decline in its value has already been substantial, but it is nevertheless likely to continue. Without policy changes, cur-rency markets could even become disorderly and generate spillover effects, both political and financial."

Were those words written by a two-bit chief executive somewhere? No, War-ren Buffet, who is "only" the second wealthiest person in the world, wrote them. He warned that "A country that is now aspiring to an 'ownership society will not find much happiness…in a 'sharecropper's society'"

"This force-feeding of American wealth to the rest of the world is now proceeding at the rate of $1.8 billion daily."

"Consequently, other countries and their citizens now own a net of about $3 trillion of the U.S. A decade ago their net ownership was negligible."

But Mr. Buffet needs no reminder that those trade policies were enacted with only vociferous union "anarchists" in protest. So to use a cliché by the New York Yankees' broadcaster Michael Kay, "You cannot put the milk back in the udder." The deed has been done and the U.S. and the rest of the world have to contend with the consequences.

Multi-lateral trade agreements and laws enacted by the World Trade Organization have engendered an economic paradigm under which—as Karl Marx predicted—states have withered away. But not even the prophetic Marx envisaged replacement of the state by a new powerful suprastructure—the multinational corporation—roaming the globe, garbed in stateless robes.

Consequences of the new economic structure created by multi-lateral agreements include global competition among countries with divergent wage structures and populations, and abolition of tariffs as a rectification mechanism. Under this new umbrella, the $20 an hour American worker is supposed to compete against the 64 cents an hour Chinese worker, and the country of Togo, with barely a blip on the economies of scale, is supposed to compete against mammoth China: almost all barriers to trading of goods across borders have been wiped out.

So some multinational corporations—whose world the rest of humanity now inhabits—are treating their capital as a consumer. And like any good consumer, they are shopping for top quality labor at the lowest price. And having completely expunged patriotism from the selection criteria, some American owners of capital are in China en masse buying up cheap and more compliant labor stripped of any benefits. The message from some American owners of capital to American workers is the same as the one Michael Corleone delivered to his brother in the movie The Godfather, "It's not personal…It's strictly business."

The result of American capital buying Chinese labor instead of American labor is evident in America's $162 billion trade deficit in 2004 with China. In a sign of accelerating consumption of Chinese labor, the trade deficit with China for the first three months of 2005 was $41.02 billion, about 36 percent higher than that for the comparable period in 2004.

A good many of the millions of jobs that have disappeared from the manufacturing and service sectors in the U.S. emanate from "Buy-Chinese-Labor" in manufacturing and "Buy-Indian-Labor" in information related businesses

And where the multinational corporations tread, so do their army of suppliers, which is why small to medium sized American manufacturing companies are also flocking to China. It is also why offshore outsourcing has become a matter of survival for many small to medium sized information technology businesses.

The relentless cost pressure exerted by some multinational corporations on the American economic infrastructure has become so acute that something major has to yield to make American workers relatively more affordable to small and medium sized enterprises competing against foreign products and services. For if nothing is done, the exodus of jobs will continue inexorably until America's most valuable asset—the middle class—is severely dented.

Yale Professor of Economics Robert Shiller worries that the effect of globalization on U.S. employment could approach the bend in a hockey stick, which grows gradually until it generates explosive velocity at the point where it's supposed to make contact with the puck. Shiller is apprehensive that growth in information technology is about to combine with open markets to unleash a disruptive force on U.S. employment. He says, "The risks created by computer technology are real and frightening."

To those who claim the solution lies in U.S. workers acquiring "skills premium," he cautions that the threat "will not be seriously changed by retraining and re-education programs, which will not give most people the skills they need to remain more efficient than the new machines."

Professor Shiller advocates that the risks of the new era must be dealt with by "fundamental changes—changes that will not make individuals more productive than machines, but will allow society to manage risks better and to redistribute them."

Shiller cautioned, "It is important to start thinking about what changes lie ahead, because it may be harder to agree later on."

The American economic infrastructure of today was built to serve the typical brick and mortar business of yesteryear, not today's hyper competitive world in which new technologies are sometimes rendered redundant before installation. The system was perfected for the General Motors, Ford, US Steel and other American titans of the 1950s, not the Microsoft, 3M, Johnson and Johnson and other thriving companies of today.

The economic infrastructure assumes supremacy of American manufacturing is innate, not to be challenged by foreign competitors with lower labor cost inputs. The system assumes technology is immobile; therefore cost of manufacturing in America is irrelevant. The system assumes Made-in-America or an American nameplate ensures loyalty of American consumers; therefore quality means nothing. The system assumes information can be locked in a safe to be protected from prying eyes; therefore product development means everything. The system assumes operating in America trumps the risk to capital; therefore capital flight is not cause for concern. The system assumes American workers are the most educated in the world; therefore will always command much higher wages and benefits compared to their counterparts in the developing world. Well, the system is wrong on all counts, and certain parts must be changed because multinational corporations have changed the rules of the game.

Starting with cost inputs, American-based businesses are severely disadvantaged compared to competitors in some foreign lands, namely China and India. Besides much higher wages, an American-based business must pay health insurance, social security premium, Medicare premiums, unemployment insurance, pension plan contribution, life insurance, disability insurance, tax on capital equipment and inventory in some states, and many other overt and covert costs before it produces a single item. These costs are passed on to consumers in the form of higher prices.

For the most part, employers in China and India and some parts of Asia carry very little to nothing of these burdens. So employers in the United States start off with a huge built-in disadvantage in the form of higher costs. Plus, they have to contend with cumbersome regulations, and myriads of other impediments rarely confronted by businesses in China and India in particular.

It is no surprise that businesses—especially small to medium sized firms—in the manufacturing and service sectors are being squeezed like never before in the United States. Capital, especially that which competes against imported products, bears excessive risk operating on U.S. soil as a result of inordinately high cost inputs.

Employers began offering health care insurance as a benefit during World War II. It was a way to attract desirable employees and still comply with imposed wage and price controls. Better pensions, life insurance and disability insurance were all add-ons in pursuit of this goal. Now many companies extend health insurance to retirees as well.

Because of these expensive but desirable benefit packages, an albatross is now hampering American employers. General Motors has dug its own grave by producing shoddy cars. But when it comes to health care, GM carries a burden unlike any other manufacturer, thereby exacerbating the problems confronting this once proud American nameplate.

GM Chief Financial Officer John Devine announced in 2004 that health care costs for employees and retirees and their dependants amounted to $19.14 per hour per worker at GM, which translated into $1525 per vehicle, more than the cost of steel required to manufacture those vehicles. The total health care cost for GM amounted to $5.6 billion in 2004. More alarmingly, the costs continue to escalate. By comparison, health care costs incurred by Toyota North America amounted to $3.76 per hour per worker, which, due also to superior productivity and higher plant utilization, translated into a miniscule $200 per vehicle.

Pension cost for GM in 2004 also amounted to $675 per vehicle. So GM is smothered with health and pension costs of $2200 per vehicle produced, costs incurred *before* a single vehicle leaves the assembly floor to a showroom.

Just across the northern border into Canada, health care costs employers $800 per worker per year, due to the fact that the entire health care system is government funded.

Across the southern border into Mexico, not only are employee health care costs lower, wages are also only about a quarter of those in the U.S.

And across the ocean in China, both health care and wages are practically negligible, plus firms there do not as yet have to contend with the stringent environmental and other workplace regulations promulgated in the United States for health and safety reasons.

For small to medium sized firms without the negotiating muscle of a GM, health care costs averaged $9,950 per year in 2004 per family, compared with $3,695 for coverage of a single worker. For these firms, the average family premium increased ten to fifteen percent in 2004, compared with a 2.2 percent growth in wages and a 2.3 percent growth in inflation.

The Employment Policy Foundation reported employers spent $331 billion in 2004 for health insurance for employees, a fifty percent increase since 1998. Between 2002 and 2003, health care cost for employers was reported to have jumped 12.4 percent, five times higher than inflation.

It is a small miracle businesses in America are able to compete at all against competitors in lower wage countries in the new environment created at the behest of multinational corporations. That businesses in America competing against foreign competition operate under an oppressive cost disadvantage is not in dispute. And if nothing is done soon, many firms will go under or join the exodus overseas.

Before say 2000, extracting benefit payments *before* a product was sold was not especially disadvantageous to firms based in the United States, because similar methods were used for the most part by other competing high wage countries like Great Britain, Germany, Japan, Italy and Canada to pay for workers' benefits.

Today, the landscape is totally different. Globalization promoted by multinational corporations has integrated markets with starkly different cost structures, and high-cost countries must employ innovation and ingenuity to compete in their own markets in which proximity of suppliers to customers is a decided advantage. The fact of the matter is that a multinational corporation wearing an American name bears no allegiance to American workers; some are closing as fast as they can to relocate overseas to maximize returns for their shareholders.

Therefore, to level the playing field between all firms selling products in the U.S., whether based in the U.S. or overseas, all pre-sale externally imposed costs on firms based in the U.S. should be eliminated. This includes health insurance, unemployment insurance, pension payments, social security contributions, life insurance, disability insurance, workers compensation, taxation on capital equipment, tax on inventory, etc. These costs incurred *before* products are sold place U.S. based firms at a competitive disadvantage, since not all foreign firms incur these costs.

Elimination of these costs must be total in order to completely extinguish punitive costs imposed on operations in the U.S. This is a completely different era, and half hearted measures that do not fully and finally eliminate these destructive costs will not suffice. The United States must immediately stop punishing firms for operating in America, because multinational corporations will punish them if the cost structure does not change.

Businesses are the engines providing power and locomotion to the U.S. and they must be set free, just like in glory days of yore, to provide sustenance and hope to America's children. Doing this will unleash once again the ingenuity of Americans, springing forth latent Andrew Carnegies and Henry Fords.

There should be no misimpressions. Doctors, nurses, teachers, firefighters, police forces and government employees and other workers thought to be immune from offshore outsourcing derive their sustenance from a critical mass of thriving businesses. So America strangles itself by strangling businesses. In effect, America is suffocating itself, which is why businesses operating on American soil must be unshackled.

Many budding entrepreneurs have given up hope, the fear of losing their capital because of low cost China imprinted on their being. And it is a palpable and eminently justifiable fear under current operating conditions. The people that gave the world the Internet infrastructure must be set free once again and a complete and utter abrogation of these instruments of disadvantage is the only way to rekindle hope in the U.S.

Destruction of these costs does not mean elimination of benefits critical to Americans. On the contrary, benefits will be strengthened and enhanced by destroying these costs, for a more productive beast will be born from this destruction. Out of these inimical ashes of high costs, a Phoenix will rise again, stronger and mightier than ever to provide *enhanced* benefits to workers.

Globalization Equalization Factor (GEF)

A new, fairer, and more equitable method of generating revenues should replace the current suffocating and antiquated method. Revenues to fund benefits like health insurance, pensions and social security should be generated by levying *all* products and services at the *point of sale* in the United States. The rate should be the same regardless of the *origin* of the product or service sold in the United States.

This proposed method of revenue generation—to be known as *Globalization Equalization Factor (GEF)*—necessary to pay benefits of U.S. workers levels the playing field and eliminates the benefit cost disadvantage incurred by operating in the U.S. It removes the $5.6 billion health care albatross hanging on GM, plus the costs of all the other benefits.

The total cost of manufacturing a product or providing a service is eventually reflected in the purchase price anyway, so consumers are shouldering the costs of providing entitlements for U.S. employees under the current system. But under the current system, the U.S. employer pays these costs, builds the costs into the price and then, hopefully, recovers the costs after sale. But if the price is higher than that of a competitor as a result of embedding those costs *before* product or service is offered for sale, then the employer cannot make a sale and must vacate the marketplace to a competitor. It must close down or relocate to China, which is what most companies facing foreign competition are doing, or contemplating doing.

Or if U.S. based competitors like Toyota North America and Nissan America are not burdened to the same degree, then a company like GM must slash the price of its cars by the amount of its additional health care cost just to be competitive.

This is one of the reasons for the zero financing, cash rebates, and other financed-based marketing strategies offered by GM, Ford and Chrysler to get consumers to purchase their products.

Or it must farm out major portions of the unit for manufacture in countries with lower cost inputs. Lou Dobbs reported in his book Exporting America that GM's new Chevy, the Equinox, is assembled in Canada with a Chinese-made engine, a phenomenon which partially explains why employment in the U.S. auto industry has dropped by 200,000 in the past four years.

Ford is investing heavily in Asia not just for the purpose of making cars for that market but to ship vehicles and auto parts back to the United States. The company closed its plant in Edison, New Jersey after fifty-three years, costing 400 jobs. DaimlerChrysler is rapidly moving vehicle and parts production outside the United States, evidenced by the transfer of Tower Automotive, frames manufacturer for Dodge Ram pickup trucks, from Milwaukee to Mexico.

But when China begins exporting vehicles en masse to the U.S. in the not too distant future, the health care discount alone will not be enough. America must adopt the GEF to make staying in the U.S. economically attractive for GM, Ford and Chrysler. Otherwise, even that which remains of these names of glories past will disappear from these United States. If nothing is done to stem this tide, the United Auto Workers will find the cupboard bare and dry when current contracts come up for renegotiations in 2007. The chicken would have already flown the coop.

The current system of paying for benefits is disadvantageous to goods and services produced on U.S. soil, since products and services from many developing countries do not for the most part contain such cost inputs. Businesses in the U.S. are therefore being penalized for operating in the United States, while multinational corporations located overseas reap additional profits.

Let's look at the simple equation below:

$$P_C = P_A + B \qquad\qquad (1)$$

Where

$$PC = \text{Current market price}$$

$$PA = \text{Price for company in America excluding benefits}$$

$$B = \text{contribution of benefits to price}$$

$$PA = R + L + PR \qquad\qquad (2)$$

And

$$R \quad = \quad \textbf{Cost of raw materials and other inputs}$$

$$L \quad = \quad \textbf{Cost of labor}$$

$$PR \quad = \quad \textbf{Profit}$$

P_C is the price for a product or service sold in the U.S. whether manufactured in the U.S. or overseas. The additional profit, outside of wage differential, accruing to an overseas-based manufacturer is therefore B, the cost of benefits. But if the overseas manufacturer decides to reduce its price in the U.S. to P_A, then the U.S. based manufacturer must extract **B** from his profit.

If the U.S. based manufacturer is able to add benefits to the final price, then his profit is:

$$PR \quad = \quad PA - R - L \qquad\qquad (3)$$

If the U.S. based manufacturer is not able to add benefits to the final price, then his profit is:

$$PR \quad = \quad PA - R - L - B \qquad\qquad (4)$$

But if a company operates in a relatively low margin environment where it is already severely disadvantaged by its higher labor cost and the benefit package is its profit margin, then not being able to charge the benefit package to the final price—Equation (4)—means the company is not profitable.

For many companies in America confronted by overseas competition, not being able to retrieve benefit package has been the difference between staying in America, closing down or moving overseas. This is the environment wrought by globalization, the new economic dispensation.

But if the benefit package—social security, health, life and disability insurance—is extracted at the point of sale in the form of a **Globalization Equalization Factor,** then a barrier to business startup is removed, thus encouraging more enterprises to be formed in the U.S. to compete against suppliers from overseas.

For businesses on U.S. soil already in competition with overseas companies, this method of collecting the benefit package means an end to a cost-based discrimination, thus increasing their competitiveness.

The Globalization Equalization Factor therefore removes one glaring obstacle confronting American based business in their quest to compete against overseas-based companies, while providing sustenance to American workers.

The magnitude of the GEF can be such that it is revenue neutral: that is the rate imposed by the GEF will be such that the total cost embedded in the product or service will be the same as previously transferred by the employer into the purchase price. This way, consumers would not be asked to incur additional cost.

On May 10, 2005 U.S. federal bankruptcy judge Eugene Wedoff approved a plan by United Airlines to terminate its employees' pension plans, which made it the largest corporate-pension default in American history. Bethlehem Steel's pension default in 2002 caused by $3.6 billion in underfunding held the previous record.

The estimated $645 million a year savings was part of $2 billion in total savings necessary to line up enough financing to allow United Airlines to emerge from bankruptcy. According to Judge Wedoff: "The least bad of the available choices here has got to be the one that keeps an airline functioning, that keeps employees being paid."

But the ruling came at a heavy cost to employees. The Pension Benefit Guaranty Corporation, the government's pension agency, assumed only $5 billion of the $9.8 billion underfunded liability, causing many employees to lose over half their anticipated pension benefits.

The ruling was a shot across the bow to the entire airline industry. For it cleared the way for American Airlines and Delta Airlines, facing bankruptcy of its own, to take similar actions. Delta Airlines was scheduled to pay out $3.1 billion in pension payments over coming 3 years, putting it at a competitive disadvantage.

The solution to the pension crisis is the **Globalization Equalization Factor.** Extracting pension payments from ticket sales will restore equity to the pension system of the airline industry, and bring relief to the 134,000 United Airlines employees and previous U.S. Airways employees faced with reduced benefits.

The value of all economic activities generated in the United States, known as the GDP, amounted to $11.74 trillion in 2004. This encompassed personal consumption expenditures of goods and services produced in the U.S., gross private domestic investment and government consumption expenditures, and gross investment.

GEF of just seven percent would have generated $821.8 billion. But then imports of goods and services amounted to $1.764 trillion, for an amount of $123.48 billion at the same GEF, bringing the total to a rough estimate of $945.28 billion.

For reference, it should be noted that many countries already extract a goods and services tax, in addition to collecting contributions like social security and health insurance. But in many of these countries, the government shoulders the health care burden, so businesses are not unduly burdened.

Canada imposed a goods and services tax of seven percent in January 1991, but this was an additional tax, not one transferred from business cost input to point of sale.

The effect of the GEF on job retention and job generation in the United States would be immediate. A thousand flowers will bloom, entrepreneurship will wash ashore in these United States again, the American middle class will once again walk erect and hope will be rekindled in companies competing against imports.

With the risk to capital diminished, many businesses that have departed these shores could return, and many more from foreign lands would consider the United States once again fertile land on which to plant their business seeds.

With the GEF leveling the playing field with regards to benefit and other punitive taxes imposed on U.S. based firms, higher wages remain the only cost disadvantage for firms in the U.S. versus competitors from developing countries where benefits are not provided.

But firms based in the U.S. hold distinct advantages over those in the Pacific. These advantages include proximity to final demand or point of sale, efficient execution of just-in-time strategies, superior customization, higher level of adaptability and safer supply chain.

The most rewarding and productive relationship between a supplier and customer is one that is symbiotic, something that is inherently more difficult to achieve when separated by 6,500 miles of Pacific waters. Collaborative research, product design and development, system integration, customer visits, quality inspection, security and other systems necessary for productivity enhancement are immeasurably more difficult and complicated when supplier and customer are separated by the vast waters of the Pacific Ocean. They are much easier to accomplish when both entities are securely entrenched in these United States.

With the GEF leveling the playing field with regards to benefit costs, productivity-generating factors could support higher wages for employees of U.S. based firms.

The McKinsey Group report for the Bay Area Economic Forum summarized the advantages of proximity to point of sale to include, "Short lead time, on-time delivery, reliable quality assurance and response time, swift introduction of new products, rapid complaint resolution, and a quick response to changes in demand." As firms go offshore in search of lower costs, the report warned "their ability to compete on these fronts decays." Firms operating closer to point of sale in the United States must capitalize by incorporating these advantages into their marketing and sales presentations to offset higher wages.

Security of supply is another critical factor stampeding herds to overseas manufacturing locations do not seem to lose sleep over. America's security forces have battled successfully since September 11, 2001 against terrorist forces of hatred. Unfortunately, as has been repeated many times over, America's security forces have to be right all the time, the terrorists only once. If terrorists throw a scare into supply lines, what will happen to the $18 billion worth of goods Wal-Mart is voraciously importing from China?

With GEF leveling the playing field with regards to benefit costs, Wal-Mart would have to do the right thing and bring back the higher valued added products purchased offshore. Wal-Mart was born, fed and nurtured into adult riches with American water and resources. It was American customers, beginning in Rogers, Arkansas, who lent a helping hand to the infant crawling Wal-Mart and turned it into the giant it is today.

With GEF in place, Wal-Mart should return to the comforts of its home: it should bring suppliers back to the U.S. America wants its Wal-Mart back, and the children of Sam Walton should then heed the anguished cries of their brothers and sisters and return home. Goods in Wal-Mart should be emblazoned once again with Made-in-America labels.

Understandably, not every product can be manufactured profitably in the U.S. High labor content and relatively low value of some goods cannot be negated by higher wages and are better off being manufactured overseas. But a combination of the GEF and aggressive marketing could support the manufacture of higher value added products in the U.S., leading to retention of more American jobs.

America will need entrepreneurs to begin the "Long March" from China once GEF is in place, for America cannot afford to have critical firms enrich other countries, and then have these firms turn around to devastate those left behind trying to feed America's children.

Design and engineering jobs are moving from the U.S. to China in droves to support the advanced semiconductor industry bubbling in China. As the trend continues, the United States will lose "ecosystem of supplies," a phrase coined by the McKinsey Group in the report for the Bay Area Economic Forum.

The report said an ecosystem of 25 California companies employing 3,900 workers provide parts for the Toyota-GM New United Motors Manufacturing, Incorporated (NUMMI) plant in Fremont, California. The suppliers in the ecosystem feed off NUMMI, the anchor plant, when it expands economic activity. Plus, the workers in the ecosystem interact to create a "knowledge" platform, from which research and design, engineering, and product design emanate. Transplantation of the anchor leads not only to the dissolution of the ecosystem, it precipitates a deleterious chain reaction of software design and applications, health care resolutions and other expert business functions.

The massive transplantation of American anchor companies overseas, and subsequent dissolution of ecosystems, for the predominant objective of re-supplying the U.S. is inimical to America's interests. If the trend is not stopped, evisceration of key sectors of America's industrial base will be irreversible in the near term.

In 2003, GM paid its workers $37.25 per hour. Since GM's productivity was 36.67 hours per vehicle, the wage differential with China amounts to about $1,366 per vehicle. With the GEF in place, the cost of shipping, security and the productivity enhancing factors engendered by operating close to point of sale in the US should offset this differential.

The fact the Canadian province of Ontario, not Mexico, is now the largest producer of vehicles in North America is a vivid demonstration of the possibility of trumping lower wages with combination of lower health care cost input, dynamic ecosystem of suppliers, language commonality, supply security, and transportation efficiency, all of which are true of Ontario.

The U.S. textile and apparel industry is the largest manufacturing employer in ten key states: California, North Carolina, South Carolina, New York, Pennsylvania, Texas, Alabama, Virginia, Georgia and Tennessee. The industry has lost over 1.0 million jobs in the last decade or so, with 12,000 of these losses occurring in January 2005 alone, the first month after the agreement to end quotas went into effect. The livelihood of the remaining textile and apparel workers and the communities that depend on them is under threat as never before.

Technology-engendered productivity increases and loss of export markets caused by relocation to supply overseas markets and a rising dollar are contributing factors, but higher wages are often cited as the predominant factor. The evidence suggests this may not be entirely correct.

Firms in the textile and apparel industry worldwide operate in an environment of razor-thin margins. So the fact U.S. firms in this industry continue to shut down despite implementation of automated technologies that have diminished the importance of the cost of labor suggests elimination of benefit input costs could provide the margin of survival.

Generation after generation in small towns in the South has earned a living thanks to the textile industry. Pat Murphy, a maintenance technician, was reported to have worked at Avondale Mills' plant in Sylacauga, Alabama for thirty-seven years. His mother was also said to have retired from the same plant after forty-four years. Mark Tapley, executive vice president of Avondale, has been with the company for thirty-six years. His family worked for Avondale, too. The list is inexhaustible.

But all these families and the many more in Sylacauga and neighboring communities who depend almost exclusively on the $34 million worth of economic activity injected by the 1,253 workers employed by Avondale and expenditures by the company are under threat. The economic imperatives of the industry threaten Avondale and Sylacauga as never before.

However, assuming an average benefit package of $7500 per employee, the almost $9.5 million total benefit cost for the 1,253 Avondale employees represents one of the cost disadvantages of doing business in Sylacauga, as opposed to being in China. For Sylacauga, adding this amount to Avondale's bottom line could be the difference between a thriving community or one that meets the same devastating fate that befell South Carolina towns like Wave Shoals, Bishopville, Pendleton, Chester and Seneca, birthplace of Senator John Edwards, or Danville and Martinsville in Virginia, when the textile companies there were decimated. Higher wages for Avondale employees would be less problematic due to continuous productivity enhancement and exploitation of its point of sale proximity to full advantage.

The GEF could be the answer to the cries of workers in the remaining textile industry in Alabama towns like Alexander City, Fayette, Geneva, Jacksonville, Phenix City, Rock Mills, Scottsboro, Valley and Wetumpka; and in Virginia towns like Warsaw, Chatham, Hillsville, Stuart and Salem; and in Dalton, Georgia.

With the GEF place, the U.S. will finally be able to provide health care for all. All working people will also be provided life and disability insurance, and social security will be strengthened.

The GEF would not prevent firms from *voluntarily* topping up any available benefits. A healthy Microsoft or Johnson and Johnson or 3M may inject additional benefits, but they would be wise to do this based on profits and not as fixed cost. Employers and employees working together in a collaborative partnership can design incentive plans satisfactory to all parties.

Collaboration

All American based companies threatened by overseas competition should institute an internal collaborative process entailing constant dialogue on survival strategies. This may include employees accepting reduced wages in exchange for profit sharing, or it may involve reduced working hours. No one formula will fit all companies, but the process needs to begin in earnest to fish out productivity enhancing methodologies, best practices and bench marking. The new motto in every workplace should be "All for one and one for all." By collaborating and sharing, enthusiasm will bound in workplaces, giving companies a fighting chance against foreign competition.

Privacy Protection

India has become a hub for computer-maker Dell's software development and back-office work. To achieve this goal, Dell hired two thousand more people for a total of ten thousand, or eighteen percent of its global workforce. The road to India is being traveled at breakneck speed by other American marquee names such as IBM, Electronic Data Systems, Lehman Brothers, Merrill Lynch and Oracle. It will not come to a stop any time soon, because, like the Autobahn, there is no speed limit.

The sheer volume of programmers linked by expanding broadband has reduced the value of jobs such as bug fixing, updating of antiquated code and routine programming to the level of high school graduates, and not only have wages in the United States declined commensurably, but programmers are meeting the same unemployment fate that befell workers in the textile, steel, furniture and automobile industries.

This commodification of basic programming is illustrated by RentACoder, a website that matches employers with some thirty thousand programmers around the world. The website ranks the programmers, allowing employers to hire according to the complexity of the task at hand. According to BusinessWeek Online, the cost of hiring the eleventh ranked programmer on the whole site for a project was $250, compared to $2,000 for an American with comparable skills. This type of transaction, where input costs are essentially the same, is a true manifestation of the supply and demand principle underpinning the free enterprise system. It should not be sopped, because it cannot be stopped.

Neither should the exodus of advanced programming jobs be stopped, but it should give America cause for concern. Because, discouraged by diminishing prospects, many of America's brightest are shunning the software industry for other professions. The irony is that the same industry leaders whose slash and burn strategies are driving many Americans away from the software industry are the very same ones who complain about shortage of American software professionals.

Confirmation of American undergraduates shying away from computer degrees—a development that must bring smiles to many foreign faces—has been confirmed by several sources. According to the USA Today (May 23, 2005), "The number of undergraduates signing up for computer degrees is falling fast, making IBM and other tech companies worry that there soon won't be enough skilled U.S. workers to meet demand."

New enrollment in North American computer science and engineering programs "has dropped four years straight, falling 10 percent during the 2003-2004 school year from the year before," according to the Computing Research Association's trade group for computer professors.

In a conclusion that must surely bring shame to the same IBM complaining of possible U.S. shortages, Ohio State computer professor Stuart Zweben said, "Students are responding to the alarming rate that the job market has changed. They're also concerned about offshoring of jobs." Ironically, the shortage of expertise in the U.S. will then lead to even more offshoring.

Karen Nguyen, a senior majoring in computer science at the University of California Berkeley, reported in the same USA Today report that enrollment had dropped from 350 when she took her first class to less than 200 in her final year.

But IBM is apparently trying to stem the looming shortage of computer professionals in the U.S. by providing schools "millions of dollars in software" from the heavy profits it has garnered by shipping jobs overseas. In the same breadth, Buell Duncan, the IBM executive in charge of the program, sanguinely advised U.S. students they "need a marriage of technical skills and business acumen."

So U.S. students are being advised to forsake the tedious work of developing code, the foundation of technical development, and focus on the very high-end business sector. The fact IBM's program seemed centered around Wal-Mart, a major consumer of software products, showed the underlying objective was to increase sales, not U.S. expertise in a critical sector.

According to data supplied by the Computing Research Association, new enrollment in North American undergraduate computer science and engineering programs had dropped from 23,416 in 2000/2001 to 15,950 in 2004/2005, a decline of about 32 percent.

The evidence of America discouraging its young and obtaining its mortgage from overseas sources could not have been more transparent from the data showing the precipitous decline in computer science enrollment.

The palpable threat to America's economy is the growing possibility of loss of leadership in this critical industry, with the possibility that the Netscapes and Oracles of the future will be discovered overseas with the help of some Americans. The ultimate insult is that some of America's business leaders are now using the global Internet infrastructure built by American taxpayers to indirectly harm America's economic interests.

So while some of America's technology leaders proclaim loudly that they are compelled to ship American jobs overseas, the government of the United States must be compelled to do what it has to do.

The Internet evolved out of a requirement by the United States military for an infrastructure capable of retaining enough functional capability to avenge an attack by the Soviet Union. Today, that capability risks being compromised as a result of sabotage of the trans-oceanic communication infrastructure by terrorists. Offshore outsourcing of government work, whether in whole or in part, has therefore evolved into a threat to the national security of the United States.

The United States should therefore award government related work only to companies with fail-safe software platforms. Suppliers of critical hardware to the U.S. military are currently forbidden from using foreign inputs. The same condition should be extended to suppliers of software systems to all branches of the United States government to ensure security of the United States is not compromised. Firms engaged in offshore outsourcing should be required to set up independent units, if they choose to do the government's business. The onus lies with these firms to prove the integrity of their operating systems is immune to sabotage by terrorists.

In an article to Infosecwriters, Melanie Goodman of Sbcglobal warned of how loss of privacy, sabotage and blackmail arising from the current offshore outsourcing craze threaten Homeland Security: "When companies outsource data and processes to foreign lands that have little or no privacy laws, individual American rights to privacy are compromised. Most importantly, when design, maintenance and/or development of American infrastructure is outsourced abroad, there is a resulting exposure of sensitive and critical information that puts American Homeland Security at risk."

American companies are forwarding medical records, financial information and credit card transactions by the millions to overseas destinations without protection or privacy and without the consent of their customers. It is not inconceivable for a foreign individual to profile a customer and use loopholes in financial or medical records for blackmail.

David Lazarus in an article to the San Francisco Chronicle reiterated a case of extortion stemming from data sent overseas. A transcriber was apparently paid hundreds of dollars after threatening to post medical records of several patients' records on the Internet if not paid an amount she claimed was owed to her. Potential escalation of such a threat in the hands of hostile forces has not given practitioners of offshore outsourcing any cause for concern.

In the face of blatant disregard for privacy and confidentiality by companies engaged in offshore outsourcing and the threat this poses to Homeland Security, the Government of the United States should take the next logical step and ban the transmission of financial, medical, credit card transactions and other confidential information to offshore locations.

It is absolutely inconceivable that countries like Japan, Germany, France, or indeed even receiving countries like China and India, that place a premium on privacy, would ever permit confidential information of their citizens to be flung around like toilet paper in cyberspace, risking the possibility of interception by hostile forces.

The freedom of companies engaged in offshore outsourcing to conduct their business does not supersede the privacy of individuals, and the practice of sending private medical and financial records to vulnerable countries must be halted.

15

PRIVATE HEALTH CARE FOR ALL AMERICANS

For those with gold-plated health care packages, the United States does indeed have the best health care system in the world. For the 41 million or so Americans without health insurance and the millions more shouldering increasing cost burdens passed on by their employers, this is a myth. That it is the most overpriced health care system in the world is indisputable, but being the most expensive does not make it the best. That it is the most complicated health care delivery system is also not in doubt, but this does not make it efficient. On the contrary, the prodigious number of players, each with a requirement to be kept in the loop, makes the U.S. health system the most inefficient in the world by far.

The United States is the only economically advanced country that does not guarantee affordable health care for all its citizens. The consequences of this lack of universality includes poor preventative medical care, leading to more costly late-term intervention as patients are thrust into emergency rooms. The fact babies born in the United States are twice as likely to die during the first year of life than in 41 other countries is also a direct result of a restrictive health care system.

Like many parts of the economic infrastructure relating to competitiveness, leaving the health care system on its current path is a recipe for disaster. Providing portable and affordable health care for all citizens should be medical and economic imperatives to be implemented in the near term.

Providing health care for all citizens while putting a brake on exploding health care costs could be positive unintended consequences of consolidating collection of health care revenue through the Globalization Equalization Factor. But instead of a "socialist" system—the weapon effectively used to frighten the majority of the populace with excellent health care coverage—the health care needs of a community could be met through the private sector by competitive bidding.

There are 3,143 counties, parishes or independent cities in the U.S. Working hand in hand with states, employers, health maintenance organizations, health care providers and other stakeholders, a health care package, similar to that enjoyed by federal employees, could be prescribed for every citizen in a county. The total package for each unit would be submitted for competitive bidding by private medical organizations. Restrictions would be placed on the number of units awarded to each organization to ensure prices are not inflated by lack of competition.

The package would be designed to take into account statistical variation and population mobility for each county or parish, information currently in databases at the Census Bureau and the Internal Revenue Service.

Medicare, Medicaid, the Drug Prescription Program and their costly supporting bureaucracies would be folded, leading to significant savings for the health care system.

This program to be known as Universally Funded and Applied Health Plan (UFAAHP) will lead to the creation of a comprehensive and portable health care system for all citizens, with significant savings generated through economies of scale.

Additional savings will be generated with the elimination of the millions of corporate, organizational and individual interactions with the medical system. Reducing the number of players interacting with the health system automatically cuts down the mountain of paper work responsible for an estimated expenditure of $10 per transaction or $250 billion in total.

Americans by a wide margin support affordable health care for all citizens, and centralized collection of revenue affords an opportunity to make this a reality. The tottering health care system, projected to cost $1.9 trillion in 2005, will be salvaged.

"To be without health insurance in this country means to be without access to medical care. But health is not a luxury, nor should it be the sole possession of a privileged few. All are created b'tselem elohim—in the image of God—and this makes each human life as precious as the next. By 'pricing out' a portion of this country's population from health care coverage, we mock the image of God and destroy the vessels of God's work." Rabbi Alexander Schindler, Past President, American Hebrew Congregations [1992].

16

U.S. ENERGY INDEPENDENCE

In 1927 South Africa acknowledged its lack of crude oil reserves had turned into a vulnerability requiring closure. Initially, the impetus was pressure from foreign exchange markets, but the motivation turned to threat of sanctions as apartheid took root in the country.

Coal, which the country had in abundance, offered the only possibility of energy independence. But the technological and commercial challenges were daunting, since viability of the technology had not been established. Seeing no other alternatives on the horizon, South Africa decided to press ahead nonetheless, with parliament tabling a White Paper to investigate the establishment of an oil-from-coal industry.

The basic principle of extracting oil from coal is rather simple. Coal is subjected to a high enough temperature under controlled conditions to expel entrapped hydrocarbons, which are then cooled and separated into constituent products. But the complexity of the conversion process belies simplicity of the concept.

First, the hydrocarbons, if left untamed, escape with enough pressure to create several Hiroshimas. Second, the catalysts required for the conversion process were available only in experimental quantities. Third, scale up of the conversion technology known as Fischer-Tropsch had never been attempted, so its efficiency was not predictable. Fourth was the complicated task of stripping the hydrocarbons of the many byproducts initially thought to be superfluous. Many were a country that yielded to the frustrations of failure, but South Africa pressed on, necessity being the mother of invention.

The first eight drums of the catalyst creosote that were ordered spurred several innovations, culminating in the formation of the South African Coal Oil and Gas Corporation, SASOL, in 1950. Though not profitable from the beginning, the alternative, importing oil, was less desirable. But the breakthroughs were stupendous, including the first automotive fuel in 1955 and conversion of low-grade coal into synthetic fuels and chemicals.

With rising oil prices, SASOL's technology has become highly profitable. The company produces polymers, solvents, olefins and surfactants and their intermediates, waxes, phenolics and nitrogenous products for domestic consumption and export to over 100 countries.

With close to $9 billion in sales and a whole town—SASOLBURG—named after it, SASOL's international crowning glory came when it was listed on the New York Stock Exchange on April 9, 2003 under the symbol SOL.

Reeling forward to 2005 finds the United States of America with one quarter of the entire world's known coal deposits. Recoverable coal in the U.S. has the energy equivalent of about one trillion barrels of crude oil—comparable to all the world's known oil reserves. At today's consumption rates, the U.S. coal reserves could last at least 250 years.

During the past decade, coal prices at electric power plants actually declined about 18 percent, while crude oil and natural gas prices have more than doubled. And coal does not have to cross the Atlantic Ocean, and neither is it vulnerable to international politics.

And while environmental issues still remain, the world has made great strides with desulphurization and denitrification technologies to remove sulfur dioxide and nitrogen-based gases, the former a major contributor to acid rain and the latter a major contributor to global warming. Particulate control technologies are capable of generating emissions below one part in a thousand.

Thanks to SASOL, the technologies required to extract oil from coal are mature. Thanks to the world, most of the technologies required to remove sulfur dioxide, nitrogen oxides, mercury, chlorides and heavy metals are in play.

The now defunct New Yorker turned Caribbean astrologer notwithstanding, there is no crystal ball to predict the future. But history, the greatest teacher available, comes the closest. And when it comes to economic predictions, the factors that require relational historical analysis are money, supply and demand.

Before the onset of the Great Depression, the skyrocketing stock market had created a great deal of paper money, which accelerated demand and caused supply to respond. But the paper money vanished when the high value of the stock market was found to have been constructed on bubbles, not solid concrete. Investors on margin calls and many consumers whose purchases were built on credit were all caught with their pants down, causing demand to collapse. The slowdown mushroomed into a full-blown crisis when manufacturers slashed production (supply)—and therefore employment—in response.

From the end of the Second World War till the mid-70s, the U.S. economy enjoyed sustained growth as more goods were supplied in response to demand created by the real money of rising wages and two-parent working families. In other words, absence of bubbles—defined also as harmony between real money, demand and supply—caused solid growth.

The recession of the seventies was due to demand shortfall precipitated by higher oil prices, while the recession of the late eighties was engineered by over-supply of goods caused by a combination of incompetence and foreign competition.

In the early 90s, information technology assets laid a new foundation for harmonious growth by providing solid money in the form of rising employment and higher wages. Demand rose in response and supply answered.

Then bubble money proliferated as the dotcoms arrived, leading to artificial demand and supply. Economic diversity saved the U.S. from a full-blown depression when the bubble money vanished in 2001. Still, the adjustment was painful, exacerbated by a new phenomenon called offshore outsourcing.

Massive government spending, tax cuts and, most of all, housing refinancing combined to bail the U.S. out of the recession of 2001. But the recovery is stuffed with several anomalies. First, just as not even Keynes meant for public stimulus to be permanent, so it is that monetary policy cannot forever be the engine that drives the U.S. economy. And it will not, because at some point growing internal demand and external imperatives (current account deficits) will cause the cost of money (interest rate) to rise enough to negatively affect growth. This is where the normal expectation is that another mechanism—new technology—either takes over or supplements the power of monetary policy. There is no such technology on the horizon, and monetary policy stands unsustainably alone. Second, because of a rather large trade deficit, the effect of any fiscal stimulus is not nearly as positive as it could be. This creates the uncomfortable scenario of keeping stimulus longer than necessary. Third, the need to retain the power of monetary policy feeds through the economic platform in the form of higher demand, which then leads to "frothy" irrational exuberance. Many indicators point to the emergence—as Paul Krugman of the New York Times pointed out—of "the final, feverish stages of a speculative bubble." And history teaches that bubbles, being as fragile as they are, always burst with deleterious consequences.

To relieve the pressure on monetary policy, a new source of economic power would have to be unearthed. But if this power reduced the current account deficit as well, then an added benefit would be to diminish, or perhaps even banish, the possibility of a disruptive increase in interest rate.

In 2004 U.S. daily imports of crude oil averaged 11.8 million barrels. At an average price of $50 per barrel, the bill for U.S. oil imports would be about $215 billion, or about a third of current U.S. trade deficit.

Therefore, if it wanted to, the U.S. could achieve energy independence by spending $215 billion to extract oil from U.S. coal. The economic activities this would engender would create millions of U.S. jobs in mining, engineering, machinery, transportation and services. Extracting oil from U.S. coal will relieve the pressure on monetary policy to stimulate the economy and reduce the U.S. current account deficit, simultaneously. The stipulation for this enterprise would be the imposition of the most stringent air cleaning regulations anywhere, thereby forcing the industry to accelerate development of even more efficient remediation technologies. More efficient and cost effective remediation technologies would create their own employment streams.

Evidence is also gathering that a crude oil supply crunch is on the horizon. According to a report by The Associated Press, some observers "predict that this year, maybe next—almost certainly by the end of the decade—the world's oil production, having grown exuberantly for more than a century, will peak and begin to decline."

Princeton University geologist Kenneth S. Deffeyes is predicting "a permanent state of oil shortage," which will cause the price of oil to increase drastically. Inflation, unemployment and economic instability are predicted for major oil-consuming countries.

These predictions may be far-fetched, but with demand for oil by China and other developing countries predicted to increase dramatically in coming years, the old adage prevention is better than cure could not be more applicable to the United States.

Therefore, considering the needs of the U.S. economy and available natural resources, there has never been a more opportune time to issue a clarion call to action with the following speech from the Oval Office:

"My fellow Americans. I come to you today with two issues of critical importance to our country. In the past, these would have been tackled individually, but by a stroke of good fortune, history has placed in our hands the capability, if we do things right, to solve both issues, simultaneously."

"The first issue is our vulnerability to imports of crude oil, especially from the volatile Middle East. Our dependence on crude oil from this part of the world has exposed our country to manipulation, which culminated in the oil embargo of 1973. Our need to protect crude oil from the Middle East means we have to budget more for security operations in that part of the world. And while the attack of September 11, 2001 was primarily because we are freedom's defender, our presence in the region because of crude oil also fuelled the flames of hatred. We have a need, indeed an urgent obligation, to cut our dependence on crude oil imports, especially from the Middle East.

"As I travel this great country of ours, I sense wariness, concern and frustration, especially among our young people. There is concern about the manufacturing jobs leaving this land for other lands. There is concern about computer programming, data processing, accounting and other jobs leaving for other lands because of the Internet we funded and developed. So the second issue is about jobs that will be kept in the United States; good paying jobs that cannot be outsourced. Those concerns of yours are also my concerns. And I am here today to announce that we are going to do something about those concerns."

"One resource we have in abundance is coal. It provided warmth for our Indian forefathers who first settled this land. It warmed our mothers as they gave birth to succeeding generations. It powered our industries, placing us at the forefront of the Industrial Revolution. From the home state of Benjamin Franklin through the Appalachians and going west across the heartland, then through my home state of Texas and into the mountains of Utah and Montana, the United States has coal in abundance. The energy content of our recoverable coal is equal to all the known crude oil reserves in the world. This coal belongs to the people of the United States. It is God's gift to our people, and we intend to use it."

"And because of the coal we have in abundance and because of clean coal technologies, most of which were developed right here in these United States, I am announcing today our goal of achieving complete energy independence before the middle of the next decade. By this I mean we will not import a single drop of oil from the Middle East by the year 2015."

"I have set up a committee comprised of the best minds our country has to offer in coal production, environmental technologies, finance and non governmental organizations. The last group will act as our conscience to ensure that we spare no expense to develop and install the best environmental technologies within our capabilities. The collaborative group will set new emission standards for particulates, acid rain and greenhouse gases. If we do it right, and we will, new technologies will emerge for export to the rest of the world.

"Economic history shows that around projects of such magnitude are millions of jobs created. And these are jobs in mining, engineering, transportation and computer programming that will stay in these United States, because we will make it a requirement that those who participate in this mammoth endeavor keep the jobs generated in these United States. Those who cannot keep this promise will not be allowed to participate."

"But coal is only the beginning of this great endeavor. We will secure our energy independence initially with coal because of its abundance and because, for the most part, we have technologies to jump-start this great enterprise. But this effort will also incorporate research and development into alternative energy sources such as wind and solar. We will not let these energy sources perish on the vineyard."

"And so my fellow Americans, I am challenging all of us to pull together to convert this glorious opportunity presented to us into reality. America works best when we pull together and I am asking all of us to pull together."

"It is not going to be easy, but if it was easy it would have been accomplished a long time ago. But we shall not and we will not let this opportunity pass because it is not going to be easy. The generations that fought for our independence, and conquered space, and helped bring down the Berlin Wall did not shirk their duties because those were not easy tasks. They persevered because it was on their shoulders that responsibility had been entrusted. It is our time and our turn to come to bat, so we accept this responsibility. And we will work together to ensure not just energy independence for ourselves, but we will also expand the pool of energy available to other countries whose needs are growing by the day."

"So my fellow Americans. I inform you and the world today that this generation of Americans has accepted the baton of responsibility to achieve energy independence for the United States. It is one we will fight for, and it is one we intend to win. God Bless You and God Bless America."

17

CONTAINER INSPECTION STRATEGY

In an August 26, 2004 presentation before the center for Strategic for Strategic and International Studies, US Customs Commissioner Robert Bonner outlined a strategy by the Bush administration to secure containers entering the United States. This initiative was part of the government's heightened security awareness in the wake of the attacks of September 11, 2001.

The "Container Security Initiative" was described as a "revolutionary initiative" and "pre-emptive" strike against the smuggling of a weapon of mass destruction in one of the approximately six million containers entering US ports annually. Mr. Bonner described the detonation of such a device in a US port facility as "truly the sum of all fears," and an event that would not only extract a devastating human toll, but could potentially cripple the global economy.

Former United States Senator from Georgia Sam Nunn has formed Last Best Chance (www.lastbestchance.org), an organization dedicated to highlighting the threat posed by acquisition of nuclear weapons by terrorists. The likeliest source for these weapons is the still unsecured enriched uranium and plutonium depots in Russia, with smuggling in containers being the likeliest entry strategy.

The CSI incorporates the use of x-ray and gamma ray technology to quickly pre-screen high-risk containers, and promotes the use of more secure containers.

The enhanced port security initiatives are reflected in the non-defense budget of the Department of Homeland Security, which has seen a steep increase from $10 billion in 2001 to a proposed $30 billion in 2005. So, ironically, US citizens, who were victims of the dastardly attacks of September 11, 2001, are being asked to shoulder the added burden of trying to stop terrorists from sneaking weapons of mass destruction into containers entering the U.S.

Again, the free ride accorded goods entering the United States from foreign countries must be halted. A ***Port Inspection Factor (PIF)*** should be levied on all goods entering the United States to capture the increase in port inspection expenditure caused by implementation of the CSI, such as the $20 billion in 2005. The PSI should be made retroactive to capture the total increase adjusted for inflation since 2001, an amount of about $50 billion. In addition, all exporters to the US should pay the necessary funds to the United States Treasury before goods depart from port of origin for the U.S.

With budgetary concerns now accounted for by the PIF, the United States should then investigate and implement the most rigorous inspection of each and every container entering the United States by the fastest means possible. Specially built inspection stations should be incorporated at all points of entry and detection systems for not just nuclear weapons, but biological and chemical weapons installed as well.

It is patently unfair to ask victimized American citizens to shoulder the added cost emanating from an attack on U.S. soil by foreigners. Those who enjoy the privilege of shipping goods into the United States, not U.S. citizens, should pay to have their goods inspected to minimize the risk of an attack on U.S. soil.

18

CONCLUSION

The American people sense something is not quite right with their country. For at a time when real estate has never been a more valuable commodity and unemployment has fallen to 5.2 percent and inflation is still at historic lows, instead of euphoria, 58 percent of Americans polled by The Gallup Organization between May 2-5, 2005 said they were dissatisfied with the state of the country. Only 38 percent were satisfied with the state of the U.S. Of the "bubbling" economic indices, only 31 percent rated the economy good to excellent, while a gaping 69 percent rated the economy fair to poor.

And part of the reason for this malaise is that Americans are seeing historical places of employment close, with the jobs transferred overseas. They are witnessing their neighbors lamenting professional jobs disappearing via the Internet and their children complaining that very few jobs seem immune to offshore outsourcing. Americans are seeing hope itself dissipate.

Hope, AR, America. A kid was born there not too long ago. Despite pain and confusion in his adolescence, he never lost that after which the town of his birth was named. He carried it with him everywhere he went, and it sustained him and nourished him. He carried it with him when he went to meet his hero, President John F. Kennedy, in the White House. Why? Because he could see the possibilities, that doors of opportunity would open if he worked hard. And William Jefferson Clinton carried that hope all the way to the White House and shared that hope with his fellow Americans. When he replied, "I feel your pain," to the woman who raised the cost of living question at the town hall meeting, he meant it from his bones. And his unspoken message was, "I was in your shoes at one time and we will work together to get you out of that pain, because I did it."

Hope has always said to Americans that tomorrow will be better than today. Always, until now. For if you are a computer programmer or engineer or accountant or manager in a firm, some of the most cherished professions that carried many an American into the solid middle class, you are filled with fear, instead of hope, for your job may disappear overnight. If you are a small or medium sized entrepreneur, the big company you serviced from the beginning of your existence may call you up in the middle of the night to inform you they will no longer buy from you, they are buying from China because your price is too high. And these are the stories unfolding in community after community across the United States. Fear, not hope, is now ingrained in many an American.

But even as millions of manufacturing and information technology jobs are obliterated in the U.S., proponents of offshore outsourcing continue to stick to their blithe "Don't worry, be happy" attitude. Like an ostrich with its head buried firmly in sand, apologists remain unruffled even as food service jobs proliferate while high technology jobs remain anemic. Neither exploding current account deficits nor contraction of textile, computer manufacturing and electronics industries gives cause for concern. They remain sanguine even as a precipitous decline in enrollment in undergraduate computer science and engineering programs has been confirmed. Wholesale transfer of U.S. citizens' private and confidential medical records, financial information and credit card records to vulnerable overseas locations—information not available even to other Americans—is pushed under the rug. Potential loss of the very essence of software development—source code—to future competitors in overseas locations is treated with nonchalance.

Apologists quote the father of comparative advantage David Ricardo ad nausea to back up their support for offshore outsourcing even as he never had to contend with such steep labor cost differentials as confront the U.S. today. Others keep watch, waiting for Adam Smith's invisible hand to lift the U.S. out of a hitherto unfathomable trade deficit quagmire. These are the Hooverites who preached before and during the Great Depression that free market forces would fix the economic sinkhole engulfing the U.S. And just as another president ignored the dogmatists, the United States will do well to ignore apologists and confront reality.

Reality includes American students deserting careers in software development as they watch jobs move to other countries at $10,000 a year, thereby creating a dearth of American expertise in the future. Reality includes the capacity to understand that transferring resources to the smart people on the other side for product development at the expense of smart people in the U.S. will lead to more Kenneth Thompsons, Dennis Ritchies, Paul Barans, Lawrence Roberts—some of the Americans responsible for developing the Internet—there rather than in one's own country. Reality includes the potential for the massive amounts of confidential information going overseas being hijacked—as happened in one reported instance to the University of California at San Francisco—and held for ransom. Reality includes source code being stolen—as happened to Solidworks Plus' 3-D computer-aided package—and offered to the highest bidder. Reality includes America waking up to discover—as nearly happened to the rare-earths magnets used in the construction of "smart" bombs—that national security has been compromised because manufacture of critical weapons' components has been transferred to hostile forces. Reality includes thinking about the future.

The future is not next quarter, not next year, perhaps not even two years; the future starts at least five years from now. By then the American foundation would have been weakened, making the country vulnerable to severe damage from even the mildest of tremors. The people perpetrating this act on their fellow citizens would be retiring in droves, heaping the consequences on succeeding generations.

The IEEE-USA has counseled that the U.S. must "develop a coordinated national strategy to maintain U.S. technological leadership and promote job growth." Otherwise, it warned, "It's going to be difficult to remain technologically competitive" if offshoring of innovators continues at rates currently projected.

The peoples receiving America's largesse are ancient, intelligent and very patient. When they assume control of critical production processes, the price of their labor will not be as it is today. But it will be too late by then for America: the chicken would have already flown the coop.

It may not be too late, however, if actions are taken now. Concerned for the future of the state, the Bay Area Economic Forum, a truly collaborative group comprising every stakeholder, commissioned a study to elicit proposals to save the 1.0 million manufacturing jobs in California at risk of being moved to another state or country. The study recommended unshackling manufacturing in California—and by extension the United States—from oppressive costs and regulations to allow proximity to sale advantage to potentially overcome disadvantage of higher wages. The study made a convincing case that symbiotic relationship between supplier and customer when both are safely ensconced on these United States could trump disadvantage of higher wages. One of their recommendations was reduction of input costs.

The **Globalization Equalization Factor** is one method of reducing costs, but it is only one step in a process that should begin in earnest to also rid American business of many onerous regulations that have outlived their usefulness. The arching objective is to reduce capital risk in order to energize American based business and make it as competitive as possible.

An entrepreneur is more likely to start a business and hire workers when capital risk has been reduced to a minimum by not having to bear the burdens of healthcare, unemployment insurance and pension benefits from the outset. That same entrepreneur will be less likely to bolt for a foreign land.

When everything humanely possible is done to unshackle American business, entrepreneurs and the American middle class will emerge winners. And the shrinkage of the American middle class will be prevented.

But time and tide wait for none. The midnight hour is approaching, and America needs to give manufacturers and service providers the tools to compete for a thousand business flowers to bloom on these shores and for many of America's companies overseas to begin the "Long March" home.

For in the end, the objective should be to restore hope again to where it began for many a person two and quarter centuries ago.

"You cannot escape the responsibility of tomorrow by evading it today." Abraham Lincoln

POSTSCRIPT A
SUMMARY OF AIR
CLEANING TECHNOLOGIES

Coal combustion technologies have to contend with removal of five groups of pollutants. These are:

1) Ash particles

2) Mercury, cadmium and reconstituted metals

3) Oxides of sulfur responsible for acid rain

4) Oxides of nitrogen responsible for acid rain and global warming (greenhouse gas)

5) Carbon dioxide, a greenhouse gas responsible for global warming

Environmental engineers have developed air-cleaning technologies capable of efficient removal of all of the above pollutants from flue gases. The key for all concerned is a mind-sight that says it is impossible to remove every pollutant, but it is possible to achieve levels that are not only tolerable but in some cases lower than those emitted by family cars.

1) Ash Particles

One of the most effective industrial processes for removing particles from gases is known as a baghouse, which is a glorified scale up of a vacuum cleaner. It contains a filter medium capable of withstanding high temperatures and chemicals in the flue gas. One filter medium pioneered by Gore-Tex—same company responsible for outerwear—has a membrane or a skin with very small openings. This filter is able to reduce the amount of particles emitted into the atmosphere to virtually negligible levels. It is a mature and cost effective technology that can make most neighbors forget they have a coal burning plant in their midst.

2) Mercury, Cadmium & Reconstituted Metals

Most of these are removable by the filter medium, but an additional insurance strategy is injection of carbon particles, which bind with these metals for removal. Alternatively, the gas is forced through a tank containing carbon particles.

3) Oxides of Sulfur

Left untreated, oxides of sulfur combine with moisture to form sulfuric acid gas, which falls back as acid rain to damage vegetation and other organic matter. Power plants use lime to neutralize oxides of sulfur. The amount of lime used depends on how much oxides of sulfur are produced. Handled properly, the byproduct of this treatment can be used for construction and other applications.

4) Oxides of Nitrogen

Oxides of nitrogen combine with moisture to form nitric acid gas, an acid rain gas. They are also responsible for global warming. Oxides of nitrogen are minimized by combination of temperature and the amount of oxygen used for burning. Then a special material—catalyst—is used to break down the oxides of nitrogen.

5) Carbon Dioxide

Carbon dioxide is a greenhouse gas responsible for global warming. Students from Clarkson University in Potsdam, NY have designed an efficient method for removing and storing carbon dioxide. The team used steel slag—a waste product from steel manufacturing—to extract carbon dioxide. In effect, one pollutant of relatively little value was put to good use for the removal of another pollutant. The byproducts were calcium carbonate (limestone) and hydrated slag, both of which can be sold for other applications.

POSTSCRIPT B
INDIA

India is the world's oldest continuous civilization dating back to the third millennium BC. A highly developed civilization has been found in the Western and northwestern part of India, with the latter surrounding the river "Sindhu" or Indus, and it is from this that the country derives its name.

When the ruins were discovered in the 1920s, the main characteristic of this civilization was found to be urbanization, with the Indian version far more sophisticated than that of Egypt, Mesopotamia or anywhere else in Western Asia. The degree of planning was astonishing. Each city was divided into administrative and residential areas, with straight streets at right angles, a grid system, drainage system with ceramic pipes, covered sewers, etc. The houses were built with burnt bricks, and a governing elite composed of merchants was very much in evidence.

The civilization flourished until it was abandoned in 2000 BC due to drought and the encroachment of the Thar Desert. The people resettled in the north and northeastern parts of the continent and left their beautiful cities in ruins.

The period between 1500 and 1000 BC, known as the Verdic Age, was documented in the Vedas, a collection of sacred hymns attributed to the Aryans, a fairer complexioned people who kept large herds of cattle. The Aryans used the ox to draw their ploughs for cultivation of the land. The caste system that was later to emerge in India was not in evidence then, because the word "Varna" was used in the Veda to describe both the fairer complexioned Aryans and the darker complexioned Dasa. As the new civilization grew larger, the Aryans migrated South in search of grazing land.

Evidence of the caste system or class system emerged during the Epic Age between 1000 BC and 600 BC. At the top of the caste system were the Brahmins, who were priests responsible for passing laws and setting an example of proper living. The Kshatriyas, who were warriors, followed them, then by the Vaisyas, the merchants, with the Shudras, also known as outcastes, at the bottom to perform menial tasks.

Foreigners began invasions of India during this period, with the Persian emperor Darius taking over Punjab in 516 BC, followed by the Bactrian Greeks, the Shakas, etc. The invasions opened India to trade with foreigners, with the Old Silk Route being the most famous.

The Turks invaded India between 1200 and 1206 AD. At one time their rule cut a large swath over India, but successive wars pushed them to the West, where they practiced their Muslim religion. The bitterness, which developed during this period, persists till today, and is the main source of conflict between India and Pakistan, the Muslim-dominated area carved into an independent country by the British in August 1947.

The country continued to evolve until a company by the name of British East India Company, apparently in search of spices, landed in India with its formation on December 31, 1600. The company established trading posts across the country, but its true purpose was revealed when it began engaging in battles with the locals and as spoils demanded payment of land revenues. Using a strategy of "divide and conquer," it courted favor with some locals while unleashing brutality on others. The indignities perpetrated by the company culminated in the Doctrine of Lapse, whereby the estate of a ruler who died without a natural heir passed to the control of the British. The exception was the presence of an adopted heir pre-approved by Britain. With approval hardly granted, most of India passed to the British.

The brutality of the company led to the mutiny of 1857, after which the British crown formally took control of India. A battle for self-determination was waged continuously from then on until a meek-looking lawyer from South Africa joined it in 1917.

Ghandi's peaceful disobedience against British rule was met by brutal repression, which infuriated the locals, drawing more of them to the protest movement. In 1930 Ghandi, searching for an issue to galvanize the locals, organized a march against the salt tax.

Indians used salt in great quantities to cook, feed their cattle, and as inputs for manufacturing of many products. Indians had been manufacturing salt from seawater since time immemorial. But to raise revenue and support industry in the motherland, Britain imposed heavy taxation on locally manufactured salt, shutting down the local industry and allowing salt to be imported from Liverpool. Any one caught with the tiniest amount of illegal local salt was subject to imprisonment and heavy fans, laws that were enforced rigorously. The burden of the salt tax fell on all Indians, but the poor suffered disproportionately.

On March 12, 1930, Ghandi launched the Dandi march on foot from Sabarmati Ashram to Dandi, a journey covering 225 miles, with seventy-eight associates. He and his associates picked up a handful of local salt from the seashore. The journey was joined in transit by wild enthusiasm from his fellow citizens and was followed by boycott of foreign goods and refusal to pay taxes. It was the beginning of the end of British rule, which came to a merciful end on August 15, 1947, Indian Independence Day.

The British had departed from India, but not before they left behind two invaluable assets, which in a cruel irony compensate for the brutality dished out during the years of occupation. The first is the English language, which became the lingua franca at educational institutions. The second is the finest educational system anywhere in the world. It is with these two assets that India is dominating the information technology industry these days.

India is a very poor country, the evidence of which pervades the entire country. From the airport in Bombay, weaving through the streets to the central business district, beggars are painfully obvious. And to the dismay of animal lovers everywhere, stray dogs are in abundance everywhere. The country that started off in the third millennium BC with its sewers covered has forgotten how to handle garbage, which decays and releases its offensive odor across the city. Auto-rickshaw, three-wheeled scooter, is the most efficient way, if one has a strong nerve, to navigate the traffic, which exists in name only. A distance of 10 miles takes 2 hours, if one is lucky. A country of one billion produced only $477 billion worth of goods in 2001. It is not a country for the faint of heart.

And yet using perfectly legal means in a free economy, India is inflicting pain on America, largely because of an educational system that plays no favorites. Wealth, race, gender, or ancestry will not get one into a top university. It is an educational system designed to systematically filter out the brightest in the land to the top universities in the country, where they are tortured some more until the very brightest equal to any in the entire world emerge with a diploma from one of the vaunted institutions, like the Indian Institute of Technology (IIT). It is a dispassionate, soulless, non-apologetic educational system superior even to that of its creators, who have abandoned some its elements..

Students are subjected to standardized tests from the very beginning, with strong emphasis on mathematics and science. Placement at top high schools is based on standardized tests, and the grades of all students accepted at IIT locations are published in the top newspapers. Students at the top institutions are awarded full scholarships: the message being it is not one's ability to pay that gains admission.

After India's independence in 1947, the leadership sought to build technical institutes of higher education accessible to all. The result was the Indian Institute of Technology (IIT), patterned after Massachusetts Institute of Technology. The first IIT was born in May 1950 in Kharagpur, West Bengal at the site of a former prison. Most students find the location apt; with the claim conditions are no better at IIT.

Four others were subsequently set up at Bombay (1958), Madras (1959), Kanpur (1960) and Delhi (1961). In 1995, a sixth campus was added at Guwahati, and the most recent, Roorkee University, was converted to IIT status in 2001. IIT offers undergraduate and postgraduate degrees in 25 different engineering, technology, and business disciplines.

Candidates for IIT spend two years preparing to write the national entrance examination in May. In 1998 100,000 students prepared intensely for the exams, but in the end only 2,500 were admitted. The meritocracy practiced by IIT, plus largely free tuition and board, means that students from all backgrounds congregate on the campuses. The interaction of students from all socio-economic backgrounds imbues the graduates with the ability to operate more effectively in the increasingly diversified workforces of today.

Once on campus the students are subjected to an even more rigorous academic schedule. To survive most routinely study until 3 a.m., or "mug" in IIT lingo, but even then high grades are difficult to come by. It is not uncommon for a professor to reserve A for the best student, B for the next, and the rest following in tow with C's and D's.

Textbooks are shared, enforcing the value of cooperation. Hands-on learning is an integral part of the curriculum, with students required to learn to make machine tools and operate rotation motors. At a faculty-student ratio of 1:6 or 1:8, the students are dotted on by world-class professors.

The hands-on curriculum pays off enormously. In 1968 a group of students was forced out of necessity to write an operating system for a Russian-built mainframe. When one of the students later studied at Carnegie Mellon University he became the star called upon to fix the Univac 1108 mainframe any time it developed problems.

Once the students receive their diplomas, they are ready to take on the world. Hundreds of these graduates enter the US every year, with their skills in high demand at universities and corporations alike. For example, a full 30% of the graduating class in 1998 went to the US. The impact of these students has been phenomenal.

The influx grew in the 1970s as graduates poured out of Stanford, MIT, Carnegie Mellon and other stand out institutions in the United States into research labs at IBM, Intel, Hewlett Packard and other leading information technology companies where they excelled. Corporations and US colleges valued these students so much they launched massive recruiting drives: it was not uncommon for students to receive multiple offers before graduation.

Many IIT graduates, given the freedom and seemingly unlimited resources in the US, became engines of invention. Vinod Khosla (IIT-Delhi, 1976) co-founded Sun Microsystems, Suhas Patil (IIT-Kharagur, 1965) founded chip designer Cirrus Logic, Umang Gupta (IIT-Kanpur, 1971) founded software developer Keynote Systems, Kanwal Rekhi (IIT-Bombay, 1967) founded board-maker Excelan, and many more. A study conducted of Silicon Valley in its hey day revealed that, of an estimated 2000 start ups by immigrants, forty percent were by Indians, and half of those were IIT graduates.

The IIT graduates are the superstars, but below them are many more thousands of computer science graduates pouring out of lesser-known universities, technical institutes and colleges thousands, their activities coordinated by a stand alone Ministry of Information Technology.

India produces 2 million software professionals a year, so it is likely that the employee answering the phone to respond to basic credit card inquiries from North America clients is eminently qualified to offer more valued services. An Indian call center company reported sixty percent of its employees were graduates, while the remaining forty percent were postgraduates.

POSTSCRIPT C
CHINA

China is the most populous country on earth, with 1.3 billion people, or one-fifth of all humans. China, like India, is an ancient land, tracing its origins as a discrete political and cultural unit as far back as the second millennium BC. Traditionally, the Chinese traced their history through many dynasties to a series of legendary rulers, like the Yellow Lord (Huang Di), who invented the key features of civilization—agriculture, the family, silk, boats, carts, bows and arrows, and the calendar. The last of these kings was Yu, who was succeeded by his son, thus establishing the principle of hereditary rule. The descendants of Yu created the Xia dynasty, which began in the second millennium BC and lasted for fourteen generations before declining and being replaced by the Shang dynasty.

The Bronze Age civilization emerged independently in Northern China between 2000 and 1600 BC. Coinciding with the Xia dynasty, this civilization was marked by writing, metalwork, domestication of horses, a class system, and a stable political and religious hierarchy.

The Bronze Age was advanced by the Shang Dynasty, which lasted until the end of the first millennium BC with central coordination of a large labor force to mine, refine, and transport copper, tin, and lead ores, as well as produce and transport of charcoal. Technically skilled artisans were required to make clay models, construct ceramic molds, and assemble and finish vessels, the largest which weighed as much as 1,800 pounds.

The writing system used by the Shang is the direct ancestor of the modern Chinese writing system, with symbols or characters for each word. This writing system evolved over time, but it never duplicated a phonetic system like the Roman alphabet, which uses symbols (letters) to represent specific sounds. Mastering the written language thus required learning to recognize and write several thousand characters, making literacy a highly specialized skill requiring many years to fully master.

A frontier state called Zhou defeated the Shang Dynasty in the eleventh century BC. The Zhou kings believed in providing sacrifices to their ancestors as well as Heaven (Tian). The Zhou's version of their history was described in one of the earliest transmitted texts. It assumed a close relationship between Heaven and the king, called the Son of Heaven, explaining that the king was given a mandate to rule only as long as he did so in the interest of the people.

Confucius, one of the most influential figures in world history, came of age during the latter half of the Zhou dynasty. A man who defined humility, Confucius thought of himself as a "transmitter and not an innovator," though he was very original, starting one of the greatest intellectual traditions of all time known in China as the "School of the Scholars."

During his time, Confucius stressed the "Book of Songs," anthology of poems he compiled from a variety of sources. He encouraged his students to dig deeply into the poems in order to unearth their philosophical and ethical underpinnings. The "Book of Songs" and the "Book of Documents" are part of the group of texts from China known collectively as the Five Classics, or Confucian Classics. These texts, which cement China's place as the home of the world's longest continuous tradition of writing, are revered in China and elsewhere as guides to moral action and the correct ordering of human society.

Confucius shared a belief, common in his time, that China had in the past enjoyed almost utopian periods of peace and prosperity under the rule of wise kings, and that kings derived their power not from military power but by being virtuous. This virtue or charisma came from being a good person, which in turn engendered loyalty from others.

Confucius emphasized three key principles in his teachings. The first translated as proprietary, good manners, politeness, ceremony and worship. Part of this principle contained filial piety to "Honor one's parents." Confucius believed family was central to the survival of society.

And Jesus said: "So in everything, do to others what you would have them to you, for this sums up the Law and the Prophets." Matthew 7:12. But hundreds of years before Jesus instructed his disciples to follow the Golden Rule, Confucius had instructed his disciples in his second principle thus: "Do not do to others what you would not like them to do to you." It is the expression of altruism, righteousness and loyalty.

The third principle of Confucius emphasized the idea of a true gentleman. The gentleman displays self-respect, sincerity, persistence, and benevolence. His relationships are described as loyalty of a son, kindness of a father, loyalty and faithfulness of an official, and faithfulness and tactfulness of a friend.

A critical difference between Christianity and Confucianism is that the former places primary focus on God, while the latter is derived from the inherent goodness of the being. But the two faiths, for Confucianism did become a religion, share identical principles and virtues.

The teachings of Confucius are the foundation on which cultures in China, Japan, Korea, Vietnam, Singapore, Malaysia, Indonesia and Thailand are built.

Several other dynasties headed by monarchs and commoners alike succeeded the Zhou dynasty. So it remained until unification was achieved through force of arms in the third century BC. From then until modern times, centralized governments ruled by monarchs became the norm. Every time disorder erupted, a military strongman emerged to regain control and impose centralized rule.

The period from the first century AD to the eighth century AD was marked by periods of identity crisis, with the teachings of Confucius banned and restored several times. Buddhism arrived in China in the first century AD as the religion of merchants from Central Asia. For the next three centuries, the teachings of the Indian prince Siddhartha (Buddha) flourished in China. Kumarajiva, a Buddhist monk from India, arrived to direct thousands of Chinese monks in the translation of Buddhist texts, resulting in the building of over six thousand temples and training of over 77,000 monks and nuns in the north. The south witnessed the building of close to three thousand temples and training of over 82,000 clerics.

The influence of Buddhism in China was mitigated, however, by contradictions with Confucianism and other established Chinese thoughts. For example the Chinese found monks' vow of celibacy and jettisoning of surnames to be diametrically opposite to the traditional importance of family lines.

So Emperor Taizu had no difficulty asserting the supremacy of Confucianism when he founded the Song Dynasty in 960. The Song Dynasty (960—1279) ushered in a period of immense economic and intellectual growth in China. A tight coterie of highly educated bureaucrats ruled over a population of about 100 million. Those who aspired to hold office pursued years of intensive Confucian study, a practice retained well into the twentieth century.

The strength of the Song Dynasty was based on the power of the economy, allowing defenses to be constructed against foreign enemies. The period also benefited from a highly developed iron and steel industry and the invention of gunpowder, which was used for bombs and explosive projectiles. Rice production improved dramatically with the introduction of early ripening rice, which made it possible for farmers to harvest two crops annually. Cotton cultivation spread during the 12th century, consumption of tea increased in China and abroad, and ceramic technology became the most advanced in the world.

The earliest known printed text was a Buddhist religious book known as *Jin-gangjin (Diamond Sutra)*, which dates from 868 AD. But it was during the Song dynasty that printing took off, allowing the government to control the distribution of literature and official proclamations. The spread of printing had a profound effect on Chinese culture, as Confucian texts, drama, and laws guiding commercial activities became widely available.

China experienced unprecedented growth in commerce, arts and science, and technology during the Song dynasty, with commercial success evidenced in the prosperity of its several great cities, many of which had populations exceeding one million inhabitants.

The Song dynasty came to an end when the Mongols conquered China. The Mongols were nomadic tribes in the area of modern Mongolia who created a powerful empire when Genghis Khan was declared ruler in 1206. He embarked on wars of conquest and conquered China and much of central and west Asia within seventy years. His successful conquests led to the creation of the largest empire in the world at the time.

The Mongols visited great destruction on settled populations, confiscated Chinese land and subjected the locals to harsh taxation. Incompetents from Persia and even Russia replaced the efficient administration cultivated during the Song dynasty. With confusion and anarchy in vogue, the progress made in China during the Song dynasty was reversed.

The Mongols were overthrown by forces led by Chu Yuan-chang, an illiterate peasant who founded the Ming dynasty (1368—1644). His humble roots motivated him to balance the scholarly with the military so neither would dominate the government.

But the scholars went on to eventual domination, so that groundbreaking expeditions into the Indian Ocean involving heavily armed fleets were scrapped and all the records destroyed. Some of the ships in the expeditions were more than 400 feet long, with nine masts (the *baochuan*, "treasure ships"). The scholars, frowning on contacts with "barbarians," made it a capital offense to build anything larger than a two-masted ship, thereby crippling curtailing further expeditions. The world is left to wonder history's journey had Vasco da Gama, the famed Portuguese explorer, been confronted by the technologically advanced Chinese naval presence when he arrived in the Indian Ocean in 1498, just 65 years after the Chinese expeditions were terminated.

The Ming dynasty saw the building of the Great Wall of China, remains of which are visited often near Beijing, along the northern border in the 15th and 16th centuries to keep out the Mongols. The impressive stone and earthen fortifications of this era, estimated conservatively at 1,500 miles long, differs from the semi-legendary wall built along a different northern border in the 3rd century BC. The ancient structure of the 3rd structure has disappeared completely.

The Ming were not welcoming of foreigners, so unauthorized dealings with outsiders was prohibited. This policy could not be enforced, and many Chinese collaborated with foreigners in widespread smuggling. The riches of the Chinese reached the Portuguese who had established a beachhead at the port city of Malacca (now Melaka) on the Malay Peninsula. By 1557, they had taken control of Macao, a small trading station on China's coast. Representatives of the Dutch East India Company, unable to capture Macao from the Portuguese, took control of coastal Taiwan in 1624.

Unfortunately for the Ming scholars, their abhorrence of the military left the country woefully unprepared when peasants, chaffing under the autocratic rule of the scholars, rebelled. The Manchus called in to assist in putting down the rebellion ended up taking control of China. So in the end, the last dynasty in China, the Qing (1644—1911), was not Chinese at all.

As contacts with foreigners increased, the British attempt to pay for huge quantities of imported tea by barter proved futile, and they were forced to pay with silver. Not only that, but limited access prevented expansion of Sino-British trade, leaving the balance of trade in favor of the Chinese.

British merchants reversed the balance of trade by introducing Indian opium during the 1780s. The opium became popular with a large segment of the population, causing addiction and social disorder and tipping the balance of trade in favor of the British. The initial Chinese attempt to stop the opium trade was rebuffed by the militarily superior British during the first Opium War of 1839 to 1842. The British extracted huge commercial and territorial advantages when the Chinese signed the Treaty of Nanjing at gunpoint in 1842. The British obtained the rights to the Chinese island of Hong Kong, unlimited access to the ports of Shanghai, Guangzhou and others, and residence for foreigners answerable only to British laws.

The Treaty of Tianjin, concluded after the Second Opium War (1856—1860), ratified the total humiliation of the Chinese. Britain, joined by France, Russia, Japan and the United States, imposed its own laws, including prevention of the Chinese from setting tariffs to protect its industries. The result was that imported goods flooded into China to compete against locally manufactured products, thereby destroying a wide range of industries. The foreigners came and went as they pleased, with Shanghai in particular assuming an international identity.

The Chinese believe the roots of the humiliation suffered by the enactment of the two treaties, also known as the unequal treaties, were planted during the Ming dynasty when supremacy of the scholars caused the military to be virtually disarmed. Had the military not been disarmed, the Chinese believe subsequent defeats at the hands of the British (Opium Wars) and the Japanese (Sino-Japanese Wars) would have been averted. The people who invented gunpowder were vanquished with their own ingenuity.

History books in China are filled with pictures of rampaging Japanese, burning and looting in the city of Nanjing in 1938, with the refrain "Never Again" burned into the minds of all Chinese. Never again will they disarm to the point of being pummeled by another foreign power.

Chinese Nationalists eventually overthrew the weakened Qing dynasty in 1911. The Communists, led by Mao Zedong, in turn defeated the Nationalists, leading to proclamation of the People's Republic of China (PRC) in the capital city of Beijing on October 1, 1949. The Nationalists, Kuomintang, fled to the island province of Taiwan, where it established a pro-western capitalist government.

The new Communist government allied itself with countries of the emerging Soviet bloc, throwing a chill on relations with the United States. The chill thawed when the American and Chinese table tennis teams exchanged visits, leading after months of "Ping-Pong" diplomacy to President Nixon's visit to China in February 1972. That visit, one of the most epochal events in world history, led to the rapprochement manifested in the establishment of commercial relations between China and the United States.

Operating a pseudo market based economy since 1980, the Chinese economy grew at an annual rate of 10.2 percent in the 1980s and by 9.6 percent annually between 1990 and 2003, among the highest in the world. In 2004 China's gross domestic product was $1.65 trillion, making it the seventh largest economy in the world; but it remains relatively poor due to its large population.

INDEX

www.nsf.gov/statistics

http://www.cra.org/info/education/us/women

www.cra.org/info/taulbee/bachelors

http://www.thocp.net/companies/microsoft/microsoft-company.com

http://www.thocp.net/companies/microsoft/microsoft_company_part2

www.city.pittsburgh.pa.u

www.pghhistory.org

www.skidmore.edu/-bturner/history

http://www.heinz.com/jsp/history.jsp

http://www.hfp.heinz.org/aboutus/heinzhistory

www.carnegie.org/sub/about/biography

http://encarta.msn.com/encyclopedia_761558094/Carnegie_Andrew

http://encarta.msn.com/encyclopedia_761567245/Ford_Henry

http://www.britannica.com/eb/articletocId=9051466

http://inventors.about.com/library/weekly/aa041897

http://encarta.msn.com/article=AfricanAmericanInventors

http://www.galegroup.com/free_resources/bhm/bio/carver_g

http://encarta.msn.com/encyclopedia_761584403/Great_Depression

http://www.pbs.org/wgbh/amex/carnegie/peopleevents/pande01

http://www.post-trib.com/steelinfo/history/history10

http://charlotte.bizjournals.com/charlotte/2003/12/29

http://www.jsonline.com/bym/news/dec03/195883

www.pghtech.org

http://sev.prnewswire.com/20041028/SFTH02628102004

http://www.electrospec.com/ID=2477

http://www.sfgate/2005/04/26/BUG1RCF6541

web.mit.edu/afs/net/user/srz/www/multics

cm.bell-labs.com/cm/cs/who/dmr/hist

www.bell-labs.com/history/unix

www.isoc.org/internet/history

charlotte.com/mld/charlotte/4338944

http://news.yahoo.com/newstmpl=story=/20050506

http://www.indiainfoline.com/nevi/ture

groups.msn.com/ThePracticalFuturist/aug2003archive

http://www.financialexpress.com/id=38202

http://www.atkearney.com/C52C1C130

http://economictimes.indiatimes.com/msid-703875

http://www.cfo.com/3710367/c_3710393

http://www.bearcave.com/economics

http://www.bearcave.com/shiller

http://www.ieeeusa.org/releases/2005/030805

http://www.ieeeusa.org/releases/2004/031804

http://www.forbes.com/2004/05/27/id_0527

http://federalreservegov/boarddocs/2005/20050422

http://www.jsonline.com/nov04/271818

http://story.news.yahoo.com/gm_earnings

http://www.jsonline.com/dec03/195883

http://www.bls.gov/news.release/empsit.nr0

http://cio.com/090103

http://www.insurancetech.com/ID=14706297

http://www.ariannaonline.com/forums/20811

http://www.newstarget.com/001765

http://www.scottlondon.com/reports

http://www.nytimes.com/2005/04/29/opinion/29friedman

http://www.businessweek.com/04_09/b3872001

http://www.washingtonpost.com/A38565-2005Mar15

http://www.msnbc.msn.com/id/7678024

http://www.whitehouse.gov/omb/budget/fy2005/tables

http://japan.usembassy.gov/e/p/tp-se1624

http://www.textilenews.com/archives/040102

http://www.twbookmark.com/books/32/0446577448/chapter_excerpt19382

www.paksplace.com/outsourcing

http://www.newstarget.com/006015

http://www.technologyreview.com/articles/04/04/impact0404

http://www.dailyhome.com/2004/0502-dsinclair-5238

http://www.americanfreepress.net/Free_Trade

http://jobwatch.org

http://www.bea.doc.gov/bea/newsrel/gdpnewsrelease

http://www.todaysengineer.org/2004/Dec/benefits

http://www.pbs.org/newshour/vote2004/candidates/can_bush-sept11

http://www.americanrhetoric.com/speeches/gwbush911prayer&

http://www.whitehouse.gov/news/release/20010920

http://www.historyplace.com/speeches/jfk-space

http://www.thespaceplace.com/nasa/spinoffs

http://www.cio.com/archive/050103/staffing

http://www.news14charlotte.com/ID=48769

http://www.hq.nasa.gov/office/pao/History/sputnik

http://education.yahoo.com/id=18192

http://news.co.uk/onthisday/july21/id_2635000/2635845

http://www.presentationhelper.co.uk/president_kennedy_speech_man

http://www.roubiniglobal.com/archives/2005/04/massive_capital

http://www.iht.com//articles/2005/02/24/opinion/eddollar

http://www.bea.doc.gov/bea/newsrel/tradnewsrelease

http://www.bea.doc.gov/bea/newsrel/transnewsrelease

http://usatoday.com/Most+eco

http://atimes01.atimes.com/atimes/China/GB09Ad05

http://www.friesian.com/confuci

http://www.smithsnianmag.si.edu/smihsonian/issues02/apr02/

http://www.pbs.org/wgbh/amex/china/peopleevents/pande07

http://encarta.msn.com/encyclopedia_761557562/India

http://encarta.msn.com/encyclopedia_761573055

http://www.financialsense.com/fsu/editorials/charting/2005/0302

http://www.nhregister.com/id=7697176&BRD

http://oxrep.oupjournals.org/cgi/content/16/3/42

www.nacfam.org/PR6.3.03.pdf

http://www.morganstanley.com/GEFdata/digests/20021015

home.alltel.net/bsundquist1/www.blonnet.com/businessline/2000/08/28

http://www.infosecwriters.com/id=180

http://www.sfgate.com/chronicle/archive

http://www.msnbc.com/id/7936464/newsweek

http://www.cyber.ust.hk/internet

http://www.cio.com/archive/111503/offshore

http://www.businessweek.com/magazine/05_21/b3934053

http://www.faithfulamerica.org/display_article

http://www.msnbc.com/id/7899754

http://epi.org/id=2028

http://www.msnbc.com/id/7921011

http://commdocs.house.gov/committees/science/hsy/73323

http://www.sasol.com/id=X21R0HPKQ4CQ5G5N4

http://www.sasol.com/id=7000006

http://www.gallup.com/poll/state/Nation

http://www.nytimes.com/2005/05/27/opinion/27krugman

eia.doe.gov/pub/oil_gas/petroleum/summary2004

http://www.msnbc.msn.com/id=7997882

http://www.newswise.com/511159

978-0-595-36100-7
0-595-36100-5